Narnia and the Fields of Arbol

Culture of the Land

A Series in the New Agrarianism

This series is devoted to the exploration and articulation of a new agrarianism that considers the health of habitats and human communities together. It demonstrates how agrarian insights and responsibilities can be worked out in diverse fields of learning and living: history, science, art, politics, economics, literature, philosophy, religion, urban planning, education, and public policy. Agrarianism is a comprehensive worldview that appreciates the intimate and practical connections that exist between humans and the earth. It stands as our most promising alternative to the unsustainable and destructive ways of current global, industrial, and consumer culture.

Series Editor

Norman Wirzba, Duke University, North Carolina

Advisory Board

Wendell Berry, Port Royal, Kentucky

Ellen Davis, Duke University, North Carolina

Patrick Holden, Soil Association, United Kingdom

Wes Jackson, Land Institute, Kansas

Gene Logsdon, Upper Sandusky, Ohio

Bill McKibben, Middlebury College, Vermont

David Orr, Oberlin College, Ohio

Michael Pollan, University of California at Berkeley, California

Jennifer Sahn, *Orion* magazine, Massachusetts

Vandana Shiva, Research Foundation for Science,
Technology and Ecology, India

Bill Vitek, Clarkson University, New York

Narnia and
the Fields of Arbol

The Environmental Vision of
C. S. Lewis

Matthew Dickerson
and David O'Hara

THE UNIVERSITY PRESS OF KENTUCKY

Scholarly publisher for the Commonwealth,
serving Bellarmine University, Berea College, Centre
College of Kentucky, Eastern Kentucky University,
The Filson Historical Society, Georgetown College,
Kentucky Historical Society, Kentucky State University,
Morehead State University, Murray State University,
Northern Kentucky University, Transylvania University,
University of Kentucky, University of Louisville,
and Western Kentucky University.
All rights reserved.

Editorial and Sales Offices: The University Press of Kentucky
663 South Limestone Street, Lexington, Kentucky 40508-4008
www.kentuckypress.com

09 10 11 12 13   5 4 3 2 1

Frontispiece: Portrait of C. S. Lewis by Elisabeth Ehmann.

Library of Congress Cataloging-in-Publication Data

Dickerson, Matthew T., 1963–
Narnia and the Fields of Arbol : the environmental vision of C. S.
Lewis / Matthew T. Dickerson and David O'Hara.
  p.   cm. — (Culture of the land—a series in the new agrarianism)
Includes bibliographical references and index.
ISBN 978-0-8131-2522-0 (acid-free paper)
1. Lewis, C. S. (Clive Staples), 1898–1963—Criticism and
interpretation. 2. Environmental protection in literature.
3. Environmental policy in literature. I. O'Hara, David, 1969– II. Title.
  PR6023.E926   Z6419
  823'.912—dc22
                                            2008039350

This book is printed on acid-free recycled paper meeting
the requirements of the American National Standard
for Permanence in Paper for Printed Library Materials.

Manufactured in the United States of America.

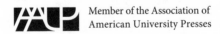
Member of the Association of
American University Presses

For Deborah and Christina, who supported us, encouraged us, helped us, and refrained from rolling their eyes too often.

The feeling about home must have been quite different in the days when a family had fed on the produce of the same few miles of country for six generations, and . . . perhaps this was why they saw nymphs in the fountains and dryads in the wood—they were not mistaken for there was in a sense a real (not metaphorical) connection between them and the countryside. What had been earth and air & later corn, and later still bread, really was in them.

—C. S. Lewis, *Letters*

The only imperative that nature utters is, "Look. Listen. Attend."

—C. S. Lewis, *The Four Loves*

Contents

❧

Acknowledgments

Just as surely as good ecological practice must be understood not as an individual but as a communal affair, so the writing of this book has depended on a greater number of people than the two authors. Together we would like to offer especial thanks to John Elder, Norman Wirzba, Robert Siegel, and an anonymous reader for helpful comments on early drafts, and for many helpful and enjoyable conversations about literature, ecology, and philosophy. Christopher Mitchell and the staff at the Marion E. Wade Center at Wheaton College (Illinois) were also tremendously helpful in our researching and writing of this book; archivist Laura Schmidt was not only a great aid, but also a joyful friendly face over the course of several visits. The library staff at Augustana College and at Middlebury College also did a superb job supporting our research.

Matthew Dickerson would like to thank Middlebury College for generously supporting his work on this project through an Ada Howe Kent grant and faculty professional development funds. He would also like to thank his Middlebury College colleagues and students (past and present) in environmental studies for numerous thoughtful discussions and lectures—especially colleagues Dan Brayton, John Elder, Laurie and Gus Jordan, Jay Parini, and Peter Ryan, and former students Andrew Haile and Devon Parish. Lastly he thanks his family (immediate and extended) as well as his church family for continued encouragement and support—including listening to him talk about the same idea over and over (and over) again. Matthew adds: *Thanks to my father, who first took me fishing and in many other ways helped form my love of nature. Thanks to my mother, who had the wisdom to bring Narnia into her elementary school classroom.*

David O'Hara similarly owes a number of debts of gratitude. Douglas R. Anderson, Stacey Ake, and John Bowen first helped him to take CSL seriously as a philosopher. He is also thankful to Frs Dale

Coleman and Larry Hofer, and to Sandy and Marion Schwartz for their examples of scholarship and hospitality; to his mother, for the gardens and the lived example of generous stewardship; to his father, for teaching him to walk quietly in the woods, and to love wild things; to Mrs. Brady, his fourth-grade teacher in Woodstock, New York, for showing him the way into Narnia; and to John Elder, who helped him get lost in the woods twenty years ago, and whose love for good writing has helped him to find his way even deeper into the woods more than once since then. Augustana College has been a wonderfully supportive community for both teaching and researching, and while David is grateful to all his colleagues for this, two merit special mention: LaMoyne Pederson, for more things than can be said briefly, and for many things said to him without words. David is especially thankful to LaMoyne for patiently showing the delicious plenitude of the prairies to one who first thought them to be empty; and Murray Haar, *O si sic omnes*. The students in David's course on Lewis and Tolkien at Augustana College in January 2007 became his fellow learners, and he was buoyed by their enthusiasm and diligence.

A handful of people, for instance Arend Smilde, also helped the authors indirectly, perhaps without knowing it. We have in mind especially Steve Bouma-Prediger and Cal DeWitt, whose books, lives, and occasional conversation at conferences have made more difference for us than they likely know. We also have in mind everyone who invited us to lecture at their churches, schools, and conferences, including the MacLaurin Institute at the University of Minnesota and L'Abri Fellowship in Minnesota, Massachusetts, Switzerland, and the United Kingdom over the last two years. It is encouraging to know that there are so many people who take the idea of a Christian ecology seriously.

Perhaps it goes without saying, but Steve Wrinn, Anne Dean Watkins, Norman Wirzba, and all the editorial and artistic staff at the University Press of Kentucky made this book a delight to write.

Conventions and Abbreviations

As might be expected, this book contains frequent references to the works of C. S. Lewis, especially the ten books in the Chronicles of Narnia and the Space Trilogy. Because of the large number of editions of both series, with different paginations, we do not give page numbers for references to the books in this series. For the seven books in the Chronicles of Narnia, as well as for *Out of the Silent Planet* and *Perelandra*, we use an abbreviation for the title (see below) and a chapter number in lowercase Roman numerals. Thus the citation (*LWW*, iii) refers to the third chapter of *The Lion, the Witch and the Wardrobe*, and (*MN*, iv) refers to the fourth chapter of *The Magician's Nephew*. For *That Hideous Strength*, we use both chapter and section numbers in Arabic numerals; thus (*THS*, 5.1) refers to section 1 of chapter 5, titled "Elasticity" (which begins "Mark woke next morning . . .").

LWW	C. S. Lewis, *The Lion, the Witch and the Wardrobe*
PC	C. S. Lewis, *Prince Caspian*
DT	C. S. Lewis, *The Voyage of the Dawn Treader*
SC	C. S. Lewis, *The Silver Chair*
HB	C. S. Lewis, *The Horse and His Boy*
MN	C. S. Lewis, *The Magician's Nephew*
LB	C. S. Lewis, *The Last Battle*
OSP	C. S. Lewis, *Out of the Silent Planet*
Per	C. S. Lewis, *Perelandra*
THS	C. S. Lewis, *That Hideous Strength*

For other citations of books and essays by C. S. Lewis, we use parenthetical references indicating the work cited using the abbreviations below. For references to *Mere Christianity*, we follow the format of published editions and give the book number in Roman numerals and chapter number in Arabic numerals; thus the citation (*MC*, III.3) refers to chapter 3 of book III of *Mere Christianity*, titled "Social Morality." For other works (where there are fewer editions in print), we give only the page number of the edition listed below.

AoL	C. S. Lewis, *Allegory of Love* (New York: Oxford University Press, 1958)
AoM	C. S. Lewis, *Abolition of Man* (New York: Touchstone, 1996)
GD	C. S. Lewis, *The Great Divorce* (New York: Macmillan, 1946)
ELISC	C. S. Lewis, *English Literature in the Sixteenth Century Excluding Drama* (Oxford: Oxford University Press, 1954)
FL	C. S. Lewis, *The Four Loves* (New York: Harcourt, Brace, Jovanovich, 1968)
L1	C. S. Lewis, *The Collected Letters of C. S. Lewis,* vol. 1: *Family Letters, 1905–1931,* ed. Walter Hooper (New York: Harper San Francisco, 2004)
L2	C. S. Lewis, *The Collected Letters of C. S. Lewis,* vol. 2: *Books, Broadcasts, and the War, 1931–1949,* ed. Walter Hooper (New York: Harper San Francisco, 2004)
L3	C. S. Lewis, *The Collected Letters of C. S. Lewis,* vol. 3: *Narnia, Cambridge, and Joy, 1950–1963,* ed. Walter Hooper (New York: Harper San Francisco, 2007)
LAA	C. S. Lewis, "On Living in an Atomic Age," in *Present Concerns: Essays by C. S. Lewis,* ed. Walter Hooper (San Diego: Harcourt, Brace, Jovanovich, 1986)
LC	C. S. Lewis, *Letters to Children,* ed. Lyle W. Dorsett and Marjorie L. Mend (New York: Simon and Schuster, 1995)
Mir	C. S. Lewis, *Miracles* (New York: Macmillan, 1947)
MC	C. S. Lewis, *Mere Christianity* (New York: Macmillan, 1943)
OSF	C. S. Lewis, "On Science Fiction," in *On Stories: and Other Essays on Literature* (San Diego: Harcourt Brace Jovanovich, 1982)
RoP	C. S. Lewis, *Reflections on the Psalms* (New York: Harcourt, Brace & World, 1958)
RPH	C. S. Lewis, "A Reply to Professor Haldane," in *Of Other Worlds: Essays and Stories,* ed. Walter Hooper (New York: Harcourt Brace Jovanovich, 1966)

RR   C. S. Lewis, "Religion and Rocketry" in *The World's Last Night and Other Essays* (San Diego: Harcourt Brace Jovanovich)

TaB   C. S. Lewis "Talking about Bicycles," in *Present Concerns: Essays by C. S. Lewis,* ed. Walter Hooper (San Diego: Harcourt Brace Jovanovich, 1986)

Introduction

Ecological Crisis, Environmental Critique, and Christian Imagination

Our only chance was to publish in the form of *fiction* what would certainly not be listened to as fact. . . . What we need for the moment is not so much a body of belief as a body of people familiarized with certain ideas.
—Dr. Ransom, in *Out of the Silent Planet*

The present ecological crisis we are facing is due in part to an impoverishment of imagination. . . . Artistic resources must be an integral part in the development of genuine creation consciousness. Art works—in every medium—can symbolize for us our deepest concerns: they can be documents of what is and is not meaningful in human existence. When we are *engaged* by a work of art, we begin to participate in a new vision of the world.
—Philip Joranson and Ken Butigan, *Cry of the Environment*

Informing the Imagination

This book asks what the late writer C. S. Lewis had to say, both directly and indirectly, about nature and ecology[1] —about the world in which we live, and about our (human) relationships with that world and with our fellow inhabitants. We address that topic by exploring Lewis's ten best-known works of fantastic fiction: the seven books of the Chronicles of Narnia and the three novels collectively referred to as the Space Trilogy. At its core, then, this is a work of literary exploration. As enjoyable as literary exploration may be, however, we hope that this book is more than an abstract intellectual and academic exercise; we hope it is also *practical,* by which we mean that it will both motivate and inform our *practices.* We want to see how the works of C. S. Lewis may help shape our thinking so that we might live in ways that are ecologically more sound, that are healthier for the broad community that is the world as well as for the local communities we inhabit.

To that end, many readers may wonder why we are writing about Lewis's fiction, and moreover about his romantic and fantastic fiction, rather than about nonfiction—or at least about what might be called "realistic fiction." Why an environmental book about *fantasy* novels? Isn't fantasy mere escapism?

One way to answer the critique of "escapism" is just to read this book. Or, better yet, read Lewis's fantasy novels with an eye to ecology and nature; those who have not done so before will be surprised at how much is there. Although ecology is generally not understood as the primary focus of his fantasy novels, Lewis shows a remarkable, consistent, complex, and healthy ecological vision in his numerous fictional worlds: Narnia, Malacandra (in *Out of the Silent Planet*), Perelandra (in the book of that name), and his imagined fictional futuristic England (in *That Hideous Strength*). We are by no means the first to explore Lewis's ecology as manifested in his fiction. Kathryn Lindskoog, in the short 1973 book *The Lion of Judah in Never-Never Land,* included a chapter on "Lewis's Concept of Nature"; while not explicitly addressing ecology, Lindskoog's work does explore metaphysical underpinnings in Lewis's view of nature.[2] Ed Chapman, explicitly recognizing the ecological aspect of Lewis's writing, wrote a short but insightful article titled "Toward a Sacramental Ecology: Technology, Nature, and Transcendence in C. S. Lewis's Ransom Trilogy."[3] Interestingly, Chapman's piece was published in 1976, before the modern genre of eco-criticism really built up steam. Other scholars, before and since, have also commented on what we might today call "ecological aspects" of Lewis's writing, though most of these addressed the issue only in passing while focusing on other subjects, and rarely used the word *ecology* or discussed (or even recognized) the ecological importance of their commentary. Thus what Chapman pointed out in 1976 is still largely true today: while much has been written about Lewis's Christian theology in his science fiction, "a good deal less attention has been devoted to Lewis's views of nature and technology, and his concern for what is now popularly called ecology."[4]

This book explores Lewis's ecology in much greater depth, not only in the Space Trilogy (or "Ransom Trilogy" as Chapman calls it), but in the Chronicles of Narnia as well. We hope that what we have to say in the next eight chapters will dispel concerns about escapism, fantasy, or even romanticism.

Nevertheless, there are a few things we can say up front in defense of our approach, and perhaps to motivate our readers to continue past this introduction. After all, even if one accepts the notion that C. S. Lewis's environmentalism is worth studying, we might note again that he wrote a large number of works of nonfiction. His second degree at Oxford was in philosophy, and many of his nonfiction works explicitly explore both the underpinnings and the practical working out of important philosophical questions, including questions about our relationship with nature. But though we touch on relevant passages from his essays and works of nonfiction, including various personal letters, we focus principally upon Lewis's two great series of fantastic fiction. The question of the value of this particular mode of story is worth addressing in our introduction.[5]

Our defense for our approach is threefold, and each of the three parts is worth elaboration in the ensuing paragraphs. First, not only is C. S. Lewis well known, but his fantasy stories, especially the Chronicles of Narnia, are his *most* known works. Far more people are familiar with *The Lion, the Witch and the Wardrobe,* for example, than with even his classic and best-known work of Christian apologetics, *Mere Christianity.* As Alan Jacobs points out, "millions of readers know [Lewis] only as the maker of Narnia." The books in this series have sold more than 85 million copies and have been translated into thirty languages.[6] Even as we began writing this book, enthusiastic viewers were watching Andrew Adamson's new and highly anticipated film adaptation of *The Lion, the Witch and the Wardrobe.* By the time our book is in print, Walden Media will have released the second film in the series, *Prince Caspian.* By writing about Lewis's best-known and most beloved stories, we can enter a dialogue with a much larger audience.

Our second point is one Lewis himself suggests: "escapism" isn't always bad; it can help us to get a breath of fresh air. By seeing in a very different light—the light, say, of the sun or moon of another world—we can often gain a new view of our own situation and our world that transcends issues such as partisan political conflicts or just our own preconceived notions and selfish ambitions. The third point is related: again, as Lewis himself argues, telling stories is sometimes more important than telling facts because of the way it provokes the imagination.

Lewis's novel *Out of the Silent Planet* (to be explored in more detail in chapter 5) provides a good introduction to all three reasons given above. In the novel, after telling a tale about a *fantastic* voyage to the planet Mars—a tale that, despite the vehicle of space travel, should be understood more as a work of fantasy than of science fiction[7]—the author intrudes into his own story. After supposedly "unmasking" himself as the author, he claims that the entire story is actually *true* (though he has changed some names to protect the innocent and disguise the guilty). Except it is not *quite* the author who claims this; it is the narrator masquerading as the author. The real author knew that the story wasn't literally true. (When C. S. Lewis wrote the story, he did not believe there was any life on Mars, or even any canals, and it seems very unlikely that he expected his readers to believe there was; what was important was that the canal myth was in the common imagination.)[8] So it is really only the author as a *fictional* character within his stories. And even then, what he tells us about story is a combination of paraphrase and "direct quote" of the novel's hero, Dr. Ransom—a hero whom scholars have suggested was inspired by Lewis's friend J. R. R. Tolkien. Nonetheless, what the fictional Dr. Ransom tells us through the pseudo-fictional C. S. Lewis rings true to what both Lewis and Tolkien have frequently argued elsewhere.

In describing the reason for writing this work of fantasy, the pseudo-fictional Lewis writes: "It was Dr. Ransom who first saw that our only chance was to publish in the form of *fiction* what would certainly not be listened to as fact" (*OSP*, xxii). Given how many people claim to be concerned about hearing "the facts," or about trusting only what they learn through science, it is an interesting suggestion that people are sometimes willing to listen to ideas that come in the form of story that they would *not* listen to in the form of abstract arguments. When we hear abstract arguments—especially about socially charged issues like climate change—we often have our political, religious, economic, and social defenses turned on. We filter everything through lenses tinted by what we wish to believe. The state of the world today bears witness to this; thanks to the great work of active environmental scientists over the past few decades, we are not lacking in scientific *facts* about environmental problems. Though there is certainly much more scientific work to be done about myriad environmental concerns and questions, and we are profoundly glad for and grateful to the scientists who have done and continue to do this work, the truth is that we already know enough about many environmental problems to be able to act in more responsible ways than we are currently acting.

This suggests that a lack of knowledge is not the biggest problem. The greater problem is a lack of the *will* to act. In so many different arenas, our modern world ignores the scientific data. We continue to dump toxins into the soil and water, and greenhouse gases into the atmosphere, while overfishing the ocean and depleting our groundwater. We don't listen to facts. We choose not to listen. But we may be willing to listen to fiction. It is not as threatening. At least not at first. The biblical story of David, Bathsheba, and the prophet Nathan is a good example of this principle.[9] Thomas Howard suggests something along these lines in his comments on this passage in *Out of the Silent Planet*. What "animated [Lewis's] narrative art" in these works of fantasy with otherworldly settings was not a desire to "[siphon] our attention away from a gritty reality that has become intolerable in our century as a sort of opiate, but quite to the contrary," to "[shake] us all awake from the poisonous torpor that settled over human imagination a few centuries ago."[10] Later in the book, Howard goes on to add, "He does not beckon us away from our experience in his fiction. Rather, he attempts to illumine that experience with the strong light used for many centuries by the bards, and left unused for some time now."[11] This is the second of our reasons for our approach, and it relates to the first. The C. S. Lewis character in the story adds that the form of fiction "might have the incidental advantage of reaching a wider public" (*OSP*, xxii). We have written about Lewis's fantasy stories because many more people have read them—and have had a chance to be influenced by them—than have read most of his nonfiction.

Influence may be the most important concern. Lewis understood that people do not respond to mere facts until their imagination has been shaped by story to be ready to receive those facts. Thus when the character Lewis in the novel argues with Dr. Ransom that telling the story *as fiction* may prompt readers to disbelieve it, Dr. Ransom responds with the most important point: "What we need for the moment is not so much a body of belief as a body of people familiarized with certain ideas" (*OSP,* xxii). Ideas and facts are not the same thing. Facts reach only our rational mind. They come as propositions. Ideas, however, can come as stories. They can reach our rational mind, but more importantly, they can work through our imagination. They can shape our very understanding of the world. Stories, therefore, can be far more powerful vehicles for shaping how people *act* than mere facts. Among other things, stories make sense of facts and put them in context. Paraphrasing a view put forth by the nineteenth-century romantic poet Samuel Taylor Coleridge, whose thoughts on the subject certainly influenced C. S. Lewis, Robert Barth writes, "Imagination is not merely an artistic faculty, the power that enables the poet to create a poem or the painter a painting. It is also, indeed first of all, the faculty that permits the human person to give meaning to the world and to his or her life."[12]

As mentioned, there is plenty of good academic scholarship—scientific, economic, political, and so on—on ecology and the need for sound environmental practices. One can read books and papers and go to talks on global climate change, healthy agrarian practices, acid rain, sound industrial practices, economic factors in conservation, and a host of other important related topics. This scholarship is not merely worthwhile; it is vital. But mere knowledge and abstract propositions alone do not always succeed in changing how people live. Indeed, one could argue that alone they almost never succeed, for alone they do not "give meaning to the world." We are not lacking knowledge. To change how we live in relationship to the earth, we must go deeper than facts and shape our imaginations. This shaping of imaginations is done through art and story.

Relating the second and third points to the first, we believe that *part* of the reason for the success of Lewis's works of fiction and fantasy are the *ideas* behind his books. This is not to say that the stories serve only as vehicles for a message or that they are didactic in purpose or in effect. The stories of the Chronicles of Narnia are, first and foremost, just that: stories. If they were not good *as stories,* if the characters and the sequence of events were not compelling and did not capture the imagination, they would not have succeeded. But part of the reason they are such good stories is that the compelling portrayals do deal with fundamental human experiences and longings, and with ideas of great import. Among these are Lewis's portrayals of the natural world and humanity's relationship to it. If we can articulate that one of the very things that attracts readers (and filmgoers) to Lewis's works is his healthy environmental vision, then our hope is that these same readers will be drawn to the healthy lifestyles.

We can conclude with confidence—a confidence that only grew in the writing of this book—that by exploring first and foremost Lewis's fantastic fiction (rather than his nonfiction) we have made no sacrifice in our ability to investigate important ideas. As we will claim in chapter 1, what Lewis thought about everything is present in what he said about anything; his worldview as it relates to nature—what we might call his *environmental vision*—is present in every story he wrote. We will, at times in this book, trace in his nonfiction works some of the ideas found in his fantastic fiction, but the purpose of doing so is not because the ideas cannot be found in his fiction; it is more to show how integrated and comprehensive his thought was, and also to help illustrate some of the reasons and philosophical presuppositions behind his views of nature—and, at times, to defend the reading we are giving of his fiction as being in keeping with the author's ideas, and to show moreover that they are thoughtful and often intentional, and not merely accidental.

Art and Our Own Personal Narrative

Turning from Lewis, then, to the broader issues of art and ecology, we are by no means the first to suggest the importance of creative, literary, and artistic responses to current environmental crises. Fortunately, many within the environmental movement are recognizing this. Cal DeWitt, the president emeritus of the Au Sable Institute of Environmental Studies and a professor of environmental science at the University of Wisconsin, teaches environmental studies primarily via story. DeWitt (who has won the Chancellor's Award for outstanding teaching) describes coming to a point in his career at which student evaluations stopped being the primary motivating factor in how he taught; instead he decided to "just teach." And in the process of this change in mind-set, a storytelling style emerged in his teaching. The shift in styles was brought home one day after class during a regular postlecture coffee time DeWitt holds for his students. On this day sixteen students were waiting for him in the coffee area. "Cal, tell us a story," they collectively asked him. Somewhat surprised by the request, DeWitt asked "Why?" "You're always telling us stories," the students responded.

Ironically (but not surprisingly to the authors of this book) when Professor DeWitt started teaching by telling stories (and stopped teaching for the sake of teaching evaluations), his evaluations skyrocketed. Students can't wait to get to his class. "I teach environmental science from stories now," he explains. "They have within them what students should understand, but all delivered in story. Because that's the way our minds work. The only way we really comprehend things in an integrated way is through story."[13]

Philosopher and writer Peter Kreeft, a professor at Boston College, makes a complementary point in his book about the philosophy of C. S. Lewis's great myth-making friend J. R. R. Tolkien. "All literature incarnates some philosophy," Kreeft writes. "In great literature it is done by the unconscious and contemplative part of the mind, which is deeper and wiser and has more power to persuade and move the reader." This is vitally important. If an environmental movement is going to have a significant and lasting impact, it must change the way people live, and to change the way people live it must do more than supply facts; it must change the way they think—it must persuade and move people. This is what stories do particularly well: they "persuade and move the reader." That Kreeft is writing about philosophies is also important. All understandings of nature and the environment—every environmental vision, good or bad—comes from some philosophy, whether consciously or not. Good stories not only communicate these philosophies; they show whether or not they make sense by embodying them. As Kreeft goes on to write, "literature not only incarnates a philosophy; it also tests it by verifying or falsifying it. . . . A philosophy that cannot be translated into a good story cannot be a good philosophy."[14]

Philip Joranson and Ken Butigan also make a similar point explicit with respect to environmental issues, broadening the imaginative approach from just stories to art in general.

> The present ecological crisis we are facing is due in part to an impoverishment of imagination—creative solutions to admittedly complex ecological difficulties are rarely proposed and even more rarely taken seriously as "realistic."

> Artistic resources must be an integral part in the development of genuine creation consciousness. Art works—in every medium—can symbolize for us our deepest concerns: they can be documents of what is and is not meaningful in human existence. When we are *engaged* by a work of art, we begin to participate in a new vision of the world. . . . They help us to *see* our world—and our place in it—in a new way.[15]

There is a profound need for literature and art in shaping our own environmental visions. We must put our imaginations to use.

Norman Wirzba argues a similar point with regard to competing mind-sets of agribusiness and agrarianism: "First, we must recognize that an agrarian transformation of contemporary culture will require the work of the imagination. We need to be able to envision a future that is markedly different from today's world, and be creative in the implementation of economic, political, religious, and educational reforms."[16] Even were there no "crisis," there is always a need for imaginative communication of sound environmental practices and the bases for them. Had we, as a society, done a better job shaping and hallowing our imaginations, perhaps we would not be facing the present crisis. But a crisis there is, and it is hard to deny. The need for an imaginative response is all the more pressing, hence our desire in this book to pay special attention to those works of Lewis that are most imaginative.

Having said all of this, it would be a rather sad irony if what we ended up writing were a merely academic, analytical treatment of C. S. Lewis that appealed only to the intellect and never connected with the imagination of our readers. The reality is that for us the writing of this book really was a personal journey of exploration and imagination—a "fact" we hope comes across in the book. In studying Lewis, we encountered his writing in new ways, both refreshing and challenging. Moreover, in seeking to compare (and contrast) ecological aspects of the writings of C. S. Lewis with those of some of the important environmental and nature writings to have emerged since his time, we continue to have new encounters with many more contemporary writers such as John Elder, Scott Sanders, Gary Snyder, Wendell Berry, Cal DeWitt, Steven Bouma-Prediger, and Norman Wirzba. We were also led into some of the important literary sources that helped shape C. S.

Lewis's own imagination, from Greek classics to nineteenth-century romantic writers such as George MacDonald.

And, of course, our own stories are woven into this book, though more unconsciously than consciously. We hope the result is enjoyable, enlightening, and encouraging, as well as challenging and bridge building.

Building Bridges

And this brings us to the final subject of our introduction, and the one that for many readers may be the point of greatest tension in this book. Like the issue of whether romantic fairy stories are appropriate vehicles for serious environmental inquiry, there is also a question of perceived conflict between Christianity and environmentalism. For some modern environmentalists, a connection between healthy ecology and the work of a well-known Christian figure like C. S. Lewis—not merely a writer of fiction, but a Christian apologist—is at the very least surprising. Aldo Leopold, for example, in the preface to his *Sand County Almanac,* blames much of our environmental decay on the "Abrahamic concept of land."[17] Jim Nollman, in his book *Why We Garden,* argues that "neither Judaism nor Christianity teaches us that nature is alive and capable of interceding in our lives in a positive, spiritually enhancing manner." He goes on to say that under Christianity and Judaism "we have never been taught what it means for us to commune with trees, to treat other species as peers with rights, to relate to mountains as animate, to live in balance with the air, to feel the pulse of the ocean in our blood. We have never experienced a sense of give-and-take with the soil and the rocks."[18]

Sallie McFague has also written on many occasions about problems with various traditional Judeo-Christian models of God and creation, including the model of God as king. In a 2002 article for *Christian Century,* she writes, "Moreover, a king is both distant from the natural world and indifferent to it, for as a political model, it is limited to human beings. At most, nature enters this model only as the king's 'realm' or 'dominion,' not with all the complexity, richness and attention-grabbing qualities of the living, mysterious creation of which we are a part. The king-realm model shuts out the earth as earth, because it allows us to imagine the God-world relationship only in terms of a king and his subjects."[19] So, according to McFague, the metaphor of God as king (a metaphor that is certainly an aspect of the Christian understanding of the world;[20] Jesus himself, when asked if he was "King of the Jews," answers "yes") implies an indifference on the part of God to the world, and a concern only with humans. This is because, according to McFague, it also causes a shutting out of the earth as earth, meaning presumably that the world's very physicality and its "complexity" and "richness" are not important in this Christian view. Now if the model of God as king is problematic, then certainly Lewis's portrayal of the Creator of Narnia not only as king but also as the Emperor-over-the-Sea is doubly problematic.

Similarly, in an earlier 1990 address titled "A Square in the Quilt,"[21] McFague writes of ecologically unhealthy and destructive tenets of the Western worldview and notes, "Christianity is surely not alone responsible for this worldview, but to the extent that it has contributed to it and supported it, the deconstruction of some of its major metaphors and the construction of others is in order."[22] Now one of McFague's points is that Christians need to take the biblical creation account more seriously— that is, to take more seriously the view of nature as creation—and this is a point with which C. S. Lewis would certainly agree (and one we explore in this book, especially in chapter 3). Likewise, when McFague calls for "a profound acknowledgment of our complicity in the deterioration of our planet" as a fundamental "first step,"[23] Lewis might also say the same thing about the failure of Christians to practice biblical teaching. The point, here, isn't to emphasize how much McFague might disagree with Lewis, but rather to note the perception of Christianity as a culprit. The editors of the *Spirit and Nature* collection state in their introduction that, as more voices joined Lynn White and "severely criticized the Judeo-Christian tradition . . . Jewish and Christian thinkers concerned about the role of religion in the environmental crisis found themselves on the defensive."[24]

This brings us to one of the most famous articles written about the relationship between ecology and religion: Lynn White Jr.'s 1967 essay "The Historical Roots of Our Ecologic Crisis."[25] In this article, White lays most, if not all, of the blame for our modern "ecological crisis" squarely on the shoulders of Christianity and its concept of God, Man, and Nature, stating outright that "Christianity bears a huge burden of guilt."[26] Although, as a critique of the actions of many churchgoers,

White's paper certainly provided a useful prompt to many Christians or segments of Christendom (and we might wish it provided a useful prompt to many others), his *theological* premises have been refuted many times since the publication of that article.[27] Thus, readers of this book may already be groaning, "Oh no, not another response to Lynn White."

Our motivation for looking at the writings of C. S. Lewis with respect to the issue of ecology is that they are worth exploring. We feel little need to say much more in response to White, beyond the next few paragraphs of this introduction. Nonetheless, White's oft-anthologized essay manages to live on and to be frequently repeated and cited as authoritative in the environmental literature (both popular and academic). Thus the idea that Christianity and healthy environmentalism are at odds, or even at war, has persisted into the twenty-first century; many active environmentalists view Christians as "the enemy," and not surprisingly many Christians are therefore wary of "environmentalists." As a result, those who might be allies in a move toward a healthy ecology are distrustful and often antagonistic toward one another—not unlike the unfortunate strife that often arises between conservationists and preservationists, or between wilderness advocates and practitioners of healthy agrarianism or sustainable forestry. Thus some mention should be made, at least in this introduction, of just what that attack on Christianity is—in the words of Lynn White Jr., its most famous proponent—and how radically that view of Christianity differs from the *mere* Christianity understood and defended by one of the most visible proponents of that faith in the twentieth and twenty-first centuries. And we should do so realizing that Lewis's famous works were published between several years and a few decades before White's, and so Lewis couldn't possibly have been altering his view of Christianity in response to the critiques of White. Thus at the risk of rehashing an old debate—and to save ourselves and our readers from repeated references to White later in the book—we summarize here White's basic charges against Christianity, as well as a few key contrasting ideas from Lewis that will be explored in depth in this book.

"Christianity had inherited from Judaism," White claims, a concept that "God had created Adam and, as an afterthought, Eve to keep man from being lonely. Man named all the animals, thus establishing his dominance over them. God planned all of this explicitly for man's benefit and rule: no item in the physical creation had any purpose save to serve man's purposes." Thus White's first charge is that under Christianity nature is seen as worthless in itself, or as having only utilitarian value. He specifically connects this to the biblical account of Adam's naming of the animals, and also to the biblical idea of God's plan. He goes on to claim that the biblical concept of humans as God's image bearers implies the following: "Man shares, in great measure, God's transcendence of nature. Christianity . . . insisted that it is God's will that man exploit nature for his proper ends."[28] Thus White sees in Christianity an explicit call to exploitation.

Those concepts, according to White, are the theological roots of the problem. It is not surprising, then, that he thought we were better off ecologically as a pagan culture. Thus another problem with Christianity, he argues, is simply that it replaced paganism. "By destroying paganism," he tells us, "Christianity made it possible to exploit nature in a mood of indifference to the feelings of natural objects." Again, he argues that Christianity justifies exploitation. Paganism, he claims, actually protects against exploitation; under Christianity, "the spirits *in* natural objects, which formerly had protected nature from man, evaporated. Man's effective monopoly on spirit in this world was confirmed, and the old inhibitions to the exploitation of nature crumbled." One of the most interesting ideas in White's paper—and one that is simply false if C. S. Lewis is any sort of example of a Christian—is that "to a Christian a tree can be no more than a physical fact."[29]

In sharp contrast to White, the writings of C. S. Lewis represent and defend what he calls "mere Christianity": the most fundamental tenets of historic Christianity. Many of Lewis's readers also think of the beautiful nature imagery in his poetry, his fiction, and also his nonfiction. In her chapter on Lewis's concept of nature, Kathryn Lindskoog notes, "Lewis's appreciation of geographical landscape is what one would expect of a Christian romantic—a reverent and insatiable delight."[30] But Lewis did more than merely write about nature as would a romantic poet or novelist. Lindskoog goes on to quote from Lewis's *The Personal Heresy*, noting that "nature is more than a background setting for the action of his characters. 'Either there is significance in the whole process of things as well as in human activity, or there is no significance in human activity itself.'"[31] This is just a hint of what we see. Running through the majority of Lewis's works are both the philosophical and theological underpinnings, and also the practical outworking, of what can be understood as a profound and healthy ecology: the tenets of good environmentalism. And this "environmentalism," rather than being at odds with Lewis's biblical Christian worldview, is deeply rooted in that faith. This aspect of his writing, perhaps, is often missed or overlooked.

In particular, though C. S. Lewis died in 1963, more than three years before White's paper was published, in his writings—and in his representation of biblical Christianity—can be found a clear counterexample to White's premises about Christianity and ecology before the premises were even put forward. Probably the clearest case is in Lewis's eschewing of anything resembling exploitation: whether of fellow humans, or of fellow nonhuman creatures, or of plants, or of the earth itself. One of the most important Christian virtues espoused and illustrated by Lewis, and put forth as heroic in nearly all of his books, is the virtue of hospitality. Hospitality stands in direct contrast with exploitation. Hospitality demands that we care for the most vulnerable: the traveler, the stranger, the outcast, the sick, creatures who cannot defend themselves against humans. The word *hospital* shares its roots with *hospitality*—hospitality implies care and concern for well-being—and it is no surprise that Jews and Christians are world leaders in the building and running of hospitals, where the vulnerable (in this case the sick) are shown hospitality. Exploitation, by contrast, takes advantage of that which is vulnerable and powerless.

Lewis also saw in Christianity—and he illustrated in his writings—that rather than nature existing to serve humanity, humanity may be said to have been created to care for nature as a way of serving God. Contrary to White's idea that "no item in the physical creation had any purpose," Lewis saw the universe as being full of purpose and order; it was wrought with purpose and it is full of purpose. It is also full of relationships, or relations: real, profound relations; the earth is not just about utility, but about mutual care, and mutual life. The world is good, and its goodness does not reside in its usefulness to humanity. Equally important, Lewis understood the Bible as being far more concerned with moral *responsibilities* than with *rights* (unlike most of twentieth-century Western culture in which he wrote). He understood that for humans to bear God's image imparts to us not the *right* to *exploit*—it is God's image we bear, and the Bible does not describe God as being exploitive—but rather the *responsibility* to *serve*. As bearers of God's image, we are moral creatures who must behave morally; hence there is an objective basis for our profound ecological responsibility. It is the materialist, Lewis argued, for whom a tree is never more than a tree; it is the Christian who can see a tree as good, purposeful, spiritual, and part of a great plan.

Here is the important part. Readers who take Lewis's ideas seriously are called to live lives in harmony with the earth; they are called to a healthy ecology and a respect of all of creation. Lewis's ideas are practical. The reader who is imaginatively moved to imitate the heroes of Lewis's tales should be living out a responsible life on this earth, showing great care for the rest of the living and even the nonliving earth. This is a point that can also be made about the Christian who takes Christianity seriously. Lewis argues and illustrates forcefully and frequently that care for creation is both a vital part of the Christian tradition and inseparable from true Christianity. Thus readers from many different religious beliefs should find in C. S. Lewis's writing and thinking common ground in how we ought to live, even if they disagree about some of Lewis's underlying Christian tenets. The unfortunate hostility that has grown between some segments of Christendom and some elements of the environmental movement should, and indeed *must,* be laid to rest.

That is one of the main senses in which we hope that this book builds bridges. Indeed, C. S. Lewis and Lynn White Jr. themselves would agree on many basic points. When White writes, "As we now recognize, somewhat over a century ago science and technology—hitherto quite separate activities—joined to give mankind powers which, to judge by many of the ecological effects, are out of control," he is stating something that Lewis certainly would have agreed with. This is a central subject of *That Hideous Strength* (to be explored in chapter 7 of this book). Now White's call to action is that Christian doctrine must be rejected, but this call to action stems from his premise about what that Christian doctrine, or "axiom" is: "Hence we shall continue to have a worsening ecologic crisis until we reject the Christian axiom that nature has no reason for existence save to serve man."[32] As we shall show in this book, Lewis would also strongly urge us to reject the axiom that nature has no purpose other than utilitarian use for humanity in large part precisely because it is *not* a Christian doctrine, and he also warned (long before White) that such an axiom would lead to ecological disaster. But the argument from Lewis is that White is wrong to call for the rejection of

Christian doctrine, at least on any ecological terms; Christian doctrine may in fact be the strongest possible ally of a sound ecological view.

In a similar vein, consider White's comment that "both our present science and our present technology are so tinctured with orthodox Christian arrogance toward nature that no solution for our ecologic crisis can be expected from them alone. Since the roots of our trouble are so largely religious, the remedy must also be essentially religious, whether we call it that or not."[33] C. S. Lewis also wrote of the arrogance of technology. His call was to a Christian humility. For humility *is* one of the central virtues of Christianity, and one that is most clearly modeled by Jesus, the central hero of Christianity.[34] It is also one of the virtues most needed by our race if we are to move toward a healthier ecology. Thus Lewis might well have said—and the idea can certainly be seen in his writing—that "our present science and our present technology are so laden with arrogance toward nature, and so lacking in basic Christian humility, that no solution for our ecologic crisis can be expected from them alone."

Returning to Lynn White's remark about the tree, and about paganism, the complaint really is not against Christianity, but against whatever disenchanted the world. C. S. Lewis also argued against the disenchantment of the world. As seen in his essay "The Empty Universe," he would agree with precisely this point that disenchantment is bad, but would then tell White that it is not Christianity but a false worship of something else that removes the enchantment and the spiritual value from woods and streams.

Perhaps where White was most in agreement with C. S. Lewis can be seen in White's statement: "What people do about their ecology depends on what they think about themselves in relation to things around them. Human ecology is deeply conditioned by beliefs about our nature and destiny—that is, by religion."[35] Lewis knew that how we think, and especially how we think about ourselves in relationship with God, with others, and with the world around us, has a strong impact on how we live. As the editors of *Spirit and Nature* wisely note, "if a religion is in harmony with the creative spiritual energies of the times, its myths, symbols, and rituals have the power to touch the heart and awaken faith. Ideas of God and teachings about the relation between God and the world shape human attitudes toward nature. A theology can obstruct development of a respect for nature or foster it."[36] That is at least one major reason Lewis was so concerned with how we think.

A major premise of this book is that Christianity leads to a profound, practical, and powerfully healthy ecology—and it does so in large part because of its teaching about nature and destiny, and about relationships. And this gets to our deeper reasons for writing this book, beyond the mere enjoyment found in the study of good literature. Though much of the book takes the form of literary criticism—that is, a (we hope) careful reading of Lewis's fantastic fiction—ultimately it is far more than just another work of literary criticism or even eco-literary criticism. To repeat what we said in the first paragraph, we hope that it has practical applications for all the readers.

One last thing. In case it is not obvious to our readers, we should explain the title of this book. Most readers will know that "Narnia" refers to the world in which the greater part of the seven books of the Chronicles of Narnia take place. The phrase "the Fields of Arbol" may be less familiar, however. The three books of the Space Trilogy take place on Mars, Venus, and Earth, respectively. When the protagonist of the first two Space Trilogy books, Elwin Ransom, travels to Mars and Venus, he learns that the true name of the sun is "Arbol," and that the true name for our solar system is "the Fields of Arbol." As should become plain later in this book, Lewis intended to use this sylvan and agrarian nomenclature to suggest that we stop thinking of what lies beyond our atmosphere as inert and empty "outer space," and that we begin to think of what lies within it as in fact lying under the gaze of the heavens. Our world, Lewis held, is, in fact, part of a cosmos that is charged with life; that life is charged with meaning; and that meaning entails ethical relations among all living things.

Chapter 1

What He Thought about Everything

To write a book on miracles . . . has made me realize Nature herself as I've never done before. You don't *see* Nature till you believe in the Supernatural: don't get the full, hot, salty tang of her except by contrast with pure water from beyond the world. Those who mistake Nature for All are just those who can never realize her as a *particular creature* with her own flawed, terrible, beautiful individuality.
—C. S. Lewis, *Letters*

What's really remarkable about Lewis is not the *diversity* of his writings, but the *unity*—the sense that something ties them all together. Certain Lewisian themes, ideas, concerns, and convictions can find their way into almost anything he writes, for almost any audience.
—Alan Jacobs, *The Narnian*

In a preface to a volume of essays about C. S. Lewis, the late philosopher and writer Owen Barfield makes an interesting comment. "There was something in the whole quality and structure of his [Lewis's] thinking, something for which the best label I can find is 'presence of mind.' And if I were asked to expand on that, I could only say that somehow what he thought about everything was secretly present in what he said about anything."[1] Though Barfield's remark may sound like hyperbole, the more one reads of Lewis the more one realizes what an accurate statement it is, which is perhaps why so many scholars have since voiced their agreement with Barfield. Even in Lewis's children's fairy tales, such as *The Lion, the Witch and the Wardrobe*—and perhaps *especially* in these books—one can find expressions of the same ideas and principles he explores and articulates in his most thoughtful nonfiction essays and books for adults.

To turn Barfield's phrase slightly, one could also say that what C. S. Lewis thought about *anything* touched on what he thought about *everything*.

Alan Jacobs, in *The Narnian: The Life and Imagination of C. S. Lewis,* summarizes Barfield's observation as follows. "And yet the chief point of Barfield's essay is that what's really remarkable about Lewis is not the *diversity* of his writings, but the *unity*—the sense that something ties them all together." He then adds, "Certain Lewisian themes, ideas, concerns, and convictions can find their way into almost anything he writes, for almost any audience."[2] Bruce L. Edwards makes a related point when he describes Lewis's life as being "thoroughly integrated." He was "a man whose presuppositions about life, faith, and reality . . . manifested themselves in all that he attempted." Edwards goes on to say that "those who try to read through the entire Lewis corpus confess that they receive an education in history, philology, sociology, philosophy, and theology so extensive and exhilarating that others seem thin and frivolous in comparison."[3] This may be less surprising if one considers the breadth and quality of Lewis's own academic studies and what he accomplished as a student and a scholar. As an undergraduate at Oxford University, Lewis earned a rare and remarkable *triple first:* achieving highest honors in three different fields of study. He earned a first in Greek and Latin, then in history and philosophy, and finally in English literature.[4] Working toward his second of the three degrees, known informally as *Greats,* Lewis studied philosophy under the tutelage of E. F. Carritt. At the time Lewis began this study, he had "settled on becoming a philosopher,"[5] and his first professional appointment was teaching philosophy at Oxford as a one-year replacement for Carritt. His third degree proved providential, however, as his second (and lasting) appointment at Oxford was in English literature, and he eventually went on to hold the chair in medieval and Renaissance English literature at Cambridge University.

As an adult, Lewis published more than thirty books in a wide range of genres. These include seven fantasy novels for children and three adult fantasy novels, as well as an autobiographical allegory titled

A Pilgrim's Regress; a fictional collection of letters from a senior devil to his pupil, titled *The Screwtape Letters;* numerous influential works of literary criticism; a number of published poems; and a handful of books and essays of philosophy, most of which—including the well-known *Mere Christianity*—fit the category of Christian apologetics. His final novel, *Till We Have Faces,* is a retelling of a famous Greek myth. But this categorization of his works is somewhat artificial, for in nearly all of these books one can find philosophy and literary criticism (even in his fiction), narrative and story (even in his nonfiction), thorough knowledge of the classics (even in his children's stories), and even poetry.

In short, C. S. Lewis had a consistent and thoroughly integrated worldview wherein all thought was intimately tied together and interrelated.[6] For Lewis, the fields of literature, education, philosophy, and theology all flowed together. As is evident in his writing, what he thought about literature both influenced and was influenced by what he thought about philosophy. What he thought about education related to what he thought about theology. And—more to the point of this book—this unity is also present in what Lewis thought and wrote about nature. Lewis understood all the disciplines as having a real connection to nature; he would have thought it absurd to attempt to develop an intellectual discipline that had no connection to some view of the natural world. All literature develops to some degree as a response to our varied experience of and attempts to understand the natural world, and Lewis was certainly conscious of this. Education has to take into account both the nature of the learner and the nature of the thing learned. Philosophy and theology are concerned with the underlying nature of things. As such, these are not isolated disciplines.

Lewis also held that one ought to lead a life consistent with one's beliefs. Ideas and actions are really connected to each other, and the ideas we hold have consequences for us, for our neighbors, and for our world. Furthermore, Lewis held that the world is orderly, and that the aim of thought is to discover this order and to live according to it, rather than to attempt to impose an arbitrary order upon the world. To ignore the inherent order of nature, and instead to attempt to impose one's own order on the world, leads necessarily to bad mental, spiritual, and ecological consequences. These features make Lewis's works very interesting to explore for somebody interested in environmental thought and action.

Lewis as Environmentalist?

Nonetheless, although Lewis's famous Chronicles of Narnia have appeal as pastoral narratives and frequently touch on themes of environmental ethics, animal rights, and agrarian practices, Lewis is not generally thought of as a nature writer, and certainly not as an environmentalist. He is known as a novelist and mythopoet, a literary scholar, a poet, a philosopher, an essayist, and a teacher. But few if any of the seemingly countless works of scholarship written about Lewis in the past fifty years have added *agrarian* or *environmentalist* to that description. Only a few works of Lewis scholarship or biography even contain *nature* or *wilderness* in their indexes (though many contain entries for *naturalism*); perhaps none contain entries to such words as *ecology, environment, conservation,* or *preservation.* Yet much can and should be said about Lewis's environmental vision: about the profundity of his thinking about nature, and about humankind's relationship with the rest of creation, with earth and all of its other inhabitants. As Ed Chapman, one of a few writers to focus on Lewis's ecology notes, "readers familiar with Lewis's works need hardly be reminded of Lewis's love of landscape as an entity in itself, and his pleasure in the fruitful relationship of humans to landscape." And he makes an even more pointed note about the Space Trilogy (to be explored in chapters 5–7 of this book): Lewis's "imagery of ecology and technology [in the Space Trilogy] is supported not only by some thoughts in *The Abolition of Man* but by a growing body of thought produced in recent years by some biologists, anthropologists, ecologists, and cultural historians."[7] One important aspect of Chapman's observation is that Lewis was not merely *responding* to a large existing body of environmental writing, but really was *prefacing* much of that work—and the need for it—with almost prophetic foresight.

Consider, for example, that decades before mass deforestation was widely recognized as a serious environmental problem of disastrous consequences (and subsequently popularized as an iconic ecological issue),[8] C. S. Lewis wrote not just one but two remarkable series of fantasy books in which the dangers of deforestation play a significant role in the narrative. Specifically, in the finale of both series, a fatal or nearly fatal danger to the world is symbolized and prefaced by a project of deforestation. In *The Last Battle,* the beginning of the end of Narnia is a major clear-cutting project in western Narnia, with the harvested lumber intended for commercial export to the country of Calormen. In *That Hideous Strength*, the first step of a process that nearly results in the destruction of England (and the world) is the wanton annihilation of the centuries-old Bracton Woods, ostensibly in order to pave the way for development (though the reader later learns there are several other motives as well). The connections Lewis makes in these books—connections extending well beyond a romantic concern for forests and trees—are both profound and prophetic. And they are the focus of this book.

Before we begin to delve into these works of fantastic fiction, however, it is important to discuss three important and traceable influences on Lewis's thinking about nature and ecology. That is, in asking how the environmental and ecological aspects of Lewis's writing may shape *our* imagination, we consider (at least briefly) how Lewis's own imagination was shaped. The three influences we introduce are: (1) previous mythic and fantastic literature, especially that of George MacDonald, the nineteenth-century writer of fairy-tale and Victorian fantasy; (2) classical philosophy and in particular Platonism; and (3) the Christian faith to which C. S. Lewis converted in his late twenties.

Entire volumes could be devoted to exploring the importance of any one of these influences on Lewis (and entire volumes *have* been devoted especially to the third). We offer here only a few brief summaries of ideas as they relate to the topic of the book. The reason for doing so is twofold: first it will help provide some background for the reader not familiar with Lewis's biography or the body of Lewis scholarship, and the second is to save us (and our readers) the tedium of repeatedly reintroducing the same ideas in several subsequent chapters focusing on specific works. Certainly all three of these influences will be explored in more detail.

Lewis as Mythopoet

Since we are exploring Lewis's fantastic writing, we begin with the influence on Lewis of myth and fairy tale, and especially of George MacDonald. Clive Staples Lewis was born in Ireland in 1898 to Albert and Flora Lewis. He always retained warm memories of the Irish countryside: romantic images that certainly helped shape his appreciation of nature. Most of his schooling and his entire adult life, however, were spent in England, and by most accounts he had lost even his Irish accent before he was thirty. Jack—a self-chosen nickname that Clive Staples Lewis took after the death of his beloved dog Jacksie, and which he would retain all his life—had one sibling, a brother named Warnie, four years his elder. The two shared a close, lifelong friendship. However, their mother died before Jack's tenth birthday, and his relationship with his father deteriorated quickly and cannot be said by any stretch of the imagination to have been a particularly good or close relationship.

As already mentioned, C. S. Lewis was first a student and then a tutor at Oxford University, and he later held a distinguished chair at Cambridge University. Because he is such an important figure, there are several excellent biographies of his life that do justice to the details of this period, including his brief period of military service in the First World War, and the injury he sustained from friendly mortar fire. George Sayer's biography, *Jack: C. S. Lewis and His Times,* follows a traditional chronological style and is an excellent introduction to Lewis's life from somebody who knew him well. William Griffin's *C. S. Lewis: The Authentic Voice* is also largely chronological (rather than thematic), but it skips Lewis's early youth and begins in 1925 with his election as fellow of Magdalen College at Oxford; it approaches Lewis's life as a series of episodes—an enjoyable choice of narrative from a biographer who is also a playwright. More recently, Alan Jacobs's *The Narnian: The Life and Imagination of C. S. Lewis* (which we have already cited) gives fewer general biographical details, but does a wonderful job connecting the important influences on Lewis's life with his creative writing, and especially (as the title of the biography suggests) with the Chronicles of Narnia. Armand Nicholi's *The Question of God: C. S. Lewis and Sigmund Freud Debate God, Love, Sex, and the Meaning of Life,* though not strictly a biography, is worth mentioning also, and is as interesting as its title; because of what it emphasizes and what it leaves out, it might give a strange and skewed impression of Lewis's background if read out of context of a more complete biography, but it does a fascinating job of contrasting Lewis's thinking with that of his contemporary Sigmund Freud, while drawing interesting biographical comparisons between the influences that shaped their thinking. Given the influence of

J. R. R. Tolkien on C. S. Lewis, and the similarities in their views of nature, readers may also be interested in Diana Glyer's book, *The Company They Keep: C. S. Lewis and J. R. R. Tolkien as Writers in Community.*

What we summarize here is that Lewis, as a teenager, abandoned his childhood Christian faith—a faith described by Nicholi as "nominal"[9] and by Jacobs as "rather bland."[10] Nicholi suggests that some of Lewis's rejection of Christianity may have come in response to a very strained relationship between Jack and his father, Albert. "His father encouraged him to attend church and to become a believer. . . . Lewis appears to be aware of some relationship between his atheism and his negative feelings toward his father. He not only associated the spiritual worldview with his father, but knew that his embracing atheism would be in defiance of and disturbing to his father."[11] After his mother's death, Lewis also had a very unpleasant experience in two different boarding schools in England, before being brought home to Ireland to be tutored by William Kirkpatrick, referred to by Lewis as the "Great Knock." Kirkpatrick was an ardent atheist who held a worldview of strict rationalism and naturalism. Part and parcel with this rejection of Christianity—perhaps both a cause and an effect of it—Lewis came to accept a materialist and rationalist view of the universe.

What is especially interesting is that Lewis's rationalism led him intellectually to reject literature in general, and myth and imagination in particular, as valid means of acquiring knowledge. Indeed, he sought to reject the imagination altogether, despite his personal love of myth and poetry. For example, though Lewis had always enjoyed Greek classics more than Greek philosophy, and was considered by his tutor as more gifted in the former, his new rationalist worldview led him to concentrate instead on Greek philosophy.[12] Jacobs makes several references to this aspect of Lewis's years as a student at Oxford, particularly during his study of philosophy. "It would seem that he was striving to make himself into a different sort of person than, by natural inclination, he truly was. I have already noted that his education and experience had combined to stifle his imaginative side; he seems to have been determined, at this stage of his life, to extinguish it altogether."[13] Lewis himself saw this as an effort to disenchant and cut off the creative part of himself. Jacobs writes a little later that "Jack had gone a long way toward turning himself into someone who wouldn't even *read* books such as the Narnia stories, much less write them."[14]

What might have happened had Lewis succeeded in starving his imagination and disenchanting himself—in removing all influence of myth and imagination in his understanding of the world—is difficult to imagine. The reasons he failed are many (and ecologically speaking we can be thankful for them). Jacobs has done a wonderful job telling the story that fills in much of the complex picture, and we won't seek to repeat all of the influences here. Certainly one reason has to do with how deeply Lewis was rooted in classical myth, and how much he loved it—too much to easily excise it completely, even when he sought to study it merely rationally. That Lewis did not get a tutoring and lecturing job immediately after earning his degree in philosophy was probably also important as well as providential, because it prompted him for pragmatic reasons to go on for a third degree, this one in English literature, and particularly in "medieval and Renaissance literature, where the mountains were especially delectable and the gardens profusive, where a path to Faery lay always nearby." As a result, Jacobs explains, "whether [Lewis] intended to or not, he would be feeding his imagination too. Of course he would be doing so under the guise of rigorous, analytical, academic study—but he would still be reading the kinds of books that had always brought him delight. And for a young man trying to protect himself—trying to disenchant himself—this flirting with delight was a dangerous thing."[15]

Yet again, Jacobs comments (and this is perhaps the best summary of this section): "In studying philosophy—philosophy, let me hasten to say, as he conceived of it, not as it necessarily is—Lewis had tried to turn himself into something like [George Bernard] Shaw, an analytical creature capable of sharp-edged distinctions and clearly delineated, if dark, pictures—someone impervious to the mystifications of fantasy and Faery, of battles and journeys and riddles. Yet when given free time to read, it was just such stories that he invariably chose, completely ignoring and even despising the modern literature that fit his professed opinions more closely."[16]

Most biographies will point out the influence of J. R. R. Tolkien, Lewis's friend and colleague at Oxford, who contributed immeasurably to Lewis's recovered high view of myth and imagination. (Thus an occasional comment in this book about Tolkien's own views on issues pertaining to ecology and story will be helpful in understanding Lewis.) Lewis's conversion to Christianity—a process that began in his

late twenties and concluded about the time he was thirty—was both
prompted by, and ultimately encouraging to, his appreciation for myth
and for mythic and imaginative ways of knowing.

So what were these imaginative influences Lewis sought to starve, or
disenchant himself from, and that ultimately ended up enchanting him
so deeply? At least one worth considering here is George MacDonald. It
may seem arbitrary to pick just this one source on which to focus. There
were certainly numerous classical and Norse myths that were both profoundly inspiring and influential on Lewis and on his writing; he particularly loved the story of Balder, and referred to it often. And many
somewhat more contemporary writers had an undeniable influence.
The list would include the nineteenth-century fantasist William Morris,
as well as the fantasy writings of Lewis's own friends J. R. R. Tolkien
and Charles Williams. Among the three books in the Space Trilogy, the
change in narrative style between the two novels from the era before the
blossoming of Lewis's friendship with Williams (*Out of the Silent Planet*
and *Perelandra*) and the novel written after the start of the friendship
(*That Hideous Strength*) is marked, with the style of the third of these
bearing the influence of Williams's fantastic fiction. As for an influence
on Lewis's critical thinking during his twenties leading up to his conversion to the Christian faith, the writings of G. K. Chesterton are arguably
more important than those of George MacDonald.

Nonetheless, so many features in George MacDonald's writings keep
reappearing in Lewis—especially in the Chronicles of Narnia—that they
are difficult to ignore.[17] And so, though some scholars of MacDonald
have argued that he had little *real* influence on Lewis, we accept as a
clue what Lewis himself wrote: "I have never concealed the fact that
I regarded [George MacDonald] as my master; indeed I fancy I have
never written a book in which I did not quote from him."[18] We briefly
summarize a few key ideas about nature to be found in MacDonald's
writing, and how those ideas were influenced by his Christian faith; we
will later see many similar ideas in Lewis's writing.

During a forty-year period from 1855 to 1895, MacDonald wrote
some twenty conventional novels, mostly set in the Scottish Highlands.
In his own time, he was probably best known for these novels. But he
also wrote a number of original fairy tales and fantasy stories for adults.
These include nine periodical-length works and the following five

book-length works: *Phantastes* (1858), *At the Back of the North Wind* (1871), *The Princess and the Goblin* (1872), its sequel *The Princess and Curdie* (1883), and finally *Lilith* (1895). Though most of MacDonald's Victorian novels are coming back into print, it is his fairy tales and fantasy stories that seem to have had the greatest influence and to have best endured the test of time. *Phantastes* was Lewis's first taste of MacDonald's writing, and it was a delicious taste. In the same preface to a collection of excerpts of George MacDonald's sayings in which he claimed MacDonald as his "master," Lewis also comments that shortly after he began reading *Phantastes* he knew that he "had crossed a great frontier."[19] This is likely *not* mere hyperbole written to promote a book. In March 1916, Lewis wrote a personal letter to his friend Arthur Greeves describing his reading of *Phantastes* as "a great literary experience." He goes on to say, "I enjoyed the book so much. . . . Whatever book you are reading now, you simply MUST get this at once."[20] Such a passionate response surely suggests, if not an influence, at least an openness on Lewis's part to *be* influenced.

There have been many fascinating studies of George MacDonald's writings, and much more could be said; MacDonald's own vision of nature is probably deserving of a book-length work. We begin by noting that MacDonald had a deep and profound love of the created world, and this was evident in his novels, his sermons, and especially in his fairy tales and fantasy novels, and his poems. From a fairy-tale writer, we may especially expect an element of the *enchantment* of nature. In his book *The Harmony Within: The Spiritual Vision of George MacDonald*, Roland Hein notes that MacDonald associates Faery with "harmonious interaction with nature."[21] The novel *Phantastes* is full of nature imagery as the hero Anados travels through the realm of Faery, delighting in its landscape and creatures. Anados is a clear inspiration for J. R. R. Tolkien's character Smith in the short story "Smith of Wootton Major"—a story that began as an introduction to a new edition of the George MacDonald fairy tale "The Golden Key." When we read in Tolkien's story that "some of [Smith's] briefer visits he spent looking only at one tree or one flower," we are seeing in the writings of J. R. R. Tolkien reflections of MacDonald's appreciation for the beauty and value of nature expressed in his nineteenth-century fairy tales, which helped inspire the later fantasy.

Given that MacDonald was a nineteenth-century writer, contemporary with Wordsworth and Coleridge, one would also expect to see some romantic nature imagery in his poems as well. An excerpt from the poem "My Room" gives us a taste of this romantic imagery, and his penchant for enchanting creation and charging it with life and religious or spiritual meaning. The poem speaks of:

> Awful hills and midnight woods;
> Sunny rains in solitudes;
> Babbling streams in forests hoar;
> Seven-hued icebergs; oceans frore.—
> See them? No; I said
>   enchanted—
> That is—hid away till wanted.
> Do you hear a voice of singing?
> That is Nature's priestess flinging
> Spells around her baby's riot,
> Binding it in moveless quiet:—
> She at will can disenchant them,
> And to prayer believing grant them.[22]

In this poem, enchanted Nature literally sings. And while the "Spells" and the "binding" add to the sense of enchantment, the imagery of a priestess and the granted prayers adds a religious and spiritual undertone. One sees in these lines that for MacDonald the sense of enchantment in nature heightens his awe and delight at the world around him.

At times, MacDonald also gives voice to nonhuman creatures, including trees. This is something we will also see in poems and fairy tales of C. S. Lewis, as well as in the writing of J. R. R. Tolkien. Consider Tolkien's ents—an important component of his own environmentalism—as well as Lewis's naiads, or wood nymphs, in relation to MacDonald's poem "The Tree's Prayer," which gives voice to a tree lamenting the long winter and looking forward to spring. The tree laments,

> Alas, 'tis cold and dark!
> The wind has all night sung a wintry tune!
> Hail from black clouds that swallowed up the moon,
> Beat, beat against my bark.

Oh! why delays the spring?
Not yet the sap moves in my frozen veins;
Through all my withered roots creep numbing pains,
That I can hardly cling.

The sun shone yester-morn;
I felt the glow down every fibre float,
And thought I heard a thrush's piping note,
Of dim dream-gladness born.[23]

Of course the levels of meaning here are deep; the poem does much more than give voice to a tree, for in the tree's longing for spring we also see a profound human response to our own "winters." MacDonald may well have been writing more about the human experience than the arboreal one. (He certainly *knew* human experience more clearly than arboreal experience.) It may also seem slightly arbitrary to point specifically to MacDonald's use of such imagery. Many other poets, especially romantic poets, have used similar devices. Timothy Bleeker connects MacDonald's own view of nature with those of the romantic poets. "In thus closely linking God and nature, MacDonald is of course akin to Wordsworth and Coleridge. . . . a total correspondence exists between the natural world and the spiritual world, making it logically fruitful to draw spiritual lessons—as MacDonald often does in his fiction—from close observations of nature." As for spirits of trees, Lewis had much older literary examples than MacDonald from which to draw. What Lewis may have especially appreciated in MacDonald and his particular portrayal of nature is both the *explicit* fairy-tale element and the Christian underpinnings. As Bleeker goes on to say, for George MacDonald, "both humanity and nature draw their being from God himself."[24]

Interestingly enough, at the stage in Lewis's life when he first discovered MacDonald, he might have rejected his writing if he had known of MacDonald's Christian faith. Later, however, Lewis would write, "To speak plainly I know hardly any other writer who seems to be closer, or more continually close, to the Spirit of Christ Himself."[25] It is reasonable to assume, then, that some of Lewis's later Christian understanding of nature would—consciously or unconsciously—reflect the view of nature evident in MacDonald. As we will later see was the case with Lewis as well, MacDonald's love flowed out of his religious faith.

Bleeker makes some other important observations about MacDonald's view of nature and its relationship to his faith: "True religious feeling, in MacDonald's books, always leads to a reverence for and deeper understanding of nature, the 'house of God.' When he was about twenty-two he wrote to his father: 'I find that the happiness springing from all things not in themselves sinful is much increased by religion. . . . Nature is tenfold brighter in the sun of Righteousness, and my love of Nature is more intense since I became a Christian.'"[26] That MacDonald would call nature "the house of God" is itself deeply significant. It establishes a very high view of the created world, and a high calling to care for it. To associate nature with "the house of God" is to associate it with the tabernacle of Moses, or the Jewish temple in the time of the nation of Israel, and therefore with all the laws pertaining to the honoring of that temple. One ought not mistreat or exploit nature any more than one should mistreat or exploit the temple, or house of God. His comment that his love of nature became far more intense after his conversion is also something we see in Lewis, as we explore in the next two sections.

Indeed, we might say that the love of nature not only was intensified by the Christian faith but also helped lead Lewis to that faith. In an article titled "C. S. Lewis's Debt to George MacDonald," Gregory Wolfe makes this point in drawing comparisons between the two writers: "Both were born in the Celtic perimeter of Britain, Lewis in Ireland and MacDonald in Scotland. Both lost their mothers at an early age, and both had strong fathers, though MacDonald's was more loving and sensitive. Both made life-long commitments to living in England and identifying with English culture, but they remained conscious of their role as outsiders. In their youth, Lewis and MacDonald had a strong love of nature and literary romance, that led them to Christianity and shaped their faith."[27] Roland Hein, a respected MacDonald scholar, also notes some important features of George MacDonald that have particular relevance to the next two sections on Lewis's Platonism and his Christian faith. Hein writes that MacDonald has a "view of the sacramental character of nature" that "solidly challenges the essentially Platonic assumptions." A few sentences later he explains what he means. "MacDonald could not accept the view that there exists an irreconcilable enmity between body and spirit, and that the body must be severely checked and chastised for the good of the soul."[28] Of course one's view of the value of the physical world has profound implications on our ecology. As a Christian later in life, Lewis would certainly be drawn to MacDonald's spiritual world-view. But Lewis was also a Platonist. Would he have seen this rejection of Plato in MacDonald? And if so, how did he view it?

Lewis as Platonist (but Not a Gnostic)

Perhaps the most famous refrain of Professor Kirk in *The Lion, the Witch and the Wardrobe* is his rhetorical question "What *do* they teach them at these schools?" He says this to Peter and Susan near the start of the story when they come to ask advice about Lucy (*LWW*, v), and again at the end when their adventures have ended and they wonder if they will ever get back to Narnia (*LWW*, xvii). However the refrain takes new meaning—and elicits friendly laughter from the others—when it is repeated in *The Last Battle* (with the same emphasis on the word *do*), but with an added preface. "It's all in Plato, all in Plato: bless me, what *do* they teach them at these schools!" (*LB*, xv).

It is easy to see, then, why many have described Lewis as a Platonist. To understand this, and to answer the questions posed at the end of the previous section, we should begin by asking, *What do scholars mean when they describe Lewis as a Platonist?* One difficulty in using this label is that each different age has its own interpretations of Plato. Lewis's Plato was primarily the medievalist's Plato. This does not mean that Lewis read only what the medieval writers wrote *about* Plato and did not read Plato himself. Lewis was a classics scholar; he could certainly cite large passages of Plato in the original Greek. Likewise, we are also not suggesting that these different ages' interpretations of Plato have nothing in common. To the extent that they all begin with Plato, they share fundamental underlying ideas. But each may emphasize differ-ent aspects of Plato's writing, and so for the sake of this book when we speak of Platonism we are trying to get at what Lewis *understood* to be Platonic thought. This is important in understanding both what Lewis ultimately agreed with in Platonism and what he disagreed with.

For example, there are many similarities between the writing and thinking of Lewis and his friend Tolkien, including in their underly-ing views on what today could be called *ecology* and *environmental-ism*—similarities stemming from their shared Christian faith as well as their common medievalist outlook. The similarities between the ideas of these two are so startling that Peter Kreeft, in his book *The*

Philosophy of J. R. R. Tolkien, for each of the fifty philosophical questions he poses and answers from Tolkien's writing, also provides "a quotation from C. S. Lewis . . . showing the same philosophy directly stated."[29] Thus Kreeft's book is as much a philosophical critique of Lewis as it is of Tolkien. But there are also subtle differences, many of which stem from the fact that Lewis was an Anglican Platonist and Tolkien a Catholic Aristotelian. Some might say that Lewis viewed Christianity through the eyes of Platonism and Protestantism, while Tolkien viewed Christianity through the eyes of Aristotle and Catholicism. We believe it is probably more accurate to say that Lewis viewed Plato, and Tolkien viewed Aristotle, through the eyes of Christianity, and therefore their similarities are far more striking and important than their differences— as was noted by Kreeft, who also points to Platonic ideas (and Ideals) in Tolkien's writing as well.[30] This Platonism—the sort of neo-Platonism that can be seen in medieval literature from Chaucer on—doesn't so much *devalue* the physical world in favor of a separate spiritual realm as it sees the spiritual *permeating* the physical. This view helps interpret many of the concepts associated with Plato.

One of the most famous concepts of Plato is one now known as *Platonic Ideals:* the belief that the physical reality is just an imperfect reflection of perfect ideas. In this thinking, a specific chair in my living room is just an example of the perfect concept of Chair or of Chairness. In some interpretations of Plato, the Ideal reality exists independent of the imperfect material examples of it, and the material reality is both less true and less good, and even less real, than the Ideal reality. Many Lewis scholars have observed the concept of the Ideal at work in much of Lewis's writing, both his fiction and nonfiction. Evan Gibson comments on Lewis's imaginative portrayal of heaven in *The Great Divorce,* which describes the "diamond-hardness of the grass" and the "apples which take more than human (or ghostly) strength to life." In these descriptions Gibson sees what he takes as "an extension of Plato's famous allegory of the cave, in which he describes the world that we know through our senses as only the flickering reality of shadows on a wall cast by that ultimate and infinite reality which exists out of our sight on a supernatural plane of being."[31]

In Lewis's two fantasy series, the Platonist elements come most clearly to the foreground in the final books. In *The Last Battle,* the movement "further up and further in" can be seen simultaneously as a movement toward heaven and as movement toward the Platonic Ideals, which certainly relates to what Lewis wrote about heaven in *The Great Divorce*. The concept also appears several times in *That Hideous Strength*. Describing the bear, Mr. Bultitude, the narrator notes that "sometimes there returns to us from infancy the memory of a nameless delight or terror, unattached to any delightful or dreadful thing, a potent adjective floating in a nounless void, a pure quality" (*THS*, 14.3). This is a description of the Ideal in the words of Lewis's narrator. As an Ideal, it is unattached to any particular. It is an adjective describing a property, without the need for any particular object that might have that property even incompletely. It is not a specific example, but the "pure quality" from which all examples come. A little later, the character Ransom describes to Jane the Ideal of the masculine: "The male . . . exists only on the biological level. But the masculine none of us can escape" (*THS*, 14.5). Ransom's words suggest that the particulars of a biological male are merely an incomplete and imperfect reflection of that Ideal of maleness, or masculinity. And the Ideal is so much higher and superior to the biological particular that the particulars cannot even compare. Modern readers may chafe at the specific example, but the underlying Platonism seems clear. It is perhaps most clear in the chapter titled "The Descent of the Gods," in which spiritual beings associated with other planets descend to the earth as Platonic Ideals.

Another idea important to Plato, and especially to medieval neo-Platonism, is the belief in a nonmaterial reality. In particular, it is the belief that a spiritual reality is present in the physical reality, or more particularly that the *natural* world has its source in something (or some-*one*) *super*natural. This aspect of Platonism certain influenced Lewis at a time when he did not believe in a Christian idea of spirit. Now it may seem arbitrary to point to Plato as a source for a belief in a spiritual world; many worldviews other than Platonism affirm some spiritual reality. But Lewis saw something in Plato that he did not see even in the myths he loved—something he would specifically call "theological." He would later write about this in his *Reflections on the Psalms*. "We do of course find in Plato a clear Theology of Creation in the Judaic and Christian sense; the whole universe—the very conditions of time and space under which it exists—are produced by the will of a perfect, timeless, unconditioned God who is above all that He makes. But this is an amazing leap . . . by an overwhelming theological genius; it is not ordinary Pagan religion" (*RoP,* 79–80). So Platonism and Christianity both affirm that there is something beyond the material world. These worldviews differ on what that other reality is, and Lewis would ultimately adhere to the details of the latter. But at a time when he had rejected Christianity, and was doing his best to reject the spiritual and imaginative, nonrational, and mythic altogether, Plato was still there affirming an otherworldly reality to a young Oxford student, and then a young Oxford tutor.

It is this otherworldliness, the idea of a real nonmaterial world in both these worldviews, that can be troublesome environmentally. In certain strands of Platonic thought, especially in the first-century theology of Gnosticism—a belief that is a blending of aspects of dualist Platonic thought with aspects of Christian spirituality, and was viewed by the early church as a heresy distinct from true Christian belief—this dualism between spirit and body is emphasized. Norman Wirzba summarizes the Platonic version:

> The *Phaedo* expresses in direct, simple form an idea more completely expressed in the mature work of Plato's *Republic,* one of the most influential of the Platonic dialogues. Here Plato constructs a metaphysical picture of reality in which otherworldliness is central: what is ultimately real and truly good cannot be understood in terms of our natural lives or through ordinary human experience, since this world is characterized by mutability and flux, instability and contingency, limits and partiality, i.e., imperfection. Owing to the inherent dissatisfaction that must inevitably follow from our experience with things in this life, the true philosopher must instead seek eternal goodness, beauty, and truth in another realm, a realm that transcends this world and its faults.[32]

In Gnosticism and certain other forms of Platonism, it is believed that goodness resides *only* in the world of ideas, or Ideals, or in the spiritual world. The physical world, according to these beliefs, has no inherent value. This applies both to human flesh—our own bodies—as well as to the physical substance of the earth: its "flesh" including grass, flowers, trees, and animals, as well as rivers and oceans, rocks, dirt, and mountains. In some forms of Platonism, the physical is actually viewed as evil; our flesh, as well as the grass beneath our feet, is seen as an impediment to pure pursuits.

It is difficult to conceive how any healthy environmental perspective can come out of a worldview that believes that the earth is at best worthless and at worst evil. A reasonable consequence of such a belief is to view the earth as the enemy, which does not suggest any safeguards against exploitation. Wirzba gives a good summary:

> When this mature metaphysical account of reality was combined with Greek Orphic religion espousing a rigid soul/body distinction, it became clear that the goal of all human life must be to downplay, literally degrade, bodies and material things, for they are at their best merely the temporary prisons of a divine soul, and at their worst they are the obstinate impediments to the soul's salvation, the soul's release from the body so that it can enjoy eternal life with the gods. On this Greek account, human life is good and praiseworthy insofar as it signifies a carefully measured and reasoned disdain for a fluctuating and impermanent world.[33]

Whether this interpretation of Plato is correct or not, it is certainly an aspect of many forms of Platonism—and strands of Christianity emphasizing the *other*worldly while denying the importance of *this* world have also been linked to Platonism.[34] Yet it is also a belief that Lewis rejected later in life when he became a Christian. In a letter written in January 1940, he comments: "But I fear Plato thought the concrete flesh and grass bad, and have no doubt that he was wrong" (*L2*, 326).

Lewis as Christian (the Deepest and Most Profound Influence)

How did Lewis, who appreciated and affirmed Plato so often, come to disagree with what he understood to be an aspect of Platonism, and come to agree instead with George MacDonald and with Christianity? Lewis did not always think that Platonism was wrong in regard to the "concrete flesh and grass" being "bad." The shift in his thinking after his conversion to Christianity is interesting and important to understand. About twenty years before the previously cited letter, a decade before his conversion, Lewis wrote to his close friend Arthur Greeves: "My views at present . . . are getting almost monastic about all the lusts of the flesh. They seem to me to extend the dominion of matter over us. . . . I have formulated my equation Matter=Nature=Satan. And on the other side Beauty, the only spiritual and not-natural thing that I have yet found" (*L1*, 371). Here, Lewis is affirming a Platonic viewpoint with which he disagreed in his later letter. It is only the nonmaterial ideals, he claims, things outside of nature, that can be beautiful: beauty as an Idea is good, but there are no beautiful particulars. Again, it is easy to see that a stated belief like this would not support a healthy environmentalism. If nature is evil, why nurture it? In this view, it not only has no inherent value; it isn't even beautiful. Interestingly, despite the reference to monasticism, Lewis did not have an active faith in God or a belief in Satan at the time he wrote this. (This can be seen in the quote itself, in that he refers to the abstract idea of Beauty, and not to God, as the "only spiritual . . . thing" he has found.) He seems to be using the name *Satan* only as a popular symbol of evil, to illustrate his point that matter and nature are evil. It is his particular form of Platonism, then, and not a Christian faith, that leads to his rejection of matter.

Ideas like this surface repeatedly in Lewis's pre-Christian thinking. In a letter written the next month, he repeats this formula that matter is evil. And just two weeks after that, he writes again to Greeves with yet another argument that nature cannot be beautiful:

> You say that nature is beautiful, and that is the view we all start with. But let us see what we mean. If you take a tree, for instance, you call it beautiful because of its shape, colour and motions, and perhaps a little because of association. Now these colours etc are sensations in my eye, produced by vibrations on the aether between me and the tree: the real tree is something quite different—a combination of colourless, shapeless invisible atoms. It follows then that neither the tree, nor any other material object can be beautiful in itself: I can never see them as they are, and if I could it would give me no delight. (*L1*, 374)

For the young C. S. Lewis, the pre-Christian materialist, a tree could never be more than a tree. As we see, however, a tree is just one example from nature. The materialist viewpoint he espouses here has a much broader generalization: the things of nature are never more than *things*. They have no intrinsic worth or beauty. All has been reduced to mere invisible atoms, and our interaction with nature is just a series of sensory perceptions. Again, those who have any concern for nature—any desire for good environmentalism—should count ourselves fortunate that Lewis did not devote his life to defending this viewpoint.

The clearest explanation for the change in Lewis's thinking about nature is his conversion to Christianity. Like most shifts in thinking, it was probably not immediate. But by the 1940s, when Lewis was writing books defending the Christian faith, he was also expressing a high view of the value of nature, and he explicitly associates his shift with his Christian thinking. In September 1943, for example, referring to his book titled *Miracles*—a philosophical defense of Christianity and of a worldview that accepts the supernatural—he writes in a letter, "Did I tell you that this attempt to write on the Supernatural has turned many chapters into sorts of hymns on Nature!" (*L2*, 591). Two years later he repeats this idea in more detail in another letter: "To write a book on miracles . . . has made me realize Nature herself as I've never done before. You don't *see* Nature till you believe in the Supernatural: don't get the full, hot, salty tang of her except by contrast with pure water from beyond the world. Those who mistake Nature for All are just those who can never realize her as a *particular creature* with her own flawed, terrible, beautiful individuality" (*L2*, 648). For Lewis, a belief in the Christian understanding of the supernatural greatly enhanced his appreciation for the beauty of nature and the natural—as opposed to his earlier pre-Christian interpretation of Platonic spirituality, which diminished his appreciation of the "imperfect particulars."

It is also important to note, in reference to this letter, that when Lewis speaks of nature as "flawed," he certainly does not mean it is evil. Lewis states this explicitly in a personal letter written in December 1961, in which he describes the earth as "a creature . . . not an evil creature but a good creature corrupted: retaining many beauties, but all tainted. And certainly not a creature made for our benefit (think of the spiral nebulae)" (*L3*, 1303). Lewis's new understanding, here, and his rejection of the Platonic view of the physical world as evil, certainly drew on the writing of the Apostle Paul. In the same letter in which he suggests that Plato was wrong to think of "concrete flesh and grass" as "bad," he prefaces this comment with reference to Paul's writing.

The Platonic and neo-Platonic stuff has, no doubt, been rein-forced (a) By the fact that people not very morally sensitive or instructed but trying to do their best recognize temptations of appetite as temptations but easily mistake all the spiritual (and worse) sins for harmless or even virtuous states of mind: hence the illusion that the "bad part" of oneself is the body. (b) By a misunderstanding of the Pauline use of σάρξ ["flesh"], wh. in reality cannot mean the body (since envy, witchcraft, and other spiritual sins are attributed to it) but, I suppose, means the unregenerate manhood as a whole. (You have no doubt noticed that σῶμα ["body"] is nearly always used by St. Paul in a good sense.) (*L2*, 326)

In distinguishing between Paul's use of the Greek words for *flesh* and *body*, and pointing out that the latter is "nearly always used . . . in a good sense," Lewis provides his own careful interpretation of Paul. Nature—including the physical world as well as our physical bodies—in Lewis's Christian understanding is inherently good. He describes those who reinforce Platonic and neo-Platonic ideas to the contrary as either morally insensitive or poorly instructed; they may be well intentioned, Lewis says, but they have misunderstood Paul. It is the spirit that causes us to fall, and not the body. This idea appears often in Lewis's writing. In a letter written about a year before his death, he complains that his body is failing him and "wearing out" like an "old automobile." But then he goes on to speak about just how important that body is, and how much he values it, even as it ages: "I have a kindly feeling for the old rattle-trap. Through it God showed me that whole side of His beauty wh. is embodied in colour, sound, smell and size. No doubt it has often led me astray: but not half so often, I suspect, as my soul has led *it* astray. For the spiritual evils wh. we share with the devils (pride, spite) are far worse than what we share with the beasts: and sensuality really arises more from the imagination than from the appetites: which, if left merely to their own animal strength, and not elaborated by our imagination, would be fairly easily managed" (*L3*, 1384). It is through the body that Lewis has appreciated so much of the beauty of God's creation, and even the beauty of God's creation is appreciated for its physical qualities of color, sound, smell, and size.

Lewis also argues that, though nature (the physical world) certainly benefits humanity, its goodness is independent of any usefulness to us; it was pronounced "good" (in Genesis 1) before humans even appeared. Rather, nature has suffered—it has become "flawed"—because of the evil of humanity, and also (as Lewis also notes in his letter) because of the devil who can make nothing but "has *infected* everything" (L3, 1303). In other words, unlike the Gnostics or various strains of Platonists, Lewis views nature not as evil but rather as the *victim* of evil. In doing so, he is echoing another Christian doctrine also found in the epistles of Paul, who writes in his letter to the Roman church: "The creation waits in eager expectation for the sons of God to be revealed. For the creation was subjected to frustration, not by its own choice, but by the will of the one who subjected it, in hope that the creation itself will be liberated from its bondage to decay and brought into the glorious freedom of the children of God. We know that the whole creation has been groaning as in the pains of childbirth right up to the present time" (Romans 8:19–22, NIV). As Paul explains, because humans have rebelled against God's good plan to nourish creation, and have chosen to use (or, rather, abuse) our authority to exploit, all of creation suffers. The "frustration," "groaning," and "pains" of creation—the "bondage" of nature—are a result of human evil, not of any evil in nature. Paul also points out that God intends *all* of creation, the "creation itself" and not just humanity, to be redeemed and liberated.

Now Lewis not only echoes this Pauline/Christian doctrine, but elsewhere he also explicitly comments on it. In an essay (interestingly titled "Religion and Rocketry"), he writes of God's "redemption of other species" as "working through" the human species, and he attributes this suggestion to Paul and the passage cited above. The implication is that Christians who desire to be a part of God's redeeming work on earth ought to be concerned not only with redemptive work among other humans, but also with redemptive work in all of creation. Lewis even wonders if Paul's message might apply extraterrestrially. "On the conscious level," he writes, "I believe that [Paul] was thinking only of our own Earth: of animal, and probably vegetable, life on earth being 'renewed' or glorified at the glorification of man in Christ." So Paul (and God) is certainly concerned with the renewal of all life on earth. But then Lewis goes on and adds, "But it is perhaps possible—it is not necessary—to give his words cosmic meaning. It may be that Redemption, starting with us, is to work from us and through us" (RR). Whether the extraterrestrial application is there or not, the implication is the same: just as all creation suffers from humanity's evil, humans are meant to be part of redeeming work, helping rescue all of creation from the impact of our evil.

The other change we see in Lewis, following his conversion, is that nature is no longer *merely* nature; he begins to refer to it as a *creature*. In more common terms, nature is *creation*. In this book (including in its title) we use the terms *nature* and *creation* almost interchangeably, largely because Lewis viewed nature as creation. Many Christian environmentalists, however, argue for the consistent and intentional use of the word *creation* rather than *nature*. T. M. Moore, drawing on the works of Alister McGrath, summarizes the reasons. "'Nature' implies neutral, ungrounded reality—stuff of various kinds—existing, as it were, by itself, waiting to be discovered, defined, and deployed according to whatever social purposes or worldview may have possession of it at any given time."[35] In short, then, Lewis's conversion to Christianity coincides with a change in his understanding of nature; he rejects that very element of Platonism that devalues nature as evil, and instead views nature as creation, and not intended primarily for human use. "Another result of believing in Creation," he writes, "is to see Nature not as a mere datum but as an achievement"(*RoP,* 83).

Thus the idea that "a tree can be no more than a tree" would have made no sense to the Christian C. S. Lewis. He would have had to look no further than his avowed "master," and model of Christian faith, George MacDonald, for a more profound understanding of the Christian faith and what it might say about the tree. Hein summarizes MacDonald well: "If MacDonald read Blake's proverb that a fool does not see the same tree that a wise man sees, he agreed with it. The person who wills God's will sees in a tree something of the glory God is investing in it, and profits spiritually. The person who sees it only as a botanist would, or a lumberman, may have a practical view of its structure or of its uses, but does not see the truth of the tree."[36] It is the postconversion Lewis who suddenly sees a tree as a beautiful and valuable part of creation, who sees God's glory in that tree. If the tree is "useful," its primary usefulness is not economic but rather spiritual.

It is also the details of *particular* trees that become important. It is not only abstract trees or poetic trees or literary trees or the Ideal of a tree that matters; the actual tree outside the window—or the particular cloud or a specific mountain in our own country—all matter. And here again we have a connection to George MacDonald. In his article on Lewis's debt to MacDonald, Greg Wolfe also writes about the effect of Lewis's conversion on his appreciation of nature, saying, "When, as a mere Romantic, Lewis experienced a moment of Joy, he naturally associated it with another world—the North, fairy land, a story. Even when the joy was linked to clouds or mountains, Lewis said, they did not lead him to think differently about the particular clouds and mountains he knew. Instead, after the moments of joy, he experienced a dissatisfaction with the world. But in *Phantastes* Lewis was confronted by a reversal of the Romantic experience in that now moments of joy did not cause dissatisfaction; they enhanced the real world."[37] A passage from Philip Sherrard's insightful book *The Rape of Man and Nature* resonates strongly with how Lewis's spiritual view of the world enhances rather than diminishes the potential for a healthy environmentalism. Of a worldview that denies the spirit, Sherrard writes:

> Our failure to perceive the divine in man has gone hand in hand with a failure to perceive the divine in nature. As we have dehumanized man, so we have desanctified nature.... I refer to that process whereby the spiritual significance and understanding of the created world has been virtually banished from our minds, and we have come to look upon things and creatures as though they possessed no sacred or numinous quality. It is a process which has accustomed us to regard the created world as composed of so many blind forces, essentially devoid of meaning, personality and grace, which may be investigated, used, manipulated and consumed for our own scientific or economic interest.[38]

The key point can be found in the final line. Prior to his conversion, Lewis viewed the universe as composed only of "blind forces." He did not view it as a "created world" at all, but as mere "nature." It was open, therefore, to all sorts of investigation and manipulation—that is, exploitation—in the name of economics. Once he began to believe in the supernatural, however, Lewis began to see the sacredness in nature as well. It was then that it ceased to be merely an object for exploitation—"certainly not a creature made [merely] for our benefit."

Lewis and Nature (the Underlying Philosophy Summarized)

We are now in a better position to summarize our goals for this book, to address potential criticism of our approach, and to outline where we are going. To reference a just concern for the direction that some Lewis scholarship has taken, this is not a book that asks "what C. S. Lewis *would* have thought about ecology, nature, and environmentalism if he had lived long enough to see it."[39] This is a book that explores what Lewis actually *did* think about these things—or, more accurately, to explore in Lewis's writings the ideas expressed about ecology, nature, and the responsibility of humankind toward them.

If one accepts the (reasonable) premise that "one who thinks carefully about ecological ideas must also be good at ecological observance," then the conclusion would follow that "C. S. Lewis thought and wrote carefully and extensively about ideas of great ecological import, and therefore (by the implied premise) he was also a model of ecological observation." However, we are also not asking our readers to accept the opening premise that ecological ideas automatically lead to ecological observance. What this book will illustrate is *both* that Lewis was concerned with ecological ideas, and *also* that he observed and illustrated the ecological consequences of those ideas. In other words, he was a master of both the ideas and the observation, and we see both of these in his writing.

Our goals for this book are threefold. First, for readers of any ideological or philosophical background who are attracted to Lewis's imaginative work (a very large audience), we want to argue that one of the important features of that work is an environmental vision. Lewis's work is popular for a number of reasons, and has attracted a range of different audiences. We hope to make clear that Lewis's environmental vision is present in all his writing and especially in his fiction (both as ecological ideas and as ecological observation). It is, one might say, such an integral part of the landscape of his fiction that it has gone largely unnoticed. We have not seen the forest of his environmental vision for the individual trees of his fiction. His idea of what makes good literature is inseparable from his notion of moral goodness; and his environmental vision is both the fruit of that notion of moral goodness and an example of it in literature. His theory of literature, his ethics, and his landscapes are all woven tightly together. If we are right in saying this, then it follows that this is a theory with some bite to it. If we enjoy Lewis's literature, or his religion and ethics, then we would argue that this is in part because we already share his awareness that: (a) how we treat the land around us is *symptomatic of* our inner moral state; and (b) how we treat the land around us also *affects* our inner moral state. That is, our relationship to the land is at once a *sign* of our ethics and a significant force in *shaping* our ethics. In this book we are arguing that in Lewis's view, literature affects our lives and shapes both our actions and our worldviews. If literature requires us to disdain Nature in order to enjoy the book, then it is bad literature; and if we enjoy good literature without growing in our respect for Nature, then we are bad readers.

Our second and third goals relate to bridging gaps within the environmental movement. As noted in *Ents, Elves, and Eriador: The Environmental Vision of J. R. R. Tolkien,* "the modern 'environmental movement,' like any significant large-scale social development, does not represent a single monolithic agenda or set of procedures: it is, rather, a varied collection of diverse subgroups. These subgroups differ significantly not only in their means, but frequently even in the ends or goals towards which they are oriented. As such, they are often at odds; where there ought to be harmony and collaboration, we find disagreement and division."[40] Of course a certain amount of debate among different "camps" is healthy. But sadly, quarrels among those who call themselves *environmentalists* have often hindered rather than aided their work. As there is often strife between preservationists and conservationists, so is there also often distrust between those coming from different faith traditions. Since Lewis is respected as one of the most articulate and thoughtful representatives of Christian faith in the twentieth century, we hope that any readers who share Lewis's faith will also be moved toward the sort of consistent and humble environmentalism and responsible creation-care that Lewis's fiction models and even advocates, rather than distrusting environmentalists who share some of the same goals but at times different motivations; Christians should see that Christianity itself calls them to a deeper and more profound environmentalism than has sometimes been practiced in the history of Christianity. As theologian N. T. Wright has recently written,

The mission of the church is nothing more or less than the outworking, in the power of the Spirit, of Jesus' bodily resurrection. . . . The split between saving souls and doing good in the world is not a product of the Bible or the gospel, but of the cultural captivity of both. The world of space, time, and matter is where real people live, where real communities happen. . . . And the church that is renewed by the message of Jesus' resurrection must be the church that goes to work precisely in that space, time, and matter.

Thus the church that takes sacred space seriously . . . will go straight from worshipping in the sanctuary to debating in the council chamber; to discussing matters of town planning, of harmonizing and humanizing beauty in architecture, green spaces, and road traffic schemes; and to environmental work, creative and healthy farming methods, and proper use of resources. If it is true, as I have argued, that the whole world is now God's holy land, we must not rest as long as that land is spoiled and defaced. This is not an extra to the church mission. It is central.[41]

A third and related purpose is to illustrate for those readers who do not share Lewis's Christianity or even his theism that his worldview provides a strong and objective basis for healthy environmentalism including agrarian and wilderness ideals—again, if for no other reason than to make allies of different strands within environmentalism, because there is much greater strength in unity than in division.

With respect to our second and third purposes, though we do not want to turn Lewis's fictional work (or our own book) into explanations and defenses of Christianity (such as Lewis's *Mere Christianity* or *Miracles*), or into more responses to Lynn White, there is some degree to which we are *using* Lewis's writing as a *defense* of a certain Christian view of ecology. It is a defense both to Christians who appreciate Lewis but who don't see ecology as an important topic and to those who are not Christian, who see ecology as very important, and who hold a low view of Christian ecology.

In the next three chapters, we explore the Chronicles of Narnia. Chapter 2 covers the first five books of the Chronicles and addresses principles to be found in all of them. Chapter 3 focuses on Lewis's mythic creation account of Narnia in *The Magician's Nephew*, addressing some themes to be found in all of the books but focusing on the ecological importance of one's view of the source and *beginning* of nature. Similarly, chapter 4 focuses on Lewis's account of the *end* of Narnia in *The Last Battle*, again addressing some common themes, but focusing on the ecological importance of one's view of the end. The next section of this book, chapters 5–7, turns attention to Lewis's Space Trilogy, with one chapter devoted to each of those three books—*Out of the Silent Planet, Perelandra,* and *That Hideous Strength*—before our conclusion in chapter 8.

This approach has both advantages and disadvantages. The main disadvantage is that, as we claim at the start of this chapter, the same ideas can be found running through all of Lewis's writing, and so to explore his works book by book will certainly lead either to some repetition of ideas or to ignoring certain facets of particular books because those ideas are explored in more depth elsewhere. In fact, we will give in to both of these disadvantages. Nonetheless, we choose this approach in order to treat Lewis's stories *as stories.* Any time a scholar looks at a body of fiction to investigate one particular theme, it is possible, probable, and perhaps even unavoidable to confuse fiction for essay and story for sermon. As we claim in our introduction, Lewis was trying to write good stories, and not merely thinly disguised sermons. In structuring our book so that we explore Lewis's books as books rather than subdividing them into mere "themes," we at least attempt to minimize the possible violence done to stories that have enchanted countless readers including ourselves.

Chapter 2

Nature and Meaning in the History of Narnia

Humans came into the land, felling forests and defiling streams.
—Trufflehunter the Badger, in *Prince Caspian*

Very little of that good work of keeping creation will be accomplished without the concrete embodiment of the virtues. . . . The good work of earthkeeping is impossible without . . . these ecological virtues, these fundamental traits of character.
—Steven Bouma-Prediger, *For the Beauty of the Earth*

Wendell Berry's powerful novel *Jayber Crow*—published in the year 2000 at the start of a new millennium—has as its subtitle *The Life Story of Jayber Crow, barber, of the Port William Membership, as Written by Himself.*[1] And the book is, in a way, the life story of Jayber Crow. But it is also the life story of a small town, and more specifically of two characters in the town, one of whom is loved by Jayber, and one who is despised by him. The one loved by Jayber is Mattie Keith or "Mattie Chatham as she was to be" (11). The one despised by Jayber is her husband, Troy Chatham. Mattie is introduced at the start of the second chapter as the young woman who is currently a Keith, but will become a Chatham. The story ends with her death in a hospital bed.

What is at stake in the novel is the soul of the town of Port William and of its many inhabitants about whom the reader comes to care deeply. The battle—for it *is* a battle, and the narrator describes it as such many times and in many ways—is between two competing visions for what the good life is all about: the vision of Athey Keith passed on to his daughter Mattie, as opposed to that of Troy Chatham.

Athey's vision of goodness is that of the consummate agrarian. He "was not exactly, or not only, what is called a 'landowner.' He was the farm's farmer, but also its creature and belonging. He lived its life and it lived his; he knew that, of the two lives, his was meant to be the smaller and the shorter" (182). Troy's vision, by contrast, is that of the "agribusinessman"—a word used only once in the book, but used tellingly and proudly by Troy to describe himself: "It was at that time, I believe," the narrator Jayber recalls, "that Troy began to call himself an 'agribusinessman.' He would quote a great official of the government who had said, 'Adapt or die,' meaning that a farmer should adapt to the breakneck economic program of the corporations, not to his farm" (337). But even before the word *agribusiness* is used, the reader knows exactly what Troy is about. From the moment he marries into the family, and thereby into the Keith farm, "he thought the farm existed to serve and enlarge him" (182).

Athey, as a farmer, never requires more of his land than the land could give and remain healthy. "No more land would be plowed for grain crops than could be fertilized with manure from the animals. No more grain would be grown than the animals could eat" (185). But Athey's son-in-law Troy could never take *less* than he could squeeze from the land at any cost and at all possible times. Troy is always imagining replacing the old ways of doing things with grander buildings, bigger equipment, more mechanization, and faster techniques. And central to all of these other dreams is one in which Troy is in a seat of power, in a big farm office where instead of having to work the land himself he can order other people around. Not long after Mattie and Troy's marriage and the birth of their first daughter, the narrator tells us that "What [Troy] wanted, as time would reveal, was to be a sort of farming businessman, an executive who would 'manage' the 'operation' from an office with a phone while other people (and machines) did the actual work" (188).

When the Keith land comes under Troy's power, it is eventually destroyed in the name of progress and adaptation. Of course it is not only Troy who is to blame for the demise. There are many other forces at work, including the new highway, government inspectors of barbershops, and all sorts of other attacks on Athey's way of life that seemed inevitable in the mid-twentieth century. But the story makes it clear that Troy's way of life is allied with the other attacks, and is part and parcel with them in the death of Port William and of so much that Athey and Mattie hold dear.

Sadly, it is only at the end of the story that Troy Chatham begins to understand that the powers with which he has allied himself—the powers to whom he has sold his soul—have also betrayed and destroyed not only Troy's family but Troy himself. "The fulcrum had shifted. The price of land had dropped. He no longer had the equity to support his debts. He was about to lose everything that he had believed he owned by courtesy of relentless work and endless debt" (360). Yet even then, in his desperation, he clings to his vision of progress. When Mattie gets ill and is hospitalized, even as she awaits death in a hospital bed, Troy sells out the most sacred thing she owns: the small wooded lot known as the Nest Egg that was, and had always been, the most precious treasured piece of land in Port William for her father Athey Keith, herself, the narrator Jayber Crow, and for many of the old-timers of Port William. It was a piece of land that Athey not only never would have sold, but certainly never would have developed or logged for mere *money*. Nonetheless, "in his desperation to salvage something, even just a little dab of pride, [Troy] had had to look at Mattie's illness as providential. . . . As soon as she had gone into the hospital . . . he had sold the timber" (360). To Troy, the Nest Egg was just a resource: a commercial commodity. And in selling it, he moves subtly but distinctly from simply being a selfish (and self-deceived) egoist to a betrayer of his own kin.

What is perhaps most appalling is how excited Troy is by the so-called progress involved in cutting the timber—that is, in the act of betrayal. Jayber Crow, awash with grief as he witnesses the rape of this beloved piece of land, finds Troy "grinning his big in-the-know grin"; all Troy can talk about is how impressive the powerful chainsaws are, and how esteemed are the men who know how to use this power. Yet the narrator, Jayber, sees behind Troy's final horrible act not only the desperation, but also a sort of distraction; it is as if Troy not only knows how bad the betrayal he has committed is, but also that he's been self-deceived all along and is not—even by selling this land—going to be able to stave off his own destruction. As the narrator explains, "Troy was a beaten man and knew it, and was trying not to know it. You could see it in his eyes." And a few sentences later he adds, with a certain sympathy beginning to mingle with his disdain, "so there he was, a man who had been given everything and did not know it, who had lost it all and now knew it, and who was boasting and grinning only to pretend for a few hours longer that he did not know it" (360).

It was exactly half a century *earlier*, in 1950, that C. S. Lewis introduced in one of his stories a character similar to the young Troy Chatham. The story is *The Lion, the Witch and the Wardrobe,* and the character is Edmund. Of course Lewis was writing a children's story, and one much shorter than Wendell Berry's novel, and thus Edmund's character is not nearly as thoroughly developed as Troy's. Nonetheless, we see many of the same ideas at work.

There comes a point in Lewis's story when Edmund has moved from being merely a self-centered and sometimes spiteful boy who lies and bullies—and who, like Troy, easily believes flattery that he is one of the "cleverest and handsomest" of young men (*LWW*, iv)—to one who consciously betrays his own family. Edmund and his siblings, Peter, Susan, and Lucy, have finally come to Narnia together, and have been sitting in the home of beavers making plans to meet Aslan. After hearing the plans, Edmund sneaks out and heads toward the house of the White Witch, the enemy who has already imprisoned Lucy's friend Tumnus and is now seeking to capture Lucy, Peter, and Susan also. Once at her house, Edmund eventually tells the witch all he knows of his siblings' plans.

Edmund might not openly have identified his actions as a *betrayal,* any more than Troy would have acknowledged his selling of the Nest Egg as such. "You mustn't think," Lewis's narrator tells us, "that even now Edmund was quite so bad that he actually wanted his brothers and sisters to be turned into stone." Edmund had simply been lured by a promise of power, prosperity, and influence: a promise that by following this course of action he would become an important person. It is a promise very much like the one Troy believes. And like Troy, even when Edmund slowly comes to realize the promise is false, and he would be caught up in the destruction, he still forges ahead with his plan. "Deep down inside him he really knew that the White Witch was bad and cruel," but rather than turn back, he continues to make excuses for his actions (*LWW,* ix).

One thing that keeps Edmund going, even when his circumstances have became painfully unpleasant and his prospects for success seem dim, is remembering his dreams of progress. "When I'm King of Narnia," he tells himself, "the first thing I shall do will be to make some decent roads." He goes on from there to consider all the ways he can replace the wilderness and rural idyll that is Narnia with his own vision of progress, and again it is much like Troy's desire to replace his father-in-law's outdated way of doing things with modernization. Edmund imagines "what sort of palace he will have" (much like Troy's big farm office) as well as "how many cars [he will own] and all about his private cinema and where the principal railways would run." And, like Troy's awe and delight with the powerful chainsaws in the final chapter of *Jayber Crow*, Edmund's dreams of progress "cheered him up a good deal"—though only momentarily, as we soon see (*LWW*, ix).

There are many who must pay the price for Troy's ambition. His wife's parents and Troy's own son pay dearly. At some level, everybody in Port William pays a price. Although it is not clear he ever understands this, Troy himself pays a considerable price, not just in the end, but throughout his entire life. Among humans, the highest price is paid by his wife, Mattie, who continues to love him with a selfless love even though she is utterly opposed to his plans, and even though Troy responds to her love with disdain and betrayal and a lack of appreciation for all she does. And, of course, the land itself suffers grievously: the trees, and the soil, and the water, and all the creatures who live upon it.

Likewise, there are many in Narnia who must pay some price for Edmund's ambition and betrayal. The animals of Narnia suffer in the ensuing battle with the witch; it is not unreasonable to assume that had Edmund not enacted his betrayal, Aslan the Lion would have been with his followers, and Narnia would have been saved quickly and with little loss. Aslan suggests something along these lines after the battle with the witch ends, when he asks Lucy, "Must *more* people die for Edmund?" (*LWW*, xvii). But it is Aslan who pays the greatest price, sacrificing his very life in the same sort of selfless love offered by Mattie to Troy. Perhaps the one difference is that Edmund comes to repent and to appreciate that love. It is not clear that Troy Chatham ever does, though Jayber Crow hints that there might be some small move in that direction after Troy loses everything.

Prince Caspian

Again, we must note that C. S. Lewis was writing a very different type of book than was Wendell Berry; Lewis wrote the Narnia stories for children, and felt there were at least four constraints imposed by such a task: (1) a strict limit on vocabulary, (2) exclusion of erotic love, (3) cutting down on "reflective and analytical passages," and (4) having chapters of nearly equal length.[2] The third of these is probably the greatest restriction with respect to the present discussion. In any case, the explicit agrarian concerns that play such an important part in *Jayber Crow* are not present in *The Lion, the Witch and the Wardrobe*, which has neither farm nor farmer in its list of scenes and characters. Though many other important comparisons might be made between the two books, and though Berry has acknowledged his admiration of Lewis,[3] it would be a misrepresentation to call Lewis's book a work of agrarian fiction.

But *The Lion, the Witch and the Wardrobe* is only one of seven books of the Chronicles of Narnia and was the first of the seven to be written.[4] In between the creation of Narnia (described in *The Magician's Nephew*, to be explored in the next chapter) with its first king called to be an agrarian leader, and the end of Narnia (described in *The Last Battle*, and explored in chapter 4) are thousands of years of Narnian history. Lewis wrote four more books recounting important stories that take place during these middle years: *Prince Caspian, The Voyage of the Dawn Treader, The Horse and His Boy*, and *The Silver Chair*. And while none of these explore what are typically considered as agrarian concerns, all of them involve what we might call a battle for the soul of Narnia—a battle between competing worldviews, and competing ideas of what the "good life is," not unlike the battle that takes place in *Jayber Crow*. As the Chronicles of Narnia progress, Lewis develops many of these ideas more completely, exploring the importance of wilderness, the relationship of humanity to the rest of creation, and the allure of technological progress and seemingly easy solutions that don't require human labor.

Prince Caspian was the second of the seven books to be written. In it, we read of yet another battle for Narnia. Though the battle is portrayed as a physical confrontation—literally a clash of swords and spears, and of tooth and claw—Lewis shows that the more significant battle is between competing sets of ideals, many of which focus on what is the right role of humankind in relationship to nature. Though the country of Calormen to the south of Narnia and the giants to the north pose a constant external threat to Narnia, in the second book as in the first, the evil to be fought is internal to the land. The battle of *Prince Caspian* is one between the "*Old* Narnians" and the more recent occupants of the land who are really Telmarines (from the land of Telmar) who conquered Narnia ten generations earlier. Based on the name "Old Narnians," one might be tempted to see the conflict as one between nostalgia and progress. But it is really between what might be called *preservationism* (represented by the Old Narnians) and *exploitation* (King Miraz and his followers).

When *Prince Caspian* begins, the four Pevensie children (Peter, Susan, Edmund, and Lucy) have been away from Narnia for a year in their time (the time of our world), but for centuries of Narnian time (which, as readers of the series know, runs at a different pace from time in our world). They are magically drawn back to Narnia by a call for help from the Old Narnians. What the reader learns is that humans have taken over Narnia. They have driven out or into hiding the talking animals, as well as nearly all nonhuman creatures such as dwarfs, centaurs, and fauns. These new rulers also have an abiding fear of and hatred for wild places, especially forests and the sea. In other words, those portrayed by Lewis as the enemies—the *villains* of the book—have an anthropocentric view of the world; they are hostile to nonhuman life and to wilderness. They are described as "the race who cut down trees wherever they could and were at war with all wild things" (*PC*, v). This alone is important to point out in terms of an implicit environmentalism imaginatively portrayed. The humans ruling Narnia have become tyrants and oppressors, and the land and its creatures suffer. The heroes of the tale, the Old Narnians, seek to preserve the land from the devastating effects of human oppression.

Before getting to the central (and for some readers the most controversial) issues, we might make a few observations on key ideas illustrated as the story unfolds—ideas that are found in many later works by other authors who are generally accepted as important contributors to the environmental canon. One of the first is that human creations—manmade buildings and edifices, and monuments to human greatness—are not lasting. When the four children first arrive back in Narnia at the start of *Prince Caspian,* they find themselves near the ruins of an old castle. They soon discover that it is none other than their beloved Cair Paravel, from which they once ruled Narnia (in *The Lion, the Witch and the Wardrobe* and *The Horse and His Boy*). Lewis now shows us this castle from the long perspective of time. It has fallen into ruin and decay, and is no longer inhabited nor even inhabitable. Of their entire ancient castle, all that survives and remains healthy are the orchards they had planted during their reign. The apple trees have grown wild—an appropriate touch—and are probably descendants of the trees they planted rather than the trees themselves. But it is certainly *their* orchard; they still remember the planting of it aided by talking moles who dig the holes, and by "the greatest of all the woodpeople, Pomona herself," who "came and put good spells on it" (*PC,* ii). So the edifices built by humans have fallen, while living things have endured and even reclaimed some wildness. One might draw from this the same principle that Athey Keith understood: between his life and the life of his farm, "his was meant to be the smaller and the shorter."

A related point also worth noting is that the four children, and later the dwarf Trumpkin, all make several meals of the apples that come from these trees. Thus future generations of Narnia are shown to benefit from, and even to depend upon, a healthy agrarian practice of a past generation—though in a fun little twist, Peter, Susan, Edmund, and Lucy are part of both the *past* and the *future* generation. This was even foretold by the chief mole, who at the planting says, "Believe me, your Majesty, you'll be glad of these fruit trees one day." And as Peter points out, "By Jove he was right" (*PC,* ii). It is probably a stretch to see this as an example of agrarianism; it is likely an accident of narrative rather than a conscious choice of the author. But if so, it is an accident that flowed from a worldview that takes into account the value of nature and the transience of even the greatest of civilizations. And it certainly resonates with a passage written by Lewis's good friend J. R. R. Tolkien in the prologue to *The Lord of the Rings,* which notes that the agrarian success of the Hobbits in the Shire in part owes to sound practices of those who dwelt on the land thousands of years before: "The land was rich and kindly, and though it had long been deserted when they entered it, it had before been well tilled, and there the king had once had many farms, cornlands, vineyards, and woods."[5]

Lewis also demonstrates early in this story—as in countless other places in his writing—that nature is meaningful and ordered. This is not a universally shared view, even within the environmental movement. As we mention in the first chapter, it is certainly possible to practice a healthy environmental ethic while still seeing nature as merely "nature," a random event devoid of any transcendent purpose. But a worldview that sees nature as *creation,* and thus as inherently meaningful and valuable, provides a *transcendent* basis for healthy environmental vision (even if many who claim to hold this worldview often sadly ignore the implications in their care of that creation). Lewis reminds his readers repeatedly that nature has an order that comes from its meaning and purpose. For example, when Prince Caspian wonders whether two stars are going to collide, his tutor Cornelius replies, "The great lords of the upper sky know the steps of their dance too well for that" (*PC,* iv). In advocating this, Lewis was espousing a medieval view of the world that had gone out of vogue, but which many important environmental thinkers, such as Dale and Sandy Larsen, argue is critical. "In the medieval period in Europe . . . all things, from work to rock to humankind to star, were engaged in a celestial dance that glorified the Creator."[6]

Another aspect of nearly all of the Narnia stories, easy to overlook or consider as insignificant, is the prevalence of walking. Just the act of walking around Narnia and experiencing its landscape is a major part of the narratives of *The Lion, the Witch and the Wardrobe* and *Prince Caspian.* Similarly in *The Horse and His Boy* and *The Silver Chair* the characters spend considerable time walking around the lands south and north of Narnia.[7] Even in *The Voyage of the Dawn Treader,* the narrative takes several breaks from the ship at sea, and the characters go on walking tours of various islands. Gary Snyder, at least, would argue that there is an important connection between walking and healthy ecology; he explains in his essay "The Etiquette of Freedom": "Walking is the great adventure, the first meditation, a practice of heartiness and soul primary to humankind. Walking is the exact balance of spirit and humility. Out walking, one notices where there is food. And there are firsthand true stories of 'Your ass is somebody else's meal'—a blunt way of saying interdependence, interconnection, 'ecology,' on the level where it counts, also a teaching of mindfulness and preparedness."[8] Snyder connects walking not only with the important ecological virtue of humility, but also with the realization of the interdependence and interconnection of all living things, which is at the heart of the most important practices of healthy ecology.

We also begin to see how imaginatively important even this simple aspect of Lewis's writing may be when one of our present day's most gifted and influential nature writers and environmental thinkers, John Elder, describes the shaping of his own imagination in terms of Lewis's and Tolkien's walking scenes and their described landscapes: "I do not take up my hiking stick and follow a trail through the woods without remembering the quests of Frodo and his Fellowship of the Ring . . . and on a hike like today's . . . I recall Jill, Eustace, and Puddleglum's journey to the land of the giants in *The Silver Chair*, from C. S. Lewis's Chronicles of Narnia."[9]

One reason Lewis could (and did) incorporate this into his Narnia stories is that he was, when his health allowed it, an avid walker, and frequently took his own walking tours around England and Ireland—a habit he formed long before there were formal walking associations to encourage such tours.[10] So Lewis not only came to know and understand the landscapes better, but he also personally experienced this humility, interdependence, and interconnection of which Snyder writes.

Competing Visions for Narnia

So what are the competing ideas battling for the heart and soul (and land) in *Prince Caspian?* What do the two sides represent, and how do they live? Miraz is the central symbol of the new power, the Telmarines. He is depicted as a cruel tyrant, willing to murder first his own brother and later his nephew in order to gain power. Not surprisingly, Miraz seeks to remove all sense of enchantment from nature—swords and battles are what are real for Miraz, not talking animals and trees—and by removing enchantment he seeks also to remove all sense of nature's sanctity. For in disenchanting and desanctifying the earth and its creatures, he will be more justified in exploiting it. This point is one of the central ideas of Philip Sherrard's *The Rape of Man and Nature*. Writing about our world and our history, Sherrard notes that "the spiritual significance and understanding of the created world has been virtually banished from our minds." He goes on to explain the consequences of this banishment. "It is a process which has accustomed us to regard the created world as composed of so many blind forces, essentially devoid of meaning, personality, and grace, which may be investigated, used, manipulated and consumed for our own scientific or economic interest."[11] This could well be a description of Miraz's outlook, or at least the outlook he foists upon his people. When his nephew Prince Caspian speaks to him about the enchantment of nature, Miraz grows angry; he becomes especially irate when Prince Caspian speaks the name of the divine being Aslan—one to whom Miraz might be responsible.

As for the Telmarines in general, the reader learns from the wise Dr. Cornelius that they have silenced the beasts and trees of Narnia, and even its fountains. To prevent the people of Narnia from having too great a love for these things—the things of nature instead of the man-made things of the present age—King Miraz tries to cover up even the memory of the good things of old Narnia, not allowing them to be spoken of (*PC*, iv). He distorts history to hide the truth. His history is described as being both "duller than the truest history you ever read and less true than the most exciting adventure story" (*PC*, xiv). It is not surprising when we learn that Miraz and the Telmarines are descended from pirates. Describing one part of their history, Aslan explains: "There they did as pirates would: killed the natives and took the native women for wives, and made palm wine, and drank and were drunk, and lay in the shade of the palm trees, and woke up and quarreled, and sometimes killed one another" (*PC*, xv). One might wonder whether Aslan, here, is giving the history only of the pirates, or of the human race.

Trufflehunter the badger explains it more simply: "The Humans came into the land, felling forests and defiling streams." Despite appearing in a children's story, the badger's condemnation of one of the competing visions for Narnia is as simple and profound an environmental statement as one could make. (If only Trufflehunter had also mentioned what humans have done to the air in addition to the soil and water, his statement would be complete.) As a result of the felling and defiling, the dryads and naiads (the spirits of trees and rivers) "have sunk into a deep sleep" (*PC*, vi). Humans have not treated nature well, Lewis is telling us, and as a result we experience the loss of the healthy relationship that should exist between us.

Lewis also makes it clear that oppressive and exploitative practices that are bad for the earth and its creatures are also bad for humans. It is not only the land and its creatures, but also its humans who suffer. "Narnia was an unhappy country. The taxes were high and the laws were stern and Miraz was a cruel man" (*PC*, v). Whether intentionally or not, this raises two important environmental principles. The first is that when we treat the earth poorly, all humans may eventually suffer, but it is the poor and less privileged who suffer the most, while the wealthy and most powerful can often avoid (at least temporarily) many of the devastating effects on the soil and water caused by their exploitation. The second principle here is one that Wendell Berry has articulated.

> It is impossible to care for each other more or differently than we care for the earth.
>
> This last statement becomes obvious enough when it is considered that the earth is what we all have in common, that it is what we are made of and what we live from, and that we therefore cannot damage it without damaging those with whom we share it. But I believe it goes farther and deeper than that. There is an uncanny *resemblance* between our behavior toward each other and our behavior toward the earth. . . . By some connection that we do not recognize, the willingness to exploit one becomes the willingness to exploit the other. The conditions and means of exploitation are likewise similar.[12]

Lewis's writing certainly illustrates Berry's point. Even as in this book we note that throughout Lewis's stories the villains are shown to exploit nature and the earth while the heroes seek to free it from exploitation, Andrew Haile has noted "in six of the seven books, much of the action centers on the struggle for freedom against forces of oppression that enslave innocent beings."[13] The two exploitations go hand in hand: that of nature and that of our fellow humans (or rational beings.)

By contrast, Aslan and those who follow him—which is to say, the Old Narnians along with Caspian, their new king—live by a very different set of principles from those of Miraz and his people, and in doing so offer not only a contrast to exploitation but also a profound hope to the real Narnians: the animals, and trees, and rivers, and fauns, and centaurs. Of course it is the principles lived out by the wise Aslan and his followers, the story's heroes, that readers can be certain are in line with C. S. Lewis's own principles. In light of this, consider several of the steps taken by Aslan and the Old Narnians when they restore Narnia and rescue it from its oppression. One of the first acts in this restoration is the tearing down of the bridge of Beruna. Aslan himself orders this. "Deliver him from his chains," he tells demigod Bacchus, which Lucy correctly understands to mean the deliverance of the river from the bridge (*PC*, xiv). This act is both symbolic and practical. It is symbolic because it is a man-made edifice (like a dam) that gives the Telmarine humans more power over nature; with a bridge, they don't have to cross at a ford and thus are not at the whims of the river and its water levels. When the bridge is destroyed, people may cross only in harmony with the water. The destruction is also symbolic because it is done by the forces of nature, namely huge trunks of ivy—although with their work sped up considerably by the power of Bacchus so that it takes a matter of a few moments rather than decades or centuries. And it is practical, because without the bridge the armies of the Telmarines cannot escape from the Old Narnians and flee back to their castle after losing the battle.

Another interesting step taken by Aslan is the disruption of some human institutions, specifically institutions of learning where students are taught Miraz's revisionist histories that deny the truth about old Narnia and the usurping of it by Telmarines. At the first school, a young female student named Gwendolyn enjoys a rather humorous rescue from a pompous teacher who doesn't believe in lions. Lest the reader think that Lewis is merely throwing in this scene and its criticism of teachers and the school system as a cheap and easy way to get approval from children who dislike school—C. S. Lewis himself had a rather miserable childhood experience at two different schools, and he does on a few occasions in the Narnia books criticize modern education, especially so-called experimental schools—in the next school scene it is the students and not the teacher who are the beasts; the mistress (schoolteacher) must be rescued from a bunch of piglike pupils about whom it is hinted that they are turned *into* pigs as punishment for their piggishness.[14] So in both cases of school disruption, Aslan is freeing individuals from bad teaching about nature—teaching Lewis considered both wrong and ecologically unhealthy. In these scenes, the cure for the bad teaching is brought about not just by more teaching but by practice as well: Aslan quite literally reconnects people (teachers and pupils alike) with nature.

One of the most interesting aspects of the first of the two school scenes is that, after she is rescued, Gwendolyn is freed up from some of her "unnecessary and uncomfortable clothes" so that she can take part in the merry dance of the Maenads. Reading passages like this (and others in *Perelandra* and *That Hideous Strength* to be discussed later) in which females figures are unashamedly unclothed, it is hard to accept the criticism of some that Lewis is opposed to sexuality or that he sees sexual desire as evil. Rather, there is evidence of our earlier broader point about Lewis's Christianity, which is that he was firmly opposed to any Gnostic tradition. He recognized the fundamental goodness of the physical earth, including the *pleasures* of the earth, such as that of partaking in and enjoying a good harvest. Lewis once said, "There is no good trying to be a purely spiritual creature. That is why [God] uses material things like bread and wine to put the new life into us. We may think this rather crude and unspiritual. God does not: He invented eating. He likes matter. He invented it" (*MC*, II.5). Twice in *Prince Caspian*, the followers of Aslan have a feast supplied by the Greek demigod Bacchus! The first feast comes entirely from the fruit of the vine: "really good grapes, firm and tight on the outside, but bursting into cool sweetness when you put them into your mouth" (*PC*, xi). Though the feast is provided magically, and without any portrayal of the necessary agricultural work that makes it possible, Lewis does show that the food comes from the soil. Even with this magic meal, we are ultimately dependent on the earth for our provision.

The second feast, also mysteriously supplied by Bacchus, has a much broader array of fare, including peaches, nectarines, pomegranates, pears, strawberries, and raspberries as well as cream, honey, and baked goods, and a variety of wines. Bacchus even provides the trees with a feast; since all living things have worth, and trees cannot eat the food of people or of animals, he shows the moles where to dig up various different types of dirt: rich brown loams that looked like chocolate, sweet pink earth, chalky soil that looked like cheese, and more (*PC*, xv). Of course there is far more than mere pleasure involved. In giving us this scene where all creatures partake together, Lewis suggests both the community of and the value of all living things: trees, animals, and humans, and even the river. It is a scene suggestive of the richest sort of fellowship and celebration around the bounty of creation, and what might be thought of as the simple but rich fare of agrarian life.

Return then to the fact that, although this feast celebrates the harvest and the goodness of the earth, we don't actually see any harvest; it comes by magic, without farmers having to care for the earth. We don't see what healthy agrarian practices preserve the health of the soil or water. Nor does Lewis address these concerns elsewhere in the Chronicles of Narnia (though, as we see in the next chapter on *The Magician's Nephew*, the first king of Narnia comes from an agrarian background and is told to be an agrarian king). It can certainly be perceived as a shortcoming in his work, but if so it is a shortcoming inherent in the fairy-tale genre in which Lewis was writing. Rather than criticise him for not writing a different type of book, we note only what Lewis did accomplish: he provided a vision for a healthy Narnia sharply in contrast to that of those like Miraz who seek only to exploit the earth for profit at the expense of the earth, the water, the creatures of the earth, and other humans.

A Vision of Domination?

A more troublesome point for some readers is the special place Lewis gives to humans in his world of Narnia. Early in the story, the badger Trufflehunter—one of the most noble and wise, and certainly the most loyal and faithful, of the creatures in the story—tells his fellow Old Narnians, "And we beasts remember . . . Narnia was never right except when a Son of Adam was King" (*PC*, v). If there is one nonhuman creature (other than Aslan) portrayed as even wiser than Trufflehunter, it is Glenstorm the centaur, and in the next chapter Glenstorm says much the same thing. "The time is ripe," he proclaims, in reference to the good omens they have seen in the stars. "On earth a Son of Adam has once more arisen to rule and name the creatures" (*PC*, vi). So the two wisest voices among the Old Narnians both speak of the appropriateness of humanity ruling over nature. The response the dwarf Trumpkin gives regarding this idea is the same that many environmentally minded readers—those aware of the human history of exploitation—might give. "Whistles and whirligigs! Trufflehunter. You don't mean you want to give the country to Humans?" (*PC*, v).

What Lewis's words may bring to mind is a passage in the biblical creation account in the first chapter of Genesis. "Then God said, 'Let us make man in our image, in our likeness, and let them *rule* over the fish of the sea and the birds of the air, over the livestock, over all the earth, and over all the creatures that move along the ground" (Genesis

1:28, NIV; emphasis added). The most troublesome part of this passage is the idea of humanity's rule over nature. It is a broad endorsement of rulership that includes as its subjects birds, livestock, creatures on the ground, and the very earth itself—in other words, everything under heaven. What does this mean? The older King James version of the Bible uses the word *dominion*. And this idea of "rule" or "dominion" is repeated just two verses later; after a description of God making male and female humans in his image, the passage continues, "God blessed them and said to them, 'Be fruitful and increase in number; *fill* the earth and *subdue* it. *Rule* over the fish of the sea and the birds of the air and over every living creature that moves on the ground'" (Genesis 1:28, NIV; emphasis added). Here we even have an added command to "subdue" the earth, as well as "fill" it—the later term suggesting substantial human population. Taken out of context, and with no knowledge of the meaning of the original Hebrew text, it is certainly a troublesome passage. Many believe that this Genesis passage gives humans—in Narnian language the *Sons of Adam* and *Daughters of Eve*—the sacred right to exploit the earth for whatever purposes they see fit. This view has been expressed and used as a justification for exploitive practices by some claiming to adhere to the Christian faith that Lewis held most of his adult life. This sort of exploitation has even been mistakenly called "stewardship."[15] Not surprisingly, therefore, this passage has also been referenced to blame the Judeo-Christian worldview for many of the environmental woes of the twentieth and now the twenty-first centuries. What did C. S. Lewis, perhaps the most recognizable Christian figure of the twentieth century, make of this passage and its implications to humanity's treatment of the created world?

To some degree, the answer to that question can be seen throughout Lewis's oeuvre, and is explored through this entire book. For now, we look only at one narrow aspect of that topic, which is the biblical idea of humanity's dominion over nature; much of Lewis's thinking on this topic can be seen in the Narnia stories and especially in *Prince Caspian,* in the exploration of what it means for humans to be the proper kings and queens of Narnia. Even on this narrow topic, a long history of respected biblical theology—much of it from Christian theologians—has refuted the exploitive interpretations of Genesis 1 so often discussed in the environmental literature.[16] Though, as we have noted, Lewis lived and wrote many years before the modern environmental movement, and before the recent critique of these Genesis passages by those who see the Judeo-Christian worldview as being opposed to good environmental practices—as noted in our introduction, Lewis was after all a *pre*-Lynn White Christian—Trumpkin's response suggests that Lewis was profoundly aware of the ecological issues raised by the first two chapters of Genesis, and of the possibility of such a misinterpretation. That he gives voice to this concern is at least hopeful.

The answer given by the badger to the dwarf brings us further along Lewis's thinking. "'I said nothing about that [giving the country to Humans]' answered the Badger. 'It's not Men's country (who should know that better than me?), but it's a country for a man to be King of. We badgers have long enough memories to know that'" (*PC*, v). Trufflehunter's words might not comfort critics, as he still proclaims the appropriateness of Man's kingship.[17] But it does illustrate a first principle that *authority* is not the same thing as *ownership*. Humans are meant to *rule* over nature (the creatures of Narnia including animals, trees, and rivers), but Narnia does not *belong* to humans. This is made clear at the end of the story when Aslan proclaims that "Narnia would henceforth belong to the Talking Beasts and the Dwarfs and Dryads and Fauns and other [nonhuman] creatures quite as much as to the men" (*PC*, xv). This is a vitally important environmental principle our species would do well to keep in mind.

In fact, Lewis makes it clear that the sort of kingship, or dominion, that humans ought to have (in Narnia or in our world) should be associated with *responsibilities* rather than with rights and privileges. This is perhaps the most important principle of the biblical model of dominion, and it is one illustrated in several ways in the Narnia stories. It is made clear in *The Horse and His Boy* when Shasta learns he must become king, and is told that "the King's under the law, for it's the law makes him a king. . . . For this is what it means to be a king: to be first in every desperate attack and last in every desperate retreat, and when there's hunger in the land (as must be now and then in bad years) to wear finer clothes and laugh louder over a scantier meal than any man in your land" (*HB*, xv). Shasta is called to service and also to responsibility that must not be shirked. He belongs to his land, and not the other way around. When King Caspian decides to abdicate the throne to go on a private adventure in *The Voyage for the Dawn Treader*, he hears a similar lesson from several different wise and trusted followers, most poignantly the valiant mouse Reepicheep, who might be expected to appreciate Caspian's desire for adventure. "You are the King of Narnia," the mouse tells Caspian. "You break faith with all your subjects . . . if you do not return. You shall not please yourself with adventures as if you were a private person." When Caspian is obstinate, Reepicheep reminds him, "Your Majesty promised to be good lord to the Talking Beasts of Narnia." Eventually, Reepicheep is supported by Aslan himself. A king serves his land and his people, and not vice versa. The king who follows Aslan must not use his authority for his own pleasure and gain (DT, xvi).

In fact, similar scenes can be found outlining the responsibilities of kings and queens to service in nearly every book in the series. In *The Lion, the Witch and the Wardrobe*, the reign of Peter, Susan, Edmund, and Lucy is described in terms relating even more specifically to the land: "These two Kings and Queens governed Narnia well, and long and happy was their reign. . . . And they made good laws and kept the peace and saved good trees from being unnecessarily cut down, and liberated young dwarfs and satyrs from being sent to school, and generally stopped busybodies and interferers and encouraged ordinary people who wanted to live and let live" (LWW, xvii). Part of the goodness of their reign lay in preventing trees from being cut down. Aslan's charge to King Frank (explored at the start of the next chapter) is even more specific with regard to the responsibilities (even ecological and agrarian ones) of leadership. These passages make it clear that human rulership, as Lewis understood the biblical model, ought to be healthy and humble. Good human rulers not only should work to keep peace (rather than seeking war), but should protect the land as well, including protecting forests from human exploitation. This is Lewis's image of the good life: of the happy days of Narnia and how it is supposed to be, and what it means to "govern well."

Now at this point we need to make an important note. It may seem inappropriate to suggest that the badger's words about kingship apply directly to our own world. Narnia is neither England, nor the United States, nor any other realm on earth. Indeed, this raises the broader question of applicability (ecological or otherwise) of *any* of the ideas raised in these books about Narnia; Lewis was writing a fantasy novel about a fictional world, not a tract about our world. Here, and throughout our book, we need to keep in mind that we are dealing with fiction, not essay, and not even allegory (though at points the Narnia stories do come close to accepting some allegorical interpretations). With regard to the specific issue at hand, it seems pretty clear that Lewis intended Narnia to be much less of a world for humans, and more of a land for animals, than is our world, or even than the countries of Calormen or Archenland, which exist in the same world as Narnia.

If we wanted to speak hypothetically, we might argue that while Lewis would concede that *Narnia* rightly belongs more to nonhumans than to humans—and even then it has a human king—our world does not, and so it rightfully falls even more under human dominion and acceptable exploitation by humans. However in considering this possibility, we must keep in mind that Lewis intended the *underlying* principles of his work—especially the moral, theological, and philosophical principles—to be drawn *from* and applicable *to* our world. Unlike the Middle-earth stories of J. R. R. Tolkien, five of the seven Narnia stories begin and end in our world, and all seven of them involve humans from our world. Most importantly, perhaps, in all the books except *The Last Battle*, those humans will return to our world at the end of the tale and are *meant* to bring back to our world the lessons they learn in Narnia.[18] Edmund and Eustace, in particular, return from their first trips to Narnia profoundly changed, and Eustace attributes that change to his time among Narnians (*SC*, i). Aslan often warns humans returning from Narnia to our world to continue to apply (in our world) the lessons they have learned in Narnia. (In the next chapter, we will explore more fully such an instance with Digory and Polly.) At the end of *The Silver Chair*, Aslan even comes to our world in his form as a lion. And in *The Last Battle*, the two worlds come together; the blurry line of distinction is erased altogether.

Perhaps of greatest importance, Aslan makes it clear that he himself can be known in our world, though by another name. In *The Magician's Nephew* Aslan tells the London cabby Frank, "I have known you long. Do you know me?" Frank acknowledges that he does, though he is not sure how (*MN*, xi). At the end of *The Voyage of the Dawn Treader*, Lucy sobs when she learns she must leave Narnia for the last time. "It isn't Narnia, you know," she tells Aslan. "It's *you*. We shan't meet *you* [in our own world]. And how can we live, never meeting you?" To which Aslan replies, "But you shall meet me, dear one. . . . But there I have another name. You must learn to know me by that name. This was the very reason why you were brought to Narnia, that by knowing me here for a little, you may know me better there" (*DT,* xvi). One gets the sense that in the same voice Aslan uses in speaking to Edmund and Lucy, Lewis is speaking to his readers about why *we* were brought to Narnia. So while trying to find too tight of an allegorical connection would be a mistake, so also it would be a mistake to ignore the implications and applications of the Narnia stories, including many important ecological ones.

That Lewis is giving us real principles about humans in our world—that is, about Sons of Adam and Daughters of Eve—is also suggested at Caspian's coronation toward the end of *Prince Caspian.* Aslan makes it known to Caspian that he is descended from pirates in our world. Caspian replies, "I was wishing that I came of a more honourable lineage." Aslan's next words are telling. "You come of the Lord Adam and the Lady Eve. And that is both honour enough to erect the head of the poorest beggar, and shame enough to bow the shoulders of the greatest emperor in earth. Be content" (*PC,* xv). In speaking of "honour," Aslan seems to be referring to the inherent value Lewis believed humans have as God's image bearers, and also the responsibility that goes with our dominion. Humans have tremendous power. Some have noted that humans and beavers are the only creatures that reshape the landscape around them. This is not entirely true, but there are no other creatures that can change the world so dramatically as members of our species. In particular, no other creature can do so much harm to our ecosystems. Thus in the same breath in which he speaks of honor, Aslan (and, of course, Lewis also) acknowledges our shame: we have not borne God's image well, and as a human race have not properly exercised our dominion in a way pleasing to our creator. In other words, there are morally good and morally evil ways of carrying out our authority. In a personal letter written in 1941, echoing a principle found in Narnia, Lewis makes this point explicit with respect to our world. "The robin in a cage and the over-fed Peke are both, to me, instances of the *abuse* of man's authority, tho' in different ways. I never denied that the *abuse* was common: that is why we have to make laws (and ought to make a good many more) for the protection of animals" (*L2,* 460).

Earlier we said there was responsibility implied in our dominion. But more to the point, there is moral obligation in our dominion.

To exploit other creatures is to do evil. Human dominion is a fact of our existence. We don't need a biblical creation account to tell us that humans have the power to eradicate species, or often to preserve species; to pollute rivers or clean them; to heal or to hurt; to exploit or to sustain. By pointing out human authority to rule, C. S. Lewis (or the book of Genesis) is not stating anything that is not already obvious to any observer. Aldo Leopold, in a section of the *Sand County Almanac* titled "Land Health and the A-B cleavage," writes,

> In all of these cleavages, we see repeated the same basic paradoxes: man the conqueror *versus* man the biotic citizen; science the sharpener of his sword *versus* science the searchlight on his universe; land the slave and servant *versus* land the collective organism. Robinson's injunction to Tristram may well be applied, at this juncture, to *Homo sapiens* as a species in geological time:
>
> > "Whether you will or not
> > You are a King, Tristram, for you are one
> > Of the time-tested few that leave the world,
> > When they are gone, not the same place it was.
> > Mark what you leave."

Leopold is acknowledging that whether we like the notion or not, our position vis-à-vis nature is one of royalty. We act with such sovereignty over nature that the question is not whether or not we are royalty; the question is what sort of royalty we will be. The important question about a worldview is what it *makes* of this potential. How does it say that humans *ought* to respond to their power? Lewis, writing from his Christian worldview, acknowledges the fact of human dominion, but in pointing to its source and to the divinely given responsibilities associated with that dominion he provides at least the basis for a profound environmentalism: it is an environmentalism in which human authority must be exercised in imitation of the "authority" of Christ, which was always exhibited as a humble servant of creation, rather than as a usurper or exploiter. It is a worldview that gives moral weight to proper exercise of the power that we cannot deny humans have.

Steven Bouma-Prediger's commentary on the Genesis passage could be a good summary of how Lewis also understood the biblical model of human authority, at least as it is portrayed in the Aslan-given responsibilities of the kings and queens in the Narnia stories.

> The [human] earth-creature is called to subdue and have dominion over other creatures. We are called to dominion. What does this mean? Does dominion, as is often assumed, necessarily mean domination? A larger canonical perspective sheds light on this important question. For example, Psalm 72 speaks most clearly of the ideal king—of one who rules and exercises dominion properly. The psalm unequivocally states that such a ruler executes justice for the oppressed, delivers the needy, helps the poor, and embodies righteousness in all he does. In short, the proper exercise of dominion yields shalom—the flourishing of all creation. This is a far cry from dominion as domination. And Jesus, in the Gospel accounts, defines dominion in terms clearly contrary to the way it is usually understood. For Jesus, to rule is to serve. To exercise dominion is to suffer, if necessary, for the good of the other. There is no question of domination, exploitation, misuse. Humans, therefore, are called to rule, but only if ruling is understood rightly.[19]

Missing and Misguided Belief

So far, we have written about *Prince Caspian* as if there were only *two* sets of ideals: two powers with two different visions, battling over the future of Narnia. But there are at least three significant parties vying for control, each with different beliefs, different goals, and different means. Caspian, Trufflehunter, and most of the Old Narnians are one group. They are the followers of Aslan, and work toward what Lewis portrays as a positive future for Narnia, including a good and healthy ecology. We will return in the next section to the virtues Lewis portrays throughout all the Narnia books as being in keeping with this healthy vision.

A second group we have already mentioned is composed of King Miraz and those Telmarines who share his values—the descendants of pirates who have not deviated much from their roots. For example, though the lords Glozelle and Sopespian seek to kill Miraz and thus are his *rivals,* at the core they really represent the *same* view of the world as does their king; Miraz, Glozelle, and Sopespian are all what the Old Narnians might call *un*believers, in that they deny the existence of Aslan, and of old Narnia itself. They are materialists in two senses of the word: they are metaphysical materialists who believe that the material reality is the *only* reality, and thus nothing is inherently sacred, holy, or enchanted; and they are also materialis*tic* in that they love wealth and material possessions. The two lords also show from their actions that they are usurpers just as Miraz was; if they succeed in deposing the exploiter Miraz, it will only be so that they can become the new exploiters and wielders of power. As mentioned, from this unbelief comes a denial that nature has any transcendent value, which can lead (and in many cases, such as that of Miraz, *does* lead) to a justification for the exploitation of nature. Lewis observed in a 1940 letter to his brother, Warnie, that what he called the "great rebellion" against divine grace was also a rebellion against nature (*L2,* 368).

So at one level unbelief could be seen, in C. S. Lewis's view, to be at the heart of Narnia's troubles. Too few Narnians (among men or talking beasts) still believe in Aslan, and in Aslan's father, the Creator, the Emperor-over-the-Sea. More broadly put, too few believe in the enchantment of the natural world that is Narnia. Even among those who still claim to believe in Aslan, many don't really expect him to be relevant to their current troubles; they don't expect him to come to their aid. But while Lewis was a defender of theistic faith, and of the Christian faith in particular, he certainly did not suggest that belief was an instant cure-all, nor did he associate all evils with unbelief. The dwarf Trumpkin, one of the book's heroes and most noble characters, is also an unbeliever. He believes no more in Aslan than does Miraz. He might believe in Aslan even less. Miraz's denial of Aslan is a convenient excuse to accomplish his political ends. Trumpkin's unbelief is much more honest. "I think the Horn—and that bit of broken stone over there—and your great King Peter—and your Lion Aslan—are all eggs in moonshine," he tells his companions. Nonetheless, Trumpkin behaves admirably throughout the book, with the same core values as those of the first group: he is loyal, humble, and self-sacrificial. Out of love and loyalty, he willingly goes on a quest that he thinks is part of the "moonshine." "You are my

King," he tells Caspian. "I know the difference between giving advice and taking orders. You've had my advice, and now it's time for orders" (*PC*, vii). The unbeliever Trumpkin plays a crucial role in the victory of the Old Narnians.

On the other side, there are plenty of Old Narnians who profess a belief in Aslan but don't always behave in ways consistent with that belief. Even Reepicheep, though undeniably valiant and in most ways very heroic, is portrayed in at least one instance as overly proud, and that pride is often a source of tension among the Old Narnians. "I have sometimes wondered, friend," Aslan tells the mouse at one point, "whether you do not think too much about your honour" (*PC*, xv). Put in terms of ecology, then, Lewis might be suggesting that a belief in Aslan provides a transcendent basis for morality, and more to the point of this book, for healthy environmental practices, but that many *un*believers have the same healthy practices (even if they don't share the some objective basis), while many believers (who *ought* to have healthy practices) fail to live out the principles of their belief.

There is yet a third group of Narnians, represented by the dwarf Nikabrik and some of his friends. They are not unbelievers like Miraz or Trumpkin; this third group accepts the reality of *some* sort of spiritual or supernatural realm. But they don't believe in Aslan in particular—certainly not as a divine being, the son of the Creator, the great Emperor-over-the-Sea. Nikabrik represents this third view well. "I'll believe in anyone or anything that'll batter these cursed Telmarine barbarians to pieces or drive them out of Narnia. Anyone or anything. Aslan or the White Witch, do you understand?" (*PC*, vi). What Nikabrik believes in, it seems, is magic, and magical forces: the old powers. He is looking for something practical and powerful. Later, when discussing the possibility of bringing back the White Witch, he says, "There's power, if you like. There's something practical" (*PC*, xii). Ideally, he is looking for something he can control. If we were to look for an analog in our world, Nikabrik and his friends would represent a pagan or pantheistic worldview. This, we suggest, is what Lewis had in mind.

It is interesting that Lewis partly associates the pagans with the believers in Aslan as both being among the Old Narnians. In *Prince Caspian*, they are on the same side. Or *almost* on the same side. Certainly, those like Nikabrik with *some* belief in the supernatural, the spiritual, the enchanted, are closer to the true believers in Aslan than most of those who deny the spiritual altogether. Lewis makes this point explicitly in some of his other writing, including in various personal letters. In a letter written in 1936 to Dom Bede, Lewis discusses their shared "love of inanimate nature." He comments that "a Christian can see the reason that the [Pantheistic] Romantics had in feeling a certain holiness in the wood and water." Both the Christian and the pagan, or pantheist, have a high view of nature, seeing its spiritual qualities. If you view nature as holy, Lewis would argue, then you will be far less inclined to exploit it for your own pleasure. (The same holds true of our view of other humans; when we see another person as having intrinsic worth and spiritual value, we ought to respond by loving our neighbors rather than exploiting them.) So, Lewis continues, "the Pantheistic conclusions they sometimes drew are false: but their feeling was just and we can safely allow it in ourselves now that we know the real reason" (*L2*, 177–78). This is one of the clear statements Lewis makes of the similarities between Christianity and pagan pantheism, at least as it impacts their outlook on nature, and the potential impact on any environmental ethic.

The results of this view can be seen in the strange union of Old Narnians: a union of both theists and pantheists—and, counting Trumpkin and others like him, atheists. All work together for the good and health of Narnia; all work to free the animals as well as the trees and rivers from human tyranny and oppression. This may be one reason why the demigods Bacchus and Silenus appear without apology in an essentially Christian fairy tale. They not only appear, but they appear with the blessings of Aslan and on the side of Aslan. As Lewis notes in many places, he believes there was *some* truth in the worldview they represent, and some virtue in the understanding of nature that stems from it. Even the idea that we can "safely allow" certain feelings associated with pantheism—especially feelings about the holiness of nature—as long as they are understood in the context of a true understanding of creation and the creator, appears in *Prince Caspian*.[20] About the appearance of these demigods, Susan tells her sister, "I wouldn't have felt very safe with Bacchus and all his wild girls if we'd met them without Aslan." To which Lucy responds with proper horror, "I should think not" (*PC*, xi).

Ultimately, however, Lewis felt that pantheism was incomplete or insufficient as an understanding of the world. In the previous chapter, we quoted a comment in one of Lewis's letters about nature not being evil, but simply corrupted, and "certainly" not existing merely for human benefit. This comment came in the context of another reference to Romantic Pantheism. "Romantic Pantheism has in this matter led us all up the garden path. It has taught us to regard Nature as divine. But she is a creature, and surely a creature lower than ourselves. And a fallen creature—not an evil creature but a good creature corrupted; retaining many beauties, but all tainted. And certainly not a creature made for our benefit (think of the spiral nebulae)" (*L3*, 1303). Lewis makes it clear that, while nature is holy, and of intrinsic spiritual worth, it is not something to be worshiped. In his book *Reflections on the Psalms,* he makes a similar point with respect to polytheism, arguing more strongly that a theistic rather than pantheistic or polytheistic view leads to a higher appreciation of nature.

> But of course the doctrine of Creation leaves Nature full of manifestations which show the presence of God, and created energies which serve him. . . . All this is of course in one way very close to Paganism. . . . But the difference, though subtle, is momentous, between hearing in the thunder the voice of God or the voice of a god. . . . When you hear in the thunder the voice of a god, you are stopping short, for the voice of a god is not really a voice from beyond the world, from the uncreated. By taking the god's voice away—or envisaging the god as an angel, a servant of that Other—you go further. The thunder becomes not less divine but more. By emptying Nature of divinity—or, let us say, of divinities—you may fill her with Deity, for she is now the bearer of messages. There is a sense in which Nature-worship silences her—as if a child or a savage were so impressed with the postman's uniform that he omitted to take in the letters. (*RoP,* 81–83)

In short, then, Lewis tells us we must not confuse the creator with the creation. Nature, or creation, is filled with Deity, but it is not divine. And in almost the same breath, he makes it clear that this is still no excuse for exploitation. Nature may be a creature, like ourselves, but it is not to be exploited as if it existed only for our benefit.

Other Virtues on the Voyages

We could continue the chapter in this vein, and find many of the same important ideas expressed in the next three Narnia books. Of all that C. S. Lewis accomplished in his fantastic fiction, one of the most valuable aspects for many readers is his appealing portrayal of moral virtue. "How rare," notes Dick Keyes, "are writers like C. S. Lewis whose genius as a writer of fiction lay in his ability to make moral goodness attractive and heroic."[21] As mentioned, however, this has already been well explored by other writers. We would only be rehashing old territory to repeat a list of virtues and examples of them in the Chronicles of Narnia.

What we must point out, however, is that these virtues not only have applications to ecology but also are vitally important to the practice of healthy environmentalism. Steven Bouma-Prediger concludes a short article titled "Creation Care and Character: The Nature and Necessity of the Ecological Virtues" (which does an excellent job addressing the importance and development of virtue in the context of ecology) by noting that "very little of that good work of keeping creation will be accomplished without the concrete embodiment of the virtues." And again, he states more strongly, "the good work of earthkeeping is impossible without . . . these ecological virtues, these fundamental traits of character."[22] Barbara Kingsolver writes, "The values I longed to give my children—honesty, cooperativeness, thrift, mental curiosity, physical competence—were intrinsic to my agrarian childhood, where the community organized itself around a sustained effort of meeting people's needs. These values, I knew, would not flow naturally from an aggressive consumer culture devoted to the sustained effort of inventing and engorging people's wants."[23] Not only does she wish to instill in her children the sort of virtues that will *lead to* healthy ecological practices; she also recognizes that those virtues *emerge from* healthy communities—like the agrarian community of her childhood—where they are intrinsic to the way of life.

With this in mind, at least some of the virtues modeled in Lewis's work are worth further comment with specific regard to their environmental applications. Many fans of the Narnia books (including some who share Lewis's faith) have praised the virtues espoused in his writing, but failed to *practice* them in their ecology—that is, in their treatment of creation. Ultimately, healthy environmentalism is impossible without the virtues, and the virtues are incomplete if not practiced in all areas of our lives. Since we claim this book should be practical, we briefly consider five virtues (or sets of virtues) evident in Lewis's writing and make the explicit connection to their environmental applications.

One of the first and most readily apparent virtues in Lewis's writing is *humility*. The practice of humility is especially important among those in authority. Toward the end of *Prince Caspian* Aslan approaches Caspian and asks, "Do you feel yourself sufficient to take up the Kingship of Narnia?" Caspian's response is a model of true humility. "I—I don't think I do, Sir," said Caspian. "I'm only a kid." Aslan's response shows just how indispensable this virtue is in Lewis's thinking. "Good," said Aslan. "If you had felt yourself sufficient, it would have been proof that you were not" (*PC*, xv). Without the virtue of humility, Caspian would not be fit to rule; he would not make good use of his authority. This relates to our earlier discussion. Lewis portrays it as proper that humans rule Narnia, but he also makes it clear what that rule or authority should *look* like: among other things it must involve humility, quite the opposite of the arrogance we often associate with dominion. One of the virtues discussed by Bouma-Prediger is that of respect for creation, which is rooted in, and flows naturally out of humility. "*Respect* names an understanding of and proper regard for the integrity and well-being of other creatures. A respectful person shows both esteem and deference to the other, because of the unique nature of that other."[24]

Norman Wirzba, speaking of the personal responsibility that is necessary for healthy environmental stewardship, writes: "The first requirement of such responsibility is that we give up the delusion that we live in a purely human world of our own making, give up the arrogant and naive belief that human ambition should be the sole measure of cultural success or failure."[25] Lisa Zinn, who works at the Au Sable Institute of Environmental Studies, views humility as one of the most important environmental virtues. "Humans have a tendency to think it is all about them," she says. "As long as we give in to that prideful tendency, we will be justified in exploiting nature, because we will see its existence only in terms of human usefulness. Having humility as individuals as well as a race is vitally important to environmentalism." Zinn points to *The Voyage of the Dawn Treader* as a great example; in the character of Eustace, we see first the destructive effects of egocentrism, while later, after his encounter with Aslan, we see the positive impact on the world around him of a growing humility.[26] Even Kingsolver's value of cooperation is dependent on humility. We will not cooperate with others unless we are humble about our own importance.

Lewis brings many ideas about humility together in *Mere Christianity*. In a passage simultaneously about the purpose of God becoming human, the purpose of the church, and the purpose of creation, he writes explicitly about how we ought to view nature: "It says in the Bible that the whole universe was made for Christ and that everything is to be gathered together in Him. I do not suppose any of us can understand how this will happen as regards the whole universe. We do not know what (if anything) lives in the parts of it that are millions of miles away from this Earth. Even on this Earth we do not know how it applies to things other than men. After all, that is what you would expect. We have been shown the plan only in so far as it concerns ourselves" (*MC*, IV.8). This passages suggests at least two important types of humility. One is humility about our lack of knowledge; there is much that we do not understand or know, not only about the far reaches of the universe, but also about life on the earth. Another is a sort of human existential humility; humans are not the only aspects of creation that are important to God. The implication is that God has a plan for all the universe, even though we don't know what that plan is or how it applies. Lewis goes on to mention not only "higher animals," but also "dead things and plants" among the "other things" that are part of this plan, and that will be "gathered together in Him." We should live with humility in this knowledge.

On the other side, arrogance—a lack of humility—not only is at the root of many of our environmental woes, but also is a hindrance to the solution, even among many well-intentioned individuals with a commitment to environmental causes. And here, again, we mean both the arrogance of the human race, and the arrogance of its individual members. Dale and Sandy Larsen have noted the following: "Books on ecology—from all sides—tend to induce guilt within the first three pages. They present the way things ought to be, and if you don't agree with the writers' visions of utopia, you're an enemy of the good, or at best unenlightened and in need of rehabilitation. . . . Because this arrogance is inherently human, it occurs on all sides of the debate. The same arrogance that causes the exploitation of nature thus infects the discussion of what to do to heal nature."[27] The virtue of humility so well modeled by Lewis's best characters, if practiced more widely, would go a long way to enabling our race to "heal nature."

A second virtue fundamental to all of Lewis's fiction is *community*. For some this may seem odd to list as a "virtue"; a "community" is an entity, not a virtue. Perhaps, but if so it is an entity that requires work both to form and to maintain. Indeed, community requires nearly all of the virtues. To value community, and to live in a way that builds community—which in Kingsolver's terms means to *cooperate*—can be seen as yet another vital virtue to healthy environmentalism. As is obvious to even the most casual reader of Lewis's fiction, community plays a vital role. Whenever Narnia (or any of Lewis's fictional worlds) is healthy, there is always a strong, supportive, and hospitable community. And, with the exception of a healthy community onboard ship in *The Voyage of the Dawn Treader*, the important communities are rooted to the land and the landscape and a particular area of Narnia. On the flip side, where healthy community relationships are lacking—the White Witch's castle or Miraz's court, for example[28]—the land itself is unhealthy.

Consider how many joyous scenes in the Chronicles involve a stranger being welcomed to a Narnian home, and soon afterward the whole community shows up to take part in the hospitality, which almost always involves the richness of the earth and land itself. It happens with Prince Caspian when he first escapes into the wild and is found by Trufflehunter the badger. And it is repeated several more times in the story, as he later travels from home to home to meet the other creatures of Old Narnia. In *The Horse and His Boy*, Shasta gets a glimpse of this among the Narnians in Calormen, despite the danger they are in; he enjoys it more fully when he first comes to Narnia. The first person he meets in Archenland, the Hermit of the Southern March, is hospitable to the four travelers and provides succor and healing at their moment of greatest need and vulnerability—and it might be said that (despite being a hermit) he lives in a community of sorts that includes goats, whom he calls "cousins" (*HB*, x). Even under the oppression of the White Witch in *The Lion, the Witch and the Wardrobe*, the closest we see to health and joy is in the hospitality shown by the beavers to the four children, which includes the bounty of the beaver's pond (fresh trout caught through the ice).

Many important environmental writers, especially of the agrarian strain—writers including Wendell Berry, John Elder, Aldo Leopold, Norman Wirzba, and Bill McKibben—have commented on the necessity of community, and on the intimate relationship between healthy communities and healthy land practices.[29] One of the most important principles and features of the Au Sable Institute is their commitment to community, and to carrying out their educational goals in the context of healthy community. One of their governing ideas is that "creation itself is a complex functioning whole of people, plants, animals, natural systems, physical processes, social structures, and more, all of which are sustained by God's love."[30] Bill McKibben, in his article "A Deeper Shade of Green," states in clear terms the importance of community in the context of the human impact on earth. He begins by noting that "what we really seem to want, according to the economists and psychologists conducting such research, is more community." He goes on to say that this is not only good for the human spirit—"more and more it feels like our greatest wish is for more contact with other people"—but also for the earth itself. He cites the importance of such diverse ideas as community-supported farmland and shared energy sources. "Imagine a windmill at the end of your cul-de-sac, powering the ten homes along the street. You wouldn't be generating much carbon, and you would be generating lots of companionship." He concludes by noting: "Environmentalism has often been a somewhat grim business. (There is, after all, plenty to be grim about.) But a convivial environmentalism, one that asks us to figure out what we really want out of life, offers profound possibilities. . . . We don't need to erase individualism; it is one of the glories of the American character. But environmentalists desperately need to learn how to celebrate community too."[31]

A closely related virtue is contentment. And closely related to contentment is the virtue of delight. These virtues come as a pair. For part of contentment rests in delight: the ability to take delight in what one has, rather than being envious of what one does not have, and perhaps more importantly the ability to delight in things for themselves (flowers, birds, rivers, mountains, trees, and all of creation) without having to *possess* them at all. These are virtues to the extent that one doesn't merely *feel* contentment and delight; one *chooses* them. For contentment to be a virtue, it must not be dependent upon circumstances. We have probably all witnessed situations where two different people live in similar circumstances, and one chooses contentment while the other chooses discontent. The Apostle Paul explains and models contentment as a spiritual virtue when he writes to the church at Philippi: "I have learned to be content whatever the circumstances. I know what it is to be in need, and I know what it is to have plenty. I have learned the secret of being content in any and every situation, whether well fed or hungry, whether living in plenty or in want" (Philippians 4:11–12, NIV). And another time he writes in a letter to his friend Timothy, "But godliness with contentment is great gain" (I Timothy 6:6, NIV). He wrote this while in prison, and yet he was still able to speak of his contentment. Such contentment, when practiced, is the greatest safeguard against exploitation and overconsumption.

Lewis himself took great delight in nature. As mentioned in the previous chapter, his conversion to Christianity seemed to have greatly heightened his sense of delight in creation. As Alan Jacobs notes, "Lewis himself was a man to take the greatest possible delight in the pleasures put before him."[32] In a personal letter in 1948, Lewis writes, "Nature herself bids us [rejoice], the very face of the earth being now renewed, after its own manner, at the start of Spring" (L2, 843). It is important to note that this delight is not merely present in what one might think of as spectacular scenery such as pounding oceans, or distant high peaks. It is a delight also in nature at its most plain and simple. According to Jacobs, Lewis learned something of this sort of delight from his close friend Arthur Greeves. "It was from Arthur that Jack first learned to appreciate the 'homely' as much as the dramatic landscapes of Norse myth, with their mighty mountains, deep fjords, and 'sunward-sailing cranes.' Arthur taught Jack to love the sight of a row of cabbages in a farmhouse garden."[33] Lewis learned this lesson well, and reflected on the underlying reasons, as is evident in a letter he wrote back to Arthur in 1930.

> As to the business about being "rooted" or "at home every-where," I wonder are they really the opposite, or are they the same thing. I mean, don't you enjoy the Alps more precisely because you began by first learning to love in an intimate and homely way our own hills and woods? While the mere globe-trotter, starting not from a home feeling but from a guide book's aesthetic chatter, feels *equally* at home everywhere only in the sense that he is really at home nowhere? It is just like the differ-

ence between vague general philanthropy . . . and learning first
to love your own friends and neighbours [which] makes you
more, not less, able to love the next stranger who comes along.
If a man loveth not his brother whom he hath seen—etc.[34] In
other words doesn't one get to the universal (either in people or
in inanimate nature) *thro'* the individual. (*L1,* 912)

Note how *many* virtues appear in this note, either explicitly, like *love*
and *philanthropy,* or hinted at, like *hospitality to strangers.* These many
virtues are tied together and relate to virtues of delighting in nature.
And it would seem that just as contentment stems from delight, delight
also stems from contentment: the person unable to be content with the
homeliness of his own hills and woods, Lewis suggests, cannot as fully
appreciate (delight in) the awe and splendor of the faraway Alps.

The importance of contentment to a healthy ecology is probably
seen most clearly when we examine the alternative. On the other side,
discontent and dissatisfaction are the cause for many extremes of commercialism that result in so much exploitation. In discussing some of
the roots of our environmental woes, Dale and Sandy Larsen note, "Our
economy is dependent on promising satisfaction through the purchase
of goods and services, but it is even more dependent on keeping us dissatisfied so we continue to purchase more."[35] Richard Foster makes a
similar observation: "We must clearly understand that the lust for affluence in contemporary society is psychotic. It is psychotic because it has
completely lost touch with reality. We crave things we neither need nor
enjoy. . . . Covetousness we call ambition. Hoarding we call prudence.
Greed we call industry." The consequences of our "psychotic" discontent have been disastrous to both the earth itself and the communities of humans who dwell on it. Not surprisingly, part of Foster's solution—his strategy for developing the virtue of simplicity that is a cousin
of contentment—involves taking more delight in creation. He suggests
that we "develop a deeper appreciation for the creation." He later adds,
"Get close to the earth. Walk whenever you can. Listen to the birds . . .
enjoy the texture of grass and leaves."[36]

All of which is illustrated in the Chronicles of Narnia. At the start of
The Lion, the Witch and the Wardrobe, there is at least a hint that discontent is one of the vices at the root of Edmund's problems. On their first
morning in the country, they wake to rain. While his older siblings Susan

and Peter find something to be cheerful about, Edmund grumbles, "Of course it *would* be raining!" (*LWW*, i). When he later meets the White Witch, she is able to play on this discontent. The Turkish Delight she magically provides for him acts exactly like an advertisement designed to make one discontented, and then to promise satisfaction with consumption: "Anyone who had once tasted it would want more and more of it, and would even, if they were allowed, go on eating it till they killed themselves" (*LWW*, iv). And it works. Edmund is not able to take any delight in the wonder and enchantment of Narnia when he later returns with his siblings, nor is he able to enjoy the meal with the beavers. "He had eaten his share of the dinner, but he hadn't really enjoyed it because he was thinking all the time about Turkish Delight—and there's nothing that spoils the taste of good ordinary food half so much as the memory of bad magic food" (*LWW*, ix). Or, we might say, there is nothing that ruins our delight in the world or in our possessions as a commercial reminding us of what we *don't* have.

In *The Silver Chair,* the Emerald Witch accomplishes the same thing with Jill and Eustace, telling them about all the luxuries to be found at the giant city of Harfang. And in this instance, the discontent is directly connected to nature. "Whatever the Lady had intended by telling them about Harfang, the actual effect on the children was a bad one. They could think about nothing but beds and baths and hot meals and how lovely it would be to get indoors" (*SC*, vi). What Jill and Eustace become discontented about is their time in nature. Until they meet the witch, they are able to enjoy the adventure of the outdoors: wildlife, landscapes, walking, and even the loneliness of the wilderness. After the meeting, they are no longer able to appreciate weather and scenery. And as with advertising, this is almost certainly the *intent* as well as the *effect* of the witch's words.

Lucy, in contrast to Edmund as he is at the start of *The Lion, the Witch and the Wardrobe,* delights in everything. Alan Jacobs makes the following note about Lewis's fiction: "Perhaps the greatest resource on which he draws—and it is a mighty one—is, simply, *delight.* He calls us to take note of what gives us pleasure, for though our pleasures can indeed lead us astray, they are in their proper form great gifts from God."[37] In *The Voyage of the Dawn Treader,* the ship encounters numerous dangers on its voyage to the eastern edge of the world, but its mission is never in greater danger than on Goldwater Island, when the crew is overcome by the lust for treasure—a lust so great that the heroes come near to killing one another, even though it is a treasure none of them needs, and which they had been content without before they even knew it existed. In the same book, Eustace is yet another example; after his dragon-lust turns him, quite literally, into a dragon, and he is then restored by Aslan to human form,[38] readers can witness his spiritual growth at least in part as a movement from discontent to contentment. The new Eustace summarizes the change by saying of his former self, "I was hating everything then" (*DT,* vii). As we discuss in chapter 4, one of the vices of the ape Shift that leads to the destruction of Narnia is discontent.

A fourth virtue, and one that enables us to put the previous virtues into practice, is self-discipline. Self-discipline has many sides. Its most basic characteristic is the willingness to do what one *ought* to do whether it is pleasant or not, and likewise a willingness to say "no" to one's lusts—as Caspian needed to do in the scene at the end of *The Voyage of the Dawn Treader,* when he wanted to sail off the end of the world. A related aspect of self-discipline is the willingness to do hard work, even if the results are not immediate. In short, self-discipline entails a refusal to be enslaved to one's feelings or momentary desires.

One of the opposites of self-discipline is the vice characterized by instant gratification so prevalent in modern Western culture. As should be clear by this point in the book, C. S. Lewis was not an ascetic. He did not believe pleasures were evil. But neither did he believe that we should be enslaved by pleasure. Self-discipline takes the long view: it foregoes the present pleasure for the future good. We see self-discipline in *Prince Caspian* in Lucy's willingness to follow Aslan in the middle of the night, despite the strong resistance of her siblings and her own knowledge of how unpleasant it will be to obey the lion.[39] And it is a central virtue in *The Silver Chair* that Eustace and Jill must learn on their journey north to rescue Prince Rillian. This is evident in Aslan's instructions that Jill continue to repeat the "four Signs"—that she make a practice of what is described very plainly as a self-discipline: "But first," he tells her, "remember, remember, remember the Signs. Say them to yourself when you wake in the morning and when you lie down at night, and when you wake in the middle of the night. And whatever strange things may happen to you, let nothing turn your mind from following the Signs" (*SC,* ii). But it is also necessary in their long journey across the Wild Waste Land of the North, which for two children might have felt as arduous as the journey of Sam and Frodo across Mordor in *The Lord of the Rings*. Likewise, both Archenland and Narnia are saved in *The Horse and His Boy* because of the self-discipline of the hero Shasta, who must bring warning to King Lune, even though it means leaving behind his friends and the comfort and safety of the Hermit's house and running for hours when he already *feels* completely exhausted.

When we describe self-discipline as the opposite of the instant gratification culture that prompts so much Western consumerism and consumption, it is not difficult to see that self-discipline is a vital environmental virtue. Self-discipline is also necessary for those doing the hard (and often thankless) work to heal the many hurts to nature, because in these endeavors the results are almost never immediate. In many cases, we are working not for benefits we will enjoy today or tomorrow, but for benefits to be reaped in decades, perhaps by our children or grandchildren or great-grandchildren. Sustainable agriculture is based on this sort of self-discipline. On the flip side, our refusal to take the difficult and expensive steps to reduce greenhouse gases, pollution, energy consumption, and so on, often stems from a lack of self-discipline; we are not willing to endure temporary hardship or discomfort that is necessary to stem the tide of devastating effects in years to come.

Conclusion: Love, Mercy, Grace

If self-discipline is a virtue that enables the previous virtues to be practiced (even when difficult or uncomfortable), the final three virtues are the most important, for they tie together all other virtues. They are the virtue of love and the related virtues of mercy and grace. Though we may hear these words often, these are perhaps the most foreign virtues to our modern society—a society that is usually far more concerned with rights than with responsibilities. These are the virtues that are most fundamentally unselfish: the virtues enabling us to give up our own claims, including our claims upon the earth and the things of the earth, in order to seek the good of others. The importance of these virtues to our care of creation, and to our interaction with others in community, is undeniable and clear. Fred Van Dyke, David C. Mahan, Joseph K. Sheldon, and Raymond H. Brand, in an important environmental book titled *Redeeming Creation,* comment on these as biblical virtues that contrast to Western materialism with respect to our ecology. "Indeed," they write, "the Bible has precious little to say about rights, for humans or for creation. The biblical writers were much more interested, indeed, enthralled, with other concepts, like love, mercy and grace." Interestingly, the book goes on to mention Lewis's important exploration of these virtues. "As one of C. S. Lewis's characters says in *The Great Divorce*, 'I haven't got my rights or I should not be here [in Heaven]. You will not get yours either. You'll get something far better. Never fear.'"[40]

To explore the expressions of love, mercy, and grace in Lewis's writing would require many books, but we really need look no further than the character of Aslan, who in mercy toward Edmund and love for Narnia gives up his own life to save not only Edmund but all of Narnia: its animals, trees, and rivers; the creatures who love him, and even those who don't. The vices behind the worst environmental damage—greed, lust, hoarding, selfishness—are those at the extreme opposite of love. Thus love may be the greatest environmental virtue. It is love that is most able to prompt one to act for the good of others and the good of the earth, rather than always seeking one's own benefit. Wendell Berry, in the interview with Kate Turner cited earlier, comments on Lewis's portrayal of love as a discipline and a practice, and how it contrasts sharply with modern ideas. "Well we've degraded the word *love* to mean simply feeling. Which is alright except you don't feel loving all the time, you know. And what Lewis is saying is love is a practice—it is something you *do*. Whether you feel like it or not, like milking your cows. And you understand that, well that's painful."[41]

Now, we began the sections on virtue (and this chapter as a whole) by admitting that the Narnia stories are not *explicitly* environmental in the way we usually think of environmental literature. And since Lewis himself did not make the ecological connections in his Narnian stories—though as we will see later, these aspects are more explicit in his Space Trilogy—we had to take the extra step of applying his virtues to ecology. But are all these environmental applications *really* accidental, or only incidental to Lewis? Is it really a stretch to view the Chronicles of Narnia as important contributions to environmental literature? Consider that nearly all of the stories, all of the expressions of virtue, take place in the context of a Narnian world that is a mix of wilderness and rural agrarian environment, where nature (animals, trees, and even rivers) are shown to us as having moral and spiritual worth. In shaping the imagination of his readers, Lewis thus implicitly connects the virtues to this natural environment, and also presents a picture of what a healthy Narnia looks like: it is largely wilderness, with some agrarian landscapes (albeit missing scenes of working farms), and free from the ravages of modern development, industrialization, and large-scale commercial agriculture.

Was this connection accidental? It probably was at the start. The Narnia stories began, as many biographers have told us, with an image of a faun that Lewis couldn't get out of his mind. When he began writing the stories, it is unlikely he consciously planned any "message," and certainly not an "environmental message." But consider what Lewis was already thinking many years before he began the Narnia stories. In 1945, five years before he published *The Lion, the Witch and the Wardrobe*, Lewis published a poem titled "Under Sentence" (which was later reprinted as "The Condemned"). Don King describes the perspective of the poem. "It is written from the perspective of the wild animals of England, and it more directly considers the destruction of the landscape and its creatures. Instinctively the animals shrink from human progress: 'Do not blame us too much if we, being woodland folk, / Cannot swell the rejoicing at this new world you make.'"[42] In other words, half a decade before his children's story, Lewis was giving careful consideration to human destruction of creation under the name of "progress." Moreover, he was considering this *from the point of view of animals*. He was giving voice, through poetry, to important environmental concerns, including the meaning of progress, human destruction of land, and the moral issues of harm to animals. Whatever image prompted the start of his Narnia stories, these *explicit* environmental concerns were important to Lewis, and they found their way into his story. In Trufflehunter the badger, and others, we see the same thing at work: animals giving voice to concerns over the ravage of nature at the hands of humans.

But what of the dwarfs, centaurs, fauns, and especially the naiads and dryads—the creatures of Narnia that are not human, but neither are they animals? Again, at the simplest level, Lewis was drawing liberally from the myths that had for many years stirred his imagination. He was trying to tell a good imaginative story. But evidence suggests that his thinking ran much deeper, and again that it included what we might properly acknowledge as environmental concerns. In another letter to Arthur Greeves, this one written in 1930, two decades before

Narnia, Lewis mentions an interesting conversation with his friend J. R. R. Tolkien:

> Tolkien once remarked to me that the feeling about home must have been quite different in the days when a family had fed on the produce of the same few miles of country for six generations, and that perhaps this was why they saw nymphs in the fountains and dryads in the wood—they were not mistaken for there was in a sense a *real* (not metaphorical) connection between them and the countryside. What had been earth and air & later corn, and later still bread, really was in them. We of course who live on a standardized international diet (you may have had Canadian flour, English meat, Scotch oatmeal, African oranges, & Australian wine today) are really artificial beings and have no connection (save in sentiment) with any place on earth. We are synthetic men, uprooted. The strength of the hills is not ours. (*L1*, 909)

The significance of the agrarian concerns raised in this letter is remarkable for its time, even if only intuited by Lewis without a deeper appreciation for all the subsequent ramifications. Lewis addresses here the importance of agrarian communities: he writes of eating locally, and the connection to the land that arises from this practice; he writes of the artificiality of our addiction to an "international diet"; and he suggests that for him, the presence of naiads ("nymphs in the fountain") and dryads is not irrelevant or *merely* a literary device, but is explicitly connected to these agrarian concerns. In short, he argues that books like his Narnia stories are the natural sorts of stories that we should expect from an agrarian culture, and also the type of stories that imaginatively support and uplift such a culture. If Lewis is correct, then, the Chronicles of Narnia are good environmental literature. Even if he is wrong, the passage at least suggests that he *thinks* of this sort of literature in relationship to healthy ecology.

And—as we suggest at the start of the next chapter—the case seems to grow only stronger the more deeply one reads into Lewis's fiction.

Chapter 3

The Magician's Nephew

Creation and Narnian Ecology

◓❡◖

Adam's race has done the harm; Adam's race shall help to heal
it. . . . And you, Narnians, let it be your first care to guard this
Tree, for it is your Shield.
—Aslan, in *The Magician's Nephew*

Nature is meaningful, teleological, full of design and purpose.
It is ecological, arranging a fit between organism and environment, between desire and satisfaction, between appetite and
food. "Nature makes nothing in vain."
—Peter Kreeft, *Heaven: The Heart's Deepest Longing*

Narnia as an Agrarian Kingdom

Anyone doubting that Lewis's vision for Narnia is an agrarian one need
only consider the job description for the first king of Narnia, given in
The Magician's Nephew. Even though it was the sixth book in the series
to be published, *The Magician's Nephew* is the first chronologically in
the history of Narnia, and it may have been the second one Lewis imagined.[1] It recounts the story of the creation of Narnia, and of its first
inhabitants. In chapter 11, a London hansom driver named Frank and
his wife, Nell, are called to be the first king and queen of Narnia. When
Aslan pronounces that they will be king and queen, Frank protests that
he is unfit for the job, having had no education (or "eddycation" as he
says). Aslan then describes the duties of the king and, with each one,
asks Frank if he is prepared to perform it. What are those duties? He

is to farm the land with his hands ("use a spade and plough and raise food out of the earth"); to care for the animals and not to enslave them; to teach others (his children and grandchildren, the future kings and queens) to do the same (so the agrarian tradition will pass on); not to have favorites but to treat all creatures equally; and to place himself and his own life between his subjects and whatever threatens them—that is, as "ruler" he is called to be a servant of the land of Narnia, rather than to see Narnia as though it existed to serve him. Frank is understandably surprised to hear that these are the duties of a king, but he agrees to try. "'Then,' said Aslan, 'you will have done all that a King should do'" (*MN*, xi). King Frank is to be an agrarian king over an agrarian state, in which all animals are equals, all are to care for one another, and, as we soon discover, all are to be protected by a tree.

Now Lewis could certainly have begun Narnia's history with the founding of a great city, or even with the building of Cair Paravel or some other palace or castle. He chose instead a pastoral kingdom that is to be governed with agrarian principles. This world will later develop cities, but they almost always wind up as examples of ruin and corruption.[2] The peace and goodness of Narnia are associated with nature: with woods and wilderness and mountains. "Narnia of the heathery mountains and the thymy downs, Narnia of the many rivers, the plashing glens, the mossy caverns and the deep forests," remembers the horse Bree wistfully from his captivity in Calormen (*HB*, i), while the mare Hwin speaks simply of "the woods and waters of Narnia" (*HB*, iii).

Why did Lewis do this? If we are to be true to the story and its teller, we have to admit at the beginning what Lewis himself says in the eponymous essay: "it all began with a picture." Lewis describes his storytelling as his attempt to tell the stories of the pictures that grew out of the soil of his imagination. One could argue, then, that the agrarianism of young Narnia is merely an imaginative fancy. But that argument would not stand close scrutiny. While there is certainly a romantic element to Lewis's pastoral landscapes, a close inspection of *The Magician's Nephew* and its literary genesis shows that it fits into a larger pattern of Lewis's fiction in which the creation of the world is intimately tied to care of the world, and in which justice and human flourishing are closely connected to caring for what God has created. In other words, the implications of the creation—both the means of creation and the nature of that which is created—are both important and consistent with what we read elsewhere in the works of Lewis.

Lewis's imagination gave birth to a picture of a world that most made sense with agrarian principles because they are the principles that Lewis himself valued and, to a degree, attempted to live out. This is not just a fantasy with no relevance for our world. It is worth remembering that the first king of Narnia was a cab driver from one of *our* world's largest cities. That city had demeaned him and made him feel like an underclass citizen by its systems of economics and education and privilege. Once he arrives in Narnia, he discovers that the way to greatness is not paved with cobblestones but cultivated with a spade. In rising to the throne he turns to this way of life by means he learned as a country boy. Even his voice, symbolically, becomes "more like the country voice he must have had as a boy and less like the sharp, quick voice of a cockney." This country voice is somehow "richer," just as his life lived in the agricultural landscape is richer than the one he lived in the city (*MN*, xii). In embracing that way of life again—embracing not only his new role as the agrarian king of Narnia but also the landscape itself ("If my wife was here neither of us would ever want to go back to London, I reckon," he tells Aslan, "We're both country folks really")—he becomes more fully human, more regal,[3] and more refined.

Conversely, in Lewis's fiction, contempt for creation seems to be paired with an ironic fear of death, seen especially in the proud, powerful, and sophisticated Queen Jadis who is almost the antithesis of Frank. The fear is ironic because the one who is so afraid spends her energies trying *not* to cease to be part of creation and so alienates herself from the creation and leads to its downfall. That is, this fear of death manifests itself in an attempt to gain power over creation, to dominate the world and its inhabitants. This results inevitably in the abuse of other creatures, in degradation of the land, and in the dehumanization of the one who has such contempt. Thus Lewis illustrates a point made by Peter Kreeft that the attempted "conquest of death" goes hand in hand with a "conquest of nature": "Death is nature's trump card. Until death is conquered, nature is not conquered."[4] David Orr also makes a very insightful observation on the relationship between bad ecological practices and the modern fear of death and pursuit of immortality:

No day passes without news of the decline of species, seas, forests, lakes, rivers, all spiraling downward into the destabilization of the planet's biogeochemical systems. We seem paralyzed by that fact, or perhaps strangely fascinated by it. Paradoxically, we are causing death at the largest scale possible, yet no culture has ever taken greater pains to deny mortality or spent more of its treasure to ward off the mere appearance of impending mortality. It is plausible that no previous culture has had greater difficulty coming to grips with death, our fears magnified by our technology.[5]

Orr's words could be a description of Jadis in *The Magician's Nephew*. She completely destroys the world of Charn—quite literally "causing death at the largest scale possible"—while she also takes pains to "deny mortality," eventually gaining a horrible sort of immortality by stealing and eating an apple from the walled garden in the newly created Narnia. She gains her power by magic rather than the "technology" mentioned by Orr, but as we discuss later in this chapter, and again in chapter 7, this often amounts to the same thing.

For this reason, one could argue that the essential distinction between the characters in *The Magician's Nephew* is between those who reject their place in creation (and so are alienated from the creation and from themselves even while they attempt to claim it for themselves) and those who embrace their place in creation (and so live harmoniously with creation even while becoming more human). In short, Narnia is not just a place for Narnians to live; it is medicine for our world, stooped as it is under the burden of injustice, toil, and the degradations of civilization.

Frank is, of course, a minor character in the story. But the same principles are underscored by the fact that when the protagonists Digory and Polly return to London they practice what they learned in Narnia and that makes them better people, too. But we are getting ahead of ourselves. Before we say more about the story it will be helpful to recap its main events and to draw attention to several of its important features: the relationship between worlds, the centrality and symbolic importance of trees, and first and foremost the idea of *creation*.

"Watchin' and listenin's the thing": The Creation of Narnia

Despite the title of the book, the central event of *The Magician's Nephew* is not something that the eponymous magician's nephew, Digory, *does*. The central event of the book is something Digory is privileged to *witness*, namely, the creation of Narnia. Of course this is narratively important, since it fills out the history of the land of Narnia we read about in the other six books. But it is also ideologically important, because it illustrates Lewis's understanding of what nature is—not only what Narnian nature is, but what our nature is as well. Nature, Lewis believed, is best understood as creation, as the work of a creator. We mention this briefly in the previous chapter, but it is worth exploring again in more depth—appropriately, in the context of a book about Narnia's creation—because it is a central idea to Lewis's environmental vision and plays a role in each of the subsequent chapters. Because Digory along with Polly witnesses the creation of Narnia, we witness it as well. Through a variety of characters we also are allowed to see that there are several ways of regarding creation—or of choosing not to regard it.

In his book *Reflections on the Psalms*, Lewis argues that the distinction between nature and creation is one that our age easily misses. We readily assume that all mythologies have a creation story of sorts, and we equate them all, because in all of them natural things come about by some sort of divine power. However, Lewis argues that the Jewish story of creation is unique in two important ways. The first of these has to do with the history of the Jews. Those Jews who wrote the Bible (and so who have been so influential in shaping our world of ideas) lived almost exclusively in agrarian societies and so had an agrarian view of nature. In those times, "everyone was close to the land; everyone vividly aware of our dependence on soils and weather." This means that there was no special "appreciation of nature" in their literature. "What we call 'the country' is simply the world, what water is to a fish." The Jews nevertheless brought to their poetry a perspective on nature that is not readily found elsewhere. While Homer, for instance, lauds land that is useful, the Jews, in their poetry, actually notice the soil, the weather, and their dependence on it. Moreover, this dependence becomes symbolic of their dependence on God. Lewis writes, "What [the Jews] do give us, far more sensuously and delightedly than anything I have seen in Greek, is the very feel of weather—weather seen with a real country-man's eyes, enjoyed almost as a vegetable might be supposed to enjoy it" (*RoP,* 76–77) The very fact that Lewis wrote about the importance of the agrarian tradition behind the Jewish (and so the Christian) creation story is suggestive of what he was thinking about in his own creation account. Lewis also appears to have this ideal in mind in the opening passages of *Out of the Silent Planet,* as we will see later.[6]

The second way the Jewish story of creation is unique is in under-standing the whole to have come from God. Lewis recounts in some detail other creation stories, in which the gods themselves arise out of some primordial elements. In the Jewish telling, God is the origin of the elements themselves. This fact has two consequences, seemingly at odds, but actually quite significant. The first is that "the doctrine of cre-ation in one sense empties Nature of divinity." This is because "to say that God created Nature, while it brings God and Nature into relation, also separates them. What makes and what is made must be two, not one."[7] The second consequence is that "the same doctrine which emp-ties Nature of her divinity also makes her an index, a symbol, a mani-festation of the Divine" (*RoP,* 80–81). So nature is not something to be worshipped *as* divine, and yet we must see the divine *in* nature. Philip Sherrard seems to have had something very much like this in mind in *The Rape of Man and Nature* when he wrote:

> It is now possible to see the consequence of applying the Christian understanding of the sacrament to the realm of nature as a whole. It means that nature is regarded not as something upon which God acts from without. It is regarded as something through which God expresses Himself from within. Nature, or creation (the terms are interchangeable in this context), is perceived as the self-expression of the divine, and the divine as totally present within it.[8]

This idea of seeing Nature as identical to Creation—of seeing nature not as divine, but rather seeing the divine as present within nature—has important implications and is worth exploring.

Again, Lewis saw two opposite extremes in possible philosophies of nature, and saw them both as both wrong and damaging. Lewis held that both extremes—a materialistic view on the one hand and what he called "Nature worship" on the other hand—had the equal effect of silencing Nature. The doctrine of creation, however, allows Nature to be simultaneously fully an index, a symbol, and a manifestation. We will return soon to these three aspects of Nature, and look at each in more detail. But the grand upshot of this is that all of Nature is literally signi-ficant, that is, sign-making. Nature is, for Lewis, *divine semiosis,* the signs that Deity makes in the world. Thus none of it is unimportant; none of it is to be misused or scorned. Additionally, all of it is for us, but it is for us in a particular way. Just as a love letter is not, for the one to whom it is sent, merely a paper but something with deep and rich significance, so nature is for us to be enjoyed, to be used, to be cherished and nurtured. Again, just as one's regard for a love letter is intimately tied to how one views the beloved, so our regard for nature ought to be, if we love God who made it.

Steven Bouma-Prediger, in a commentary similar to Lewis's, above, writes,

> In addition, God's creatures are valuable not because of their usefulness to humans—though some are useful, indeed essential, to us. Instead, they are valuable to each other—for example, the cedars are valuable as places for birds to nest, and the mountains are valuable as places of refuge and rest for the wild goats—and, most importantly, rocks and trees, birds and animals are valuable simply because God made them. Their value resides in their being creations of a valuing God, not in their being a means to some human end.[9]

Earlier in his book, Bouma-Prediger gives a more detailed commentary on the importance of viewing nature as creation, and lists six important lessons of the biblical creation account in Genesis. All of them have important and healthy ecological implications, and at least the first five of them can be seen clearly in Lewis's creation account of Narnia: (1) God is creator of all things; "the heavens and the earth and everything in between—all things—come to be as a result of God's creative Word and energizing spirit." (2) God gives his creatures the power and ability to assist in creation; "waters bring forth swarms of living creatures. The sun and moon rule the day and night. And humans are given the delegated, royal responsibility of ruling the earth." (3) The universe is a place of order and structure. Peter Kreeft notes in *Heaven, the Heart's Deepest Longing,* a book whose central argument was inspired by C. S. Lewis: "Nature is meaningful, teleological, full of design and purpose. It is ecological, arranging a fit between organism and environment, between desire and satisfaction, between appetite and food. 'Nature makes nothing in vain.'"[10] (4) There is a goodness to creation; "as intended by God, creation is good. Indeed it is very good. . . . We have, to use Wendell Berry's phrase, a gift of good land." (5) The earth is not merely a home for humans, but a home for all earthly creatures—and Narnia is a home not only for humans and for talking beasts, but for other animals as well. "Humans are not the only creatures blessed by God, for birds and fish are also blessed. In short, humans and animals share the same house." Bouma-Prediger summarizes these points by answering the question, Where are we? He answers: we are "in a God-wrought world . . . a responsive world . . . a world of wonders, wisely ordered by God . . . a world where peace is primordial . . . a home we share with many other creatures . . . an earth not of our own making, blessed by God."[11]

The Magician's Nephew, then, is about the *creation* of Narnia, and we are witnesses of it in order to understand how the doctrine of creation is significant for all worlds. But simply a list of principles does not do Lewis's story justice. The significance and beauty of the creation of Narnia is emphasized because we see it in contrast with two other worlds at very different times in their history: namely, the world of Charn and our own world. We see Narnia at its beginning, our own world (which the story begins in, returns to, and ends at) somewhere in the middle of its history, and the world of Charn in its final moments. Let us go through the story, and observe it, perhaps with our ecological eyes more attuned to just how rich the story is regarding our proper relationship with nature—and the results of improper relationships.

Lewis's story begins with a young boy and girl, Digory and Polly, living in late nineteenth-century London. (Digory is the boy who grows up to be the Professor Kirke of the later Narnia stories.) Digory's mother is terminally ill and living with her siblings, Digory's uncle Andrew and his aunt Letty. Andrew (the magician of the title) has inherited a box from his fairy godmother, one Mrs. Lefay. Lewis thus connects this story to the Arthurian legends through the sorceress Morgana Le Fay. (The appearance of Merlin as a character in *That Hideous Strength*, discussed in chapter 7, brings us back to this Arthurian connection.) Lefay had commanded the box be destroyed, but power-hungry Andrew kept it and learned it had come from Atlantis and contained dust from another world.

It's important to note here that the dust is not from another *planet* but from another *world*, quite apart from our universe. Lewis may have several reasons for this, but for now it is enough to say that it suggests a kind of historical continuity between our world and the worlds of myth—in this case both Atlantis and Logres—that underwrites and reinforces a kind of ethical continuity between all worlds. The myths are not just stories, but they are stories within an ethical framework that is relevant to our lives.

The soil Andrew holds is endowed with some sort of power, and his possession of this box deludes him into thinking that this power has been given to him by fate because he is fated to be a great man. He experiments with the dust, hoping to use it to acquire wealth and power and somehow to prolong his own life. Here, again, we get the connection between a desire for power over nature and power over death. It is also a connection between technology (or applied science) and magic as means to power. Regarding this connection, an observation made by Alan Jacobs about Uncle Andrew is insightful, and must be kept in mind as we continue to recount the tale: "Though Andrew is the 'magician' of the title, he is more of a mad scientist: though he has inherited rings with magical powers and knows a bit of the history of magic, he calls his work with the rings 'experiments' and speaks of 'testing' his ideas. He even has guinea pigs. This conflation of magic and science is central to Lewis's thinking. . . . His 'Model' really is, in the end, more pseudo-scientific than magical."[12] Indeed, Andrew doesn't even seem to believe in magic, and when Jadis comes to London, she sees at once that he is no magician; he is looking for a *technique* (or *techn-ology*) that will gain him power. After many experiments on guinea pigs, Andrew forms the dust into magic rings that can transport people from this world to other worlds. He tricks Polly into taking one, and then devilishly plays on Digory's sense of honor to get him to go after her and so to discover if his experiment has worked.

Digory follows Polly first to a place they dub "The Wood Between the Worlds," a glade of perfect rest, full of pools, grass, and trees. By wading into pools while touching the rings they are able to enter other worlds. They enter the world of Charn and find it dead. They awaken the one remaining inhabitant, the Empress Jadis, and she tells them she has spoken "the Deplorable Word" and so destroyed all other life in order to win a pyrrhic victory in a civil war.[13] Then Jadis forces the children to return to London with her. When she attempts to conquer our world, the children use their rings to take her back to Charn, but their plans go slightly awry: they wind up not in Charn but in primeval Narnia, and they find they have brought with them Uncle Andrew, a horse named Strawberry, and the horse's cabby, Frank.

In Narnia they watch the birth of all things as the lion Aslan sings a new world into being. During this time Jadis and Andrew are concerned only with their own safety and power. They both want to escape Narnia because they do not see anything of value for themselves there. While they are disputing with the children about the rings, Frank hushes them. "Oh, stow it, Guv'nor, do stow it," he says. "Watchin' and listening's the thing at present; not talking" (MN, ix). The beauty of the lion's song and the marvel of new life springing into being is lost on Jadis and Andrew. They do not notice any connection between the song and the emergence of plants and animals from formerly barren ground. This scene illustrates a principle suggested by T. M. Moore in his book Consider the Lilies, and again it relates to nature as creation.

> Every generation of believers in the God of the Bible has acknowledged: In the works of His hands God is revealing His glory and grandeur. Sometimes it surprises us, flaming out for an instant only to recede again into what we normally regard as the commonplace. . . . Occupied with the affairs of this world, [most people] trudge through their daily routines of trade and toil, unmindful of the glory shimmering and beckoning around them. They take the creation for granted, or even abuse it. Having shod their feet with the comforts of material existence, they surfeit themselves with an abundance of things, preferring these for their own sake alone, rather than for any firsthand experience of God revealing Himself in what He has made.[14]

It isn't clear that Frank is consciously mindful of the experience as one of "God revealing himself." But we do note that moments earlier he had been singing hymns—in fact, good agrarian harvest hymns about crops being gathered in. Readers, however, should not forget that Aslan, who later gives to Frank his charge as king, is the Narnian analog to the second person of the Holy Trinity.[15] Anyway, whether he understands it or not, Frank appreciates it. He knows that the creation—in this case creation as an ongoing activity and not as a completed fact—is something to be enjoyed. He is not, as Moore would say, "unmindful of the glory shimmering and beckoning around them." He is very mindful of it. When Polly begins to pay attention to these events, she also begins to "see the connection between the music and the things that were happening" (*MN*, ix); Narnia is being created in literal harmony. But this is a fact easily missed by those who will not listen. Jadis and Uncle Andrew are so accustomed to abusing creation, and so used to an abundance of things, that they cannot appreciate the scene.

That is, Andrew cannot appreciate it until he sees a chance for exploitation. He does becomes interested when, after Jadis throws an iron bar at the lion, the bar hits the preternaturally fecund ground and grows into a lamppost. Then he claims for himself the world he had moments before wanted only to escape. "I have discovered a world where everything is bursting with life and growth. Columbus, now, they talk about Columbus. But what was America to this? The commercial possibilities of this country are unbounded. . . . I shall be a millionaire." The only problem he foresees is the dangerous lion: "the first thing is to get that brute shot." To this Polly replies, insightfully, "You're just like the witch. . . . All you think of is killing things" (*MN*, ix). Polly is correct, of course: neither Andrew nor Jadis is concerned with the beauty of creation, with the harmony of life, or with their connection to the world. Their sole relation to the landscape is that of possessor; they want to dominate the world, or exploit it for wealth and power, and are willing to kill any part of it—or, in Jadis's case, all of it—if it will benefit them to do so.

After attacking Aslan, Jadis flees, and Digory is charged with planting a tree that will protect Narnia from her. He and Polly travel to a high-walled garden to retrieve the apple that will seed this tree. Digory is tempted to use his ring to return to London with the apple to heal his mother, but he chooses to obey the lion's orders and to do things as he has been directed, rather than in the way that seems most efficient to him. He returns and plants the tree just in time to see Frank the cabby and his wife, Nell, crowned king and queen of Narnia. Polly and Digory are then sent back to London with one of the apples from the tree. Digory's mother eats the fruit and is healed. Polly gets the remaining rings, which she and Digory bury with the apple core. A great tree grows up over the rings. Many years later, the tree falls in a storm, and Digory has it made into the wardrobe through which others later enter Narnia.

"Let your world beware": Witchcraft, Science, and the Power to Destroy

Taking our hint from the title, we return for a moment from the subject of creation to that of magic. In a personal letter, written in 1941, Lewis commented:

> The Renaissance is the golden age of magic and occultism. Modern writers who talk of "medieval superstitions" "surviving" amidst the growth of the "scientific spirit" are wide of the mark. Magic and "science" are twins *et pour cause*, for the magician and the scientist both stand together, and in contrast to the Christian, the Stoic, or the Humanist, in so far as both make Power their aim, believe Power to be attainable by a technique, and in the practice of that technique are ready to defy ordinary morality. Of course, one succeeded and the other failed: but that shd. not blind us to the strong family likeness. And that, I think, is the dark side of Renaissance Platonism. Is it not mainly through it that the occultism comes? (*L2*, 475)

Now this was a personal letter, and Lewis was perhaps not as careful with his words as he is in essays. As we hope to make clear later, and as Lewis himself seeks to make clear elsewhere, his real complaint is not with pure science, but with the application of science as a means to power: science not for the sake of knowledge, but as a technological tool for exploitation. His repeated use of the word *technique*, which shares a root with the word *technology*, suggests this. Though for many readers magic and science may seem like opposites, Lewis's point is that both magic and technology (or applied science) are means of manipulating the world around us in order to gain power over it.

This has important ecological implications. We have claimed that Lewis understood Narnian ethics and ecology to be related to ours. The story offers several illustrations of this connection between Narnia and our world. One connection is the two trees Digory plants, one in Narnia and its sibling in England. Another illustration of this connection comes in the Wood Between the Worlds—which we return to below. A third illustration of this connection comes in fairly explicit terms when Aslan returns Polly and Digory to London. Before leaving them, he gives them some direct instructions concerning the care of their own world and connecting its history and ecology to those of Charn and Narnia. The worlds of Charn, Narnia, and Tellus may be entirely different in landscape, but temptations within the worlds are the same, and Aslan warns the children of this. The temptation running throughout *The Magician's Nephew* is to attempt to dominate creation for personal gain. En route back to London, Aslan takes the children to the Wood Between the Worlds one more time. There he shows them the pool through which they had first entered Charn. The pool is completely dry. Aslan says, "There is no pool now. That world has ended, as if it had never been. Let the race of Adam and Eve take warning" (*MN*, xv).

So what exactly is Aslan warning them against? Charn was destroyed by Jadis's witchcraft. She has so completely damaged the world that "you couldn't [even] imagine anything growing in it" (*MN*, vi). When she is in Charn with the children, she demonstrates her power by uttering a word that reduces a solid door to fine dust. She later tries this in London, however, and discovers that she has no such power in our world. Her magic turns out not to be a real danger for us. The greatest magician we see in our world is Uncle Andrew, and his magic is, frankly, pathetic. Andrew's "magic," as we have seen, is really more of an applied science. If he did not have the Atlantean box of soil, he would not be able to do any magic at all.

But there is nevertheless a strong parallel between Jadis and Andrew, just as Polly notes. In simple terms, what ties them together is their rejection of creation. Both Jadis and Andrew reject the idea of their own created mortality. Both are willing to sacrifice other created beings in an attempt to make themselves immortal. And both understand their efforts to prolong their own existence as legitimated by their own status as great persons. Alan Jacobs notes about Uncle Andrew, "Certainly he lacks the stature of Jadis . . . not to mention [her] vast powers and iron resolution to undermine and destroy, but for Lewis that is not really the point. He is as evil as he can be, given his limitations of intelligence and commitment. . . . Their powers are drastically different, but their orientation to the moral law is precisely the same."[16] To put this "orientation to moral law" in an ecological context, consider the way they treat the land around them. Andrew is told to destroy the box but refuses to do so because he thinks he is above the commands of others. It is symbolically significant that what he manipulates and considers his own is *soil*. We are told that the soil has a proper place and that it wants to go back there.[17] When Andrew abuses this "desire" of the soil, he is essentially enslaving the soil, exploiting it for his own ends. Jadis, similarly, regards whatever is in her grasp as something she may destroy for her own purposes. When she finds something in her way, she does not go around it or seek ways of living in harmony with it. She simply destroys it. When the children encounter her, she is in such a hurry to go with them to a new, living world, that she destroys part of her palace in her attempt to get out.

Or consider the way they treat other creatures. Andrew experiments on animals with no regard for their welfare whatsoever. When Digory confronts him about this, Andrew replies that this is what the animals were for, since, after all, they belonged to him. He adds, "No great wisdom can be reached without sacrifice" (*MN*, ii). Of course, he does not mean real sacrifice, since it costs him nothing and the guinea pigs pay the full price for him. The consequence of this is that Andrew is willing to make even greater "sacrifices," including sacrificing both the children to satisfy his lust for power. This is a subtle and important argument. Lewis is arguing that our ideas have consequences for our character. Jadis mirrors this attitude, and magnifies it. She is an illustration of what Andrew's ideas might grow into if unchecked. When she tells the children how she has destroyed Charn, Digory asks her, "But [what about] the people. . . . All the ordinary people who'd never done you any harm. And the women, and the children, and animals." Jadis replies, "Don't you understand? . . . I was the Queen. They were all *my* people. What else were they there for but to do my will?" (*MN*, v). Both Andrew and Jadis make the same claim that what binds the rest of creation does not bind them. Andrew hides behind what sounds suspiciously like a Gnostic claim: "Men like me, who possess hidden wisdom, are freed from common rules" (*MN*, ii). Jadis makes a nearly identical claim about her status: "You must learn, child, that what would be wrong for you or for any of the common people is not wrong in a great Queen such as I" (*MN*, v). Now Andrew's mistreatment of guinea pigs may be a lower crime than Jadis's abuse of humans, to the same degree that Andrew is lower than Jadis, but both are shown to be crimes—a point made also in *The Horse and His Boy* when Aslan punishes not only Aravis for mistreatment of her servant, but also Shasta for mistreatment of a cat. And it connects Andrew's applied science, and experiments on guinea pigs for the sake of power, with Jadis's use of magic as a means of power—very effective in her world, though not in ours.

These characters who reject creation serve to give a moral lesson. Again, when Aslan returns the children to London, he tells them that what they have just witnessed has consequences for their own world. He says that Charn is gone, destroyed by the lust for power of one who was willing to wholly reject creation:

> "That world is ended, as if it had never been. Let the race of Adam and Eve take warning."
>
> "Yes, Aslan," said both the children. But Polly added, "But we're not quite as bad as that world, are we, Aslan?"
>
> "Not yet, Daughter of Eve," he said. "Not yet. But you are growing more like it. It is not certain that some wicked one of your race will not find out a secret as evil as the Deplorable Word and use it to destroy all living things. And soon, very soon, before you are an old man and an old woman, great nations in your world will be ruled by tyrants who care no more for joy and justice and mercy than the Empress Jadis. Let your world beware. That is the warning." (*MN*, xv)

Guarding This Tree—and Other Trees as Well

It could be argued that Lewis is not making an ecological point here so much as a political or theological point. We won't dispute the claim that Lewis was concerned with the spread of totalitarian states and nuclear weapons, and Lewis was a Christian apologist for much of his adult life. But it seems plain to us that for Lewis these various realms of human interest are not disparate and unrelated. We hope that by the end of this book, and especially in the last two chapters, it will become plain that Lewis understood politics, mythology, ecology, and the land to be connected to one another. Bragdon Wood in *That Hideous Strength* is perhaps the culminating illustration of this in his fiction. It is a good example in another way as well. Though we have not yet discussed it, the name of the place is enough to indicate that it is a forest. It is, in fact, a long-undisturbed forest. As we've already seen above, trees are an important symbol running throughout Lewis's narratives. Perhaps they were important to him only because he was from a green, wooded island, and they reminded him of home. But it should be further added that they were important because he attended to trees in his own life, and so were just one of many possible places he could point to in his own world of the importance of attending to creation.

When Digory puts on his ring, he is instantly transported to a wooded place, where he finds one of Andrew's guinea pigs (also wearing a ring) and Polly, asleep on the grass. What is this place that the children dub the Wood Between the Worlds? We have two clues. First, in London the children live in row houses, each sharing two walls with its neighbors. Each home has its own front door and garden, but in the attic a low crawlspace joins them. We could say that in the lower, common places, they are different, and different stories play out in those rooms. But in the highest place, they are joined together. The second clue is found in Lewis's long affinity for Platonism. Platonism suggests that this world is dependent upon another world of Ideas that are more substantive and more real than the things in this world that imitate or reflect those ideas. It seems that the Wood Between the Worlds is like the attic, and both are like a Platonic realm of Ideas, a place that is not *in* any world, but that is common to all worlds in being somehow higher than all other worlds, and the place where the ideals of those worlds are most fully instantiated.

This seems to be borne out by the fact that Jadis, when she arrives in the Wood Between the Worlds, loses all her power and nearly dies. She has paid a terrible price for her magic, she says, and the implication seems to be that she has somehow given up that which was most real in her. We are told "her mind was of a sort which cannot remember that quiet place at all, and however often you took her there, she would still know nothing about it" (*MN*, vi). This is because "[witches and wizards] are not interested in things or people unless they can use them; they are terribly practical." The Wood Between the Worlds, being a complete place, has nothing that is *useful* because there is nothing yet to be made or done there. So Jadis was unable to perceive that place at all.

If we are right in how we are characterizing this Wood, then the consequences of this characterization are fascinating. What is the Wood like? It is a place where there is no conflict, where all who enter it find rest (even Jadis finds rest, but she does not like it, since it is like death for her). But it has another important feature: it is a place of *growing things*. The narrator contrasts this place with Charn: "[Charn] was at least as quiet as the Wood Between the Worlds. But it was a different kind of quietness. The silence of the Wood had been rich and warm (you could almost hear the trees growing) and full of life. [Charn] was a dead, cold, empty silence" (*MN*, iv). In other words, the ideal toward which a world strives is rest and silence, in which growth is nevertheless manifest. The ideal, as Lewis envisions it, is the stillness of a forest. A popular (but not biblical) image of heaven is of clouds, harps, and angels, a place of quietness and no activity, pure white sterility. Lewis's suggestion is that heaven is not white, but green.

Of course, trees show up elsewhere in the narrative. The Narnians are charged to protect the tree Digory plants, and told that if they do so, the tree will in turn protect them. That is, a *tree* becomes the living, growing symbol of Aslan, Narnia's real protector. Again, in London it is another tree that Digory plants that protects our world from Andrew's evil machinations, and that apparently destroys the rings. That tree, in becoming the wardrobe, then later becomes a means for others to see Narnia.

Here we may tie together what Lewis says in his *Reflections on the Psalms* with what he says about trees in *The Magician's Nephew*. It might seem from the Narnian narrative that Lewis is urging a kind of neopagan worship of trees, but he is not. The trees are not divine, but they are symbols of divinity, as is all of creation. That means that they are for us to use, but there are also limits on the ways in which we should use them. In a word, we may use them in any way that it is fitting to use something that is a symbol of divinity. It is similar to George MacDonald's association of nature with the house of God, as we discuss in the first chapter. If this is vague, we think it is nevertheless helpful. Lewis is not here offering a set of rules about trees but a doctrine of creation that concerns trees and much more. The trees are not God, and they are not eternal. Before the end of *The Magician's Nephew* the Narnians have already made great use of trees. Some trees grew gold and silver, and the dwarfs pulled off the branches of these trees to make crowns, forming the metal in fires made from tree branches. Others have eaten fruit from trees, and trees have even been used to make a cage for Uncle Andrew to keep him from harming himself or others. But plainly there are also wrong uses of trees, just as there was a prohibition in the Garden of Eden on the use Adam and Eve could make of trees. In order to retrieve the seed for the tree he must plant, Digory must seek out a walled garden. He is told that he may enter only through the gate, and that he must not take any fruit for himself—which he is tempted to do when he smells it and sees that it might be able to heal his mother. In the garden he meets Jadis, who has eaten the fruit already. We learn that eating this fruit leads both to heart's desire and to despair. Lewis's Platonistic view, running through the whole story, is that there is a hierarchy of goods. All things are good, but not all things are good in all ways. The fruit is good, but it is harmful if it is stolen. Its virtue can be had only by those who are given the fruit.

In this regard, it is interesting to note what Lewis's friend Roger Lancelyn Green said about *The Magician's Nephew.* Lewis's biographer Walter Hooper recounts that

> When Roger Lancelyn Green visited Lewis on 14 June 1949 Lewis read aloud two chapters of a new story. This was the Lefay Fragment, as it is called, and it is about a boy named Digory who lives with his Aunt Gertrude because his parents are dead. He is able to understand what animals and trees say, and he is friends with the big Oak in his garden, and a squirrel called Pattertwig who lives there. One day the girl next door, Polly, persuades him to cut a limb off the big Oak so that they can make a raft. From that moment on he is deeply saddened because by this act he loses his ability to talk with the trees and animals.[18]

Later in the "Lefay Fragment," Digory's Aunt Gertrude says that Digory "looks 'exactly like what Adam must have looked five minutes after he'd been turned out of the Garden of Eden.'"[19] Of course, the story of Digory and Polly in *The Magician's Nephew* is different from the story in the "Lefay Fragment," but in both Digory is faced with a choice like the one Adam faced in Eden. More importantly, the fragment suggests that in its earliest genesis, the protagonist of *The Magician's Nephew* was faced with a significant moral choice, and what was at stake was his relationship with creation. When he makes a choice to use creation in a way that does not respect his connection to creation, that connection is greatly damaged. Obviously Lewis is working with the story of creation in the book of Genesis. One wonders how Christians could read that story and still not see that our ethical relationship to the trees around us is intimately connected to our relationship with the one who created those trees.

In any event, it is truly the case that for those who dwell in Narnia a tree symbolizes their security. No: it more than symbolizes it; in a real sense, it *is* their security, or at least the means by which they engage in the practices that will ensure their security. Aslan leaves them with this admonition: "And you, Narnians, let it be your first care to guard this Tree, for it is your Shield. The Witch of whom I told you has fled far away into the North of the world; she will live on there, growing stronger in dark Magic. But while that Tree flourishes she will never come down into Narnia" (*MN*, xiv).

Agrarianism and Economics

We say above that Lewis wrote that nature is "an index, a symbol, a manifestation of the Divine" (*RoP*, 81). Here Lewis uses not one but three words to try to capture what nature is for us. Semioticians tell us that an *index* is something that points to something else, like an index finger. It *indicates* something but it is not the thing it points to. A *symbol* doesn't point to another thing; it *stands for* that thing, the way the word *tree* (which doesn't look like a tree at all, and does not point to any particular tree, unless it is attached to a sign with an arrow, for instance) stands for a tree. A manifestation is neither an index nor a symbol but is the *coming-to-presence* of a thing or of qualities of a thing. When something hidden becomes public or something invisible is made visible, it is made manifest. By using all three of these words, Lewis is effectively carving out a large role for nature in our lives. Nature has a kind of voice, by which it points beyond itself to creation and the creator; nature, to some degree thus represents the creator as the visible sign and product of that creator; and nature even makes manifest certain qualities of that creator. If all this is so, then attention to nature may very well be a vehicle for the expression of piety. To put it differently, the way we relate to nature is an index, a symbol, and a manifestation of our worldview.

Frank's past and Digory's future become illustrations of the way in which our modern industrial and urban economics reflect a worldview that has departed from what Lewis takes to be ideal. "Where towns are few and very small and where nearly everyone is on the land, one is not aware of any special thing called 'the country,'" Lewis writes (*RoP*, 76). But with the advent of large cities and industrialization, there is a growing sense of alienation between people and the country. Frank the cabby is a fine illustration of this. Aslan gives Strawberry the horse the gift of speech, enabling an animal who was a "slave" (this is Lewis's word) in London to tell his own story after his emancipation. "It was a hard, cruel, country. . . . There was no grass. All hard stones." In the city, the horse is made to work in an environment that is alien to its nature. Frank the cabby shows his mettle in his response to the horse he once used to make his living: "Too true, mate, too true! . . . A 'ard world it was. I always did say those paving-stones weren't fair on any 'oss. That's Lunn'on, that is. I didn't like it no more than what you did. You were a country 'oss, and I was a country man. Used to sing in the choir, I did, down at 'ome. But there wasn't a living for me there" (*MN*, x). Frank's speech is a brief but poignant retort to the claim that industrialization is progress. For horse and human alike it has resulted not in progress but in exploitation of animal labor in unnatural circumstances, decline of culture (he no longer sings in the choir), and economic decline (Frank went from being master of his land to a landless servant in the city).

It turns out that Digory's family suffers similarly. In the final chapter it is revealed that the reason he is living in a row house with his aunt and uncle and invalid mother is that his father is away in India trying to make enough money to support his family. Digory's and Frank's families are thus early sufferers of the ill effects of industrialization and globalization. They are alienated from the land, from animals, and from one another, in a culture that is showing signs of losing its social cohesion. In a sense, the whole city of London is living like the boy Digory in the "Lefay Fragment"—alienated from the nature that ought to be its friend and its security. Frank and Nell are fortunate enough to be given a new life in Narnia, where they will be able to renew their bonds with the land. Digory is "saved" from his city life as well (as is Polly, through him) but only because Digory's great uncle dies and leaves Digory's family enough money to move to the country. While this is, on the one hand, a fairy-tale perfect ending, it is at the same time a wistful one, since in order for this ending to come about, someone has to die, and then there must be great wealth. This is good news for the heir, but not for the one who dies, nor for the many who have no such hope. Is the ideal of creation only available to the wealthy?

No Mousetraps! Animals as Moral Agents and as Moral Patients

Walter Hooper has commented that most of what Lewis had to say about the Narnia stories can be found in his *Letters to Children*.[20] In addition to Lewis's comments about Narnia, the letters also offer insight into how Lewis viewed animals. Perhaps writing to children brought out an avuncular awkwardness that led him to resort to talking of animals in search of some common ground with children, or perhaps he simply thought children would understand his connection to animals better than would his adult correspondents. In his letters, Lewis frequently mentions the animals living with him and his brother at The Kilns, their home near Oxford. At various times, he speaks of having geese, chickens, a dog, a kitten, and mice (cf. *LC*, 66). He peppers his pages with his observations about the changes of seasons and their effects on local plants and animals in a way that shows that they all really matter to him. When he mentions animals, whether wild or tame, he nearly always speaks of them with noticeable affection. In several letters he mentions to various children how proud he was of the kitten, who, though small, had successfully defended her territory against several larger neighborhood dogs. In another letter he laments the loss of a goose to a local fox.

Perhaps most striking in these letters are his mentions of mice. "I love real mice. There are lots in my rooms in College but I have never set a trap. When I sit up late they poke their heads out from behind the curtains just as if they were saying, 'Hi! Time for *you* to go to bed. We want to come out and play'" (*LC*, 32). Again, there is in this letter—at least in the wording of it—probably some amount of romantic thinking, and perhaps just a response to a perceived cuteness. Yet, as we've seen elsewhere in this book, Lewis wrote enough about ethical treatment of animals, as part of human responsibility to care for creation, that this comment about mice also almost certainly reflects more serious think-ing on his part. (Think of Shasta's punishment for mistreatment of a cat.) Whether Lewis thought of dumb animals as capable of intelligent communication and moral decision making is dubious. It seems likely that he did not, since even in his imaginative worlds he distinguishes between talking or rational animals and those that do not have speech. Those that have speech are certainly moral agents, and it is these that King Frank is commanded to treat as equals. On the other hand, it's not quite plain that Lewis drew this dividing line between rational and speechless animals too sharply. Rather, throughout his books Lewis suggests that it is the obligation of those animals that have greater intel-lectual power—like humans—not only to care for those that have less, but even to try to teach and improve them. Notice again that one of the obligations laid on King Frank is *education*. Lewis plainly does not mean that Frank is to become a professor or a teacher in our usual sense. Frank has confessed he has no formal education himself and is unfit for such work. But we also see that Frank has learned a kind of *moral sym-pathy* for animals through his rural lessons in husbandry and his urban work as a cab driver. It is through this moral sympathy that both Frank and the animals in his care are improved.

So when Aslan sets aside some of the dumb animals to give them the gift of speech, he is not only making new species; arguably, he is also setting an example that is to be imitated, however feebly, by Frank and Helen and their progeny.

This peculiar privilege suggests its opposite danger, however. Just as it is possible in Narnia for the animals to grow wiser, so it is possible for the humans to grow less wise. Lewis wrote to one of his young cor-respondents about one of the Narnian mice, Reepicheep, and one of the dwarfs, Nick-a-brick: "Anyone in our world who devotes his whole life to seeking Heaven will be like R[eepicheep], and anyone who wants some worldly thing so badly that he is ready to use wicked means to get it will be likely to behave like N[ick-a-brick]" (*LC*, 45). Reepicheep the mouse is, in a way, a symbol of moral excellence. He is, by the way, also a striking example of one who loves creation. There is nothing in all of Narnian creation from which Reepicheep will shrink back. He is given to much pride, true, but his pride rises up from the deep well of his love even for his own body and for his people. In the end, his full embracing of his mortality and his full love for both the creation and the creator give him courage to explore the very limits of created being. A little mouse, through his great love, courage, and curiosity (all of which are moral sentiments, after all) does something so great no Narnian before him has done it. He willingly gives up his own life so that he might see even more of what has been created.

On the other hand we have the dwarf Nick-a-brick, who is nearly human in form but whose fear of death—and through his fear his rejection of his mortality—leads him to shameful betrayal of his fellow creatures. Here it is; here is the great danger: when we reject our place in the world, including our own mortality, something else suffers for it. In *The Magician's Nephew* we see this contrast in the difference between Digory and his uncle Andrew. Andrew's fear and loathing of animals leads to the dehumanization of the one who contemns, and also to his or her alienation from that which he or she most desires.

Andrew's guinea pigs provide a good example of what we mean here. Andrew continues to experiment on them even after he sees plainly that some of them are dying violent deaths. There is an interesting dialogue in which the ownership and care of animals is dealt with. Digory and Andrew both owned guinea pigs, but their ownership is of two entirely different types. One is characterized by care (Digory's) and the other by material possession and domination. Andrew says to Digory,

> "My earlier experiments were all failures. I tried them on guinea-pigs. Some of them only died. Some exploded like little bombs—"
>
> "It was a jolly cruel thing to do," said Digory who had once had a guinea-pig of his own.
>
> "How do you keep getting off the point!" said Uncle Andrew. "That's what the creatures were for. I'd bought them myself." (*MN*, ii)

Digory's care for one animal winds up having the effect of giving him sympathy toward all animals. By contrast, Andrew's abuse of one animal hardens him toward regarding the animals as moral patients at all. They are inert tools to him, his possessions to be used in whatever manner he sees fit. "That's what the creatures were for. I'd bought them myself," he says, as though the economic exchange freed him from any further moral obligation to the animals. When Digory objects further, Andrew retorts, "Bless my soul, you'll be telling me next that I ought to have asked the guinea-pigs' permission before I used *them!* No great wisdom can be reached without sacrifice" (*MN,* ii).

Lewis is drawing a middle position between those who argue that animals are entirely at our disposal and those who argue that animals are not at all ours to possess or to use. The principle seems to be that we may in fact possess and even make certain use of animals, but that relationship must be one of mutual benefit. Andrew is nevertheless convinced that animals cannot be moral agents. He is so convinced of this that he is unable to hear it when they speak. This leads to an interesting inversion wherein the animals are both more moral and more intelligent than he. The narrator comments, "Now the trouble about trying to make yourself stupider than you really are is that you very often succeed" (*MN,* x). This is an epistemological point that is important to keep in mind. Lewis is sometimes thought of as a dogmatist, but he is pointing out that there is often dogmatism of another kind in discussions about nature.

Again, this seems to relate to a deeper question of how we view nature, with obvious implications as to how we *treat* nature. Peter Kreeft, speaking of the worldview held by both Lewis and Tolkien, writes,

> Ever since Descartes, the Western mind has separated matter and spirit, body and soul, physical and spiritual, as two 'clear and distinct ideas' that have nothing in common. Matter takes up space and does not think; mind thinks and does not take up space. But before Descartes it was not so. The distinction was there, but not total. There was an in-between category, *life,* which Descartes eliminated. (He thought of even an animal as a complicated machine.)

Kreeft goes on to describe what (for the "modern man") are the "killers of this old cosmology," which did allow this intermediate category and the less clear distinctions. "One of them, of course, is materialism. Another is Cartesian dualism, which sells out half the world—everything made of matter—to materialism, reducing everything except mind and spirit to passivity and mechanism."[21] Now if one views an animal as merely a machine, or mechanism—as Kreeft suggests that much of the modern Western world does, whether consciously or not—without any deeper sense of underlying *life*, it becomes easier to justify tinkering with that machine, or even dismantling it. For whereas something alive can be killed, machines are not killed but merely taken apart, or turned off.

What Lewis and Tolkien do in their tales, as Kreeft points out, is "restore the ancient, pre-Cartesian cosmology in which things are not that neat. Even inorganic things like mountains are alive; the distinction between trees and Ents (thinking, treelike tree herders) is not absolute; and in general the whole world of things is more personlike, mindlike, spiritlike, than in the Cartesian machine-universe." Consider the naiads who inhabit the rivers of Narnia, or the dryads of the trees. They are "more personlike, mindlike, spiritlike."[22] In Lewis's Narnia, even the stars are personlike—indeed, they are persons! The first voices to join Aslan in his singing are the voices of stars. "The new stars and the new voices began at exactly the same time. If you had seen and heard it, as Digory did, you would have felt quite certain that it was the stars themselves who were singing, and that it was the First Voice [Aslan], the deep one, which had made them appear and made them sing" (*MN*, viii). The cosmology Lewis affirms is one that posits life and meaning in every part of the cosmos. Not only all living creatures but all *things* take part in this great song—because in this cosmology of Plenitude, the reductionist distinction between living creatures and inanimate things is blurred into a community of created things, each one with a part to sing in the celestial and cosmic chorus.

The contrast between this cosmology and a more modern and more reductionist one, as it pertains to the stars, is drawn out even more in *The Voyage of the Dawn Treader*. When Eustace meets Ramandu, a retired star, he comments, "In our world, a star is a huge ball of flaming gas." Ramandu replies, "Even in your world, my son, that is not what a star is but only what it is made of" (*DT*, xiv). To put all this in practical terms, and to move from the celestial to the earthbound, or from stars back to guinea pigs, to exploit nature or creation is to exploit fellow voices in the singing of this song: a song in the Narnian world that the stars are singing alongside Aslan.

Lewis shows the consequences of Andrew's decisions in the formation of his character and the actions that result from that character. Two points stand out: first, what he does to the guinea pigs leads to similar actions toward humans. After trying his experiments unsuccessfully on the guinea pigs he then experiments on children. His inflated sense of his own importance convinces him he has permission to do this. What we see here is that in making himself out to be so important that he deserves the sacrifices of others, he has only alienated himself from the very nature he wishes to remain in eternally. He is afraid of death, so he tries to become immortal, that is, someone who will dwell in the world forever; his quest for immortality, however, demands the destruction of the world's inhabitants. By trying to enjoy the world unnaturally he winds up destroying it and therefore alienating himself from it. This alienation is the second consequence, and it is illustrated in his inability (or unwillingness) to recognize that the animals have become intelligent at the end of the book. They try to speak to him and he cannot understand them because he clings more to the presupposition of his own superior intelligence than to what he can plainly see. He alone can be intelligent, he believes; therefore, if animals seem to be intelligent this must be a misperception. He needs the animals to be lower so he can feel higher. "He had never liked animals at the best of times, being usually rather afraid of them; and of course years of doing cruel experiments on animals had made him hate and fear them far more" (*MN*, x). Ironically, this winds up making him further alienated from the animals and, even more ironically, stupider.

This is the irony that Lewis points to in his essay "First and Second Things," and in that essay he makes our relationships with animals one of his key examples: "By valuing too highly a real but subordinate good" (Andrew's desire for immortality and his desire for power may be understood as good things desired in the wrong way),[23]

> we . . . come near to losing that good itself. . . . The woman who makes a dog the centre of her life loses, in the end, not only her human usefulness and dignity but even the proper pleasure of dog-keeping. . . . . Of course this law has been discovered before, but it will stand re-discovery. It may be stated as follows: every preference of a small good to a great, or a partial good to a total good, involves the loss of the small or partial good for which the sacrifice was made. . . . You can't get second things by putting them first; you can get second things only by putting first things first.[24]

This may be a helpful rule not only for thinking about relations with humans and companion species, but also for thinking about a Christian ecology:[25] we cannot achieve temporal goods, which are secondary to eternal goods, without placing the eternal goods first. This rules out making ecological work our sole and only objective. Both the person who wantonly destroys animals and the person who invests everything in loving an animal (thus making it a sort of idol) wind up becoming less human and losing the possibility of attaining that which they most want. But this principle also does not mean that we ignore the temporal goods of striving for healthy ecological outcomes. What it does mean is that our ecological efforts find their proper place in the context of creation and its creator. We can and should revere the creation as the product of the creator. We do not revere it *instead* of the creator, but *because* of the creator. We do not mistake it for something eternal, and so try to make it last forever. Rather, we attempt to help it to thrive to the best of our ability because we recognize it as a gift of the best sort and so see that it is to be preserved. In this way, the stewardship and care of creation—a "second thing"—receives its proper place and its best care precisely because of its relation to the "first thing," that is, the Creator and Giver.

So there are two false moves to avoid: on the one hand, making animals out to be mere property, as Uncle Andrew and Jadis attempt to do, and on the other hand, divinizing the animals, as does "the woman who makes the dog the centre of her life." How then does Lewis suggest we view animals? Lewis makes two points: first, the gift of rationality (evidenced by speech) comes with the responsibility to treat other creatures gently and kindly. Second, possession is the wrong term to describe the relationship between humans and animals. Failure to acknowledge these two points demeans both rational and nonrational animals.

Once Narnia has been sung into creation, Aslan gathers the animals and gives some of them the gift of speech. When he does so, their sizes change slightly so that all of them more approximate to one another: the elephant shrinks and the mouse grows. Otherwise they retain all their distinctive features. This physical metamorphosis illustrates the idea that rationality transcends physical bodies, and that kinship is not just with those who look like us. Aslan then speaks to the animals, saying, "Creatures, I give you yourselves. . . . I give you forever the woods, the fruits, the rivers. I give you the stars and I give you myself. The

Dumb Beasts whom I have not chosen are yours also. Treat them gently and cherish them but do not go back to their ways lest you cease to be Talking Beasts" (*MN*, x). These animals who are capable of speech are therefore capable of receiving commands; rationality entails responsibility. The chief command is to be good stewards of what they have been given, including themselves, the land, and the other animals.

But there is a catch: responsibility entails consequences. If the rational animals are unkind to the Dumb Beasts, they will themselves become Dumb Beasts. Lewis intends this, once again, as a lesson for humans from our world, not just for Narnia. Uncle Andrew's horror of seeing all these animals roaming free causes him to think of them only as threats. The end result is that the animals are able to speak, but he is not. Their roles are completely reversed. Just as the Digory of the "Lefay Fragment" loses his ability to commune with the plants and animals, so the learned magician is reduced to a Dumb Beast through his unwillingness to be in relation with the animals.

There is another way in which this lesson has some traction beyond Narnia's borders. It is easy to see why talking beasts in Narnia should receive special treatment, but we have no talking beasts, so why should we care how we treat our animals? Lewis's reply to this is that first, we are wrong to think of the animals around us as our possessions, and second, that the command to improve the animals around us is one of the ethical principles that applies to all worlds. We return to this issue of improving animals in our chapter on *Perelandra*. The evidence that we are not to think of animals as our possessions comes in a single but powerful word. When the narrator describes what Strawberry was in London, he calls him this: a *slave*. There can be no positive spin on this. Frank the cabby treated him well, but the tone of that word is unadulterated disapprobation. What is more, it is the same word that Jadis uses to describe the people she willingly slaughtered. Lewis's point—one that comes up in the previous chapter as well—is this: the way we treat animals will be reflected in the way we treat people; there is not such a great distinction between us as we might like to imagine. We are all part of God's creation, and we all flourish or suffer together.

Morality and Mortality: The World Is Not Eternal

We say at the beginning of this chapter that the essential difference between characters in *The Magician's Nephew* may be seen in whether or not any given character is willing to acknowledge his or her place in creation. Acknowledging creation (rather than mere "nature") provides us with a way of understanding our very intimate relationship with our environment, while allowing us both to admire the harmonious and even divine qualities of nature, and without diminishing human importance. In nature, there is always the question of what matters most: people and our benefit or the environment and its benefit. In creation, the two are inseparable from each other.

Jadis and Andrew both acknowledge at separate times that they have paid a terrible price for their "wisdom," but neither seems to see how terrible a price it is. Their wisdom has been the single-minded quest to gain power for themselves and so to conquer death on their own. By giving themselves wholly to this quest, they unwittingly make death the defining characteristic of their lives. Furthermore, by trying so hard not to die, they miss the fact that living (that is, not dying) means continuing to be part of a flourishing creation. Both of them are ironically willing to sacrifice the flourishing creation in order to preserve their own lives—but for what? If nature is wiped out through Jadis's Deplorable Word or through whatever it is that Aslan warns Polly and Digory about—the destruction of our own nature through powerful technologies, perhaps?—will there be anything left worth living for? Jadis's one hope after ruining Charn is to escape Charn and find a new world to conquer. Jadis and Andrew attempt to secure for themselves the dominion they desire, and in so doing, lose the very things they most want and need.

Digory and Frank provide us with another way of viewing this world. When they arrive in Narnia, Frank placidly acknowledges that "if we're dead—which I don't deny it might be—well, you got to remember that worse things happen at sea and a chap's got to die sometime. And there ain't nothing to be afraid of if a chap's led a decent life" (*MN*, viii). Frank is not interested in conquest over death, nor over nature. Digory, like the Narnians, must become a planter of trees in order to care for his mother and for his world. When he plants the first tree, he cannot see the good that will come of it. He only knows that he has been commanded to do it. He chooses to recognize that as a part of creation he cannot see the whole, and he trusts that the creator sees better than he. He must give up his immediate desire and see himself as part of a bigger plan. He gives up his power to steal the apple and heal his mother. In so doing, he winds up protecting Narnia, defeating Andrew and Jadis (at least for a while), and securing his mother's health.

The ironic upshot of this is that self-interest involves accepting one's mortality. The most beneficial thing one can do for oneself is not try to gain dominion over all creation but to acknowledge one's place in it. By caring for the Tree, the Tree cares for Narnia; by doing the will of Aslan, Digory receives his greatest desire.

Lewis is not aiming at mere utility, however. Ultimately, what drives Digory to obey Aslan is something not-quite-spoken in Aslan himself. His willingness to listen to Aslan makes Aslan clearer to him. When he chooses to obey Aslan, he sees Aslan's sorrow over his mother. Aslan sheds tears for her, and "they were such big, bright tears compared with Digory's own that for a moment he felt as if the Lion must really be sorrier about his Mother than he was himself" (*MN*, xi). In the end, Digory's actions are not driven by self-interested pragmatic decisions but by love. Good ecology—in Narnia as in all the other worlds connected by the Wood Between the Worlds—is a form of piety.

One more thing needs to be said about *The Magician's Nephew*. When Digory, Polly, and the others first arrive in dark, featureless pre-Narnia, Frank's response is to sing a hymn. Significantly, as we note, the hymn he sings is a harvest thanksgiving hymn—a surprising choice in a place that has never before borne crops. What is also surprising is that Frank's song is the first one sung in Narnia—even before Aslan sings. When he finishes, Aslan's song begins. Is Lewis suggesting that God's creation grows in response to our worship? That thankfulness and reverence beget or invoke a healthy ecology? The only response the text suggests is another that makes it plain that these Narnia stories are more about us than about Narnia. Digory, a descendent of Adam, has brought the first evil into Narnia by bringing Jadis there. Aslan's solution is to make Digory into a planter of trees. Aslan seems to think that there is reason to hope that humans can learn good ecology that will, at least for a while, undo some of the harm we have done. Or, as Aslan puts it, "Adam's race has done the harm; Adam's race shall help to heal it" (*MN*, xi).

Chapter 4

The Last Battle and the End of Narnia

"Woe, woe, woe!" called the voice. "Woe for my brothers and sisters! Woe for the holy trees! The woods are laid waste. The axe is loosed against us. We are being felled. Great trees are falling, falling, falling."
—A dryad, in *The Last Battle*

The planet itself [is] at stake—and not from a possible scenario, like nuclear war, but from the consumption of the coal and oil and gas that power most of the actions of our lives.
—Bill McKibben, "A Deeper Shade of Green"

The Last Battle, the final book of the Chronicles of Narnia, begins with the ominous phrase, "In the last days of Narnia . . ." It ends with the great heroes of all seven books entering a heavenly paradise. For some, the most important environmental critique (or condemnation) of Christianity relates to the belief in heaven and the end of the earth. If one believes nature is only temporary, why not exploit it? If heaven is all that matters, why not do to the earth whatever we want? These questions have particular force if one's view of heaven is ethereal—that is, if heaven is imagined as a place of disembodied spirits hovering on clouds (and playing harps).

To fully understand the environmental implications of Lewis's worldview, therefore, it is important to see something of his *eschatology*: his view of the "last days" of earth, and of the possibility of a heaven that might follow. Not surprisingly, given its title and opening line, of the ten works of fantasy we explore, *The Last Battle* is the most important in understanding Lewis's eschatology. But it is important for many other reasons as well. Of the seven Narnia books, it contains the most complete portrayal of many of the environmental themes we discuss in the previous two chapters. Perhaps, as the last book to be written in the series, it represents Lewis's most mature and developed thinking.[1] Thus before we turn to the unique focus of this chapter, namely Lewis's view of heaven and of the earth's end times, we look first at a number of other themes we have already addressed in the previous two chapters, and see how they are further illustrated in the final book.

Wilderness, Stewardship, and the Sacredness of Nature

Lewis continues in *The Last Battle* to provide a positive portrayal of wilderness. The book starts in, and largely takes place in or on the edge of, wilderness. There are no cities, nor even any populated settlements visited in the tale. It is also the only Narnia book that does not bring us to any castles or palaces; the closest the readers come to a castle in *The Last Battle* is a sort of tower outpost, but it is unoccupied.[2] The scene of the first chapter is a pool near a waterfall on the very edge of the wild, to the west of Lantern Waste. "There were very few Talking Beasts or Men or Dwarfs, or people of any sort, in that part of the wood." And the sense of wildness increases with the description of how the "great waterfall pours down . . . with a noise like everlasting thunder . . . swollen with all the snow that has melted off the mountains from up beyond Narnia in the Western Wild" (*LB*, i).

The remainder of the story takes place within a few miles of the stable, which is not far from the king's simple lodge on the "Eastern end of Lantern Waste." There is a hint of nearby agrarian settlement in the mention of markets, and the aforementioned stable suggests some sort of a farm, but there is little more than these hints. More important to the setting is a forest, later described as having a "thick wood" that comes right down to the water's edge (*LB*, ii). It is a beautiful wilderness—or it would be if it were not for the evil that takes place there—and Lewis's narrator pauses now and then to give the reader a sense of its beauty. In one passage, the children delight in their appreciation of nature: "The sun had risen, dewdrops were twinkling on every branch, and birds were singing" (*LB*, v). In another, the details of flora and fauna are more specific. "The young leaves seemed to be much further out than yesterday: the snowdrops were over, but they saw several primroses. The sunlight slanted through the trees, birds sang, and always (though usually out of sight) there was the noise of running water. . . . The Children felt, 'This is really Narnia at last'" (*LB*, viii). The beauty of the wilderness heightens our later sense of loss at its destruction.

Wild nature also has another effect upon Eustace and Jill, the two human characters who come from our world. King Tirian, we are told, "was surprised at the strength of both the children: in fact they both seemed to be already much stronger and bigger and more grown-up than they had been when he first met them a few hours ago. It is one of the effects which Narnian air often has on visitors from our world" (*LB*, vi). Both *Prince Caspian* and *The Voyage of the Dawn Treader* mention a similar effect upon the Pevensie children. We should not make too much of this; on the surface, it may be only a narrative device, or a statement about the specific *magic* of Narnia. Note, however, that the experience of wilderness (more than just the magic of Narnian air in general) is also shown to be valuable to those characters who are not from our world. That is, even within Narnia and its world, wilderness has particular meaning and value; it is rejuvenating to humanity, and thus worth preserving for this reason even if for no others. When King Tirian first appears at the start of the second chapter, he is spending ten days on a hunting holiday in this wilderness, living in the simplicity of a "low, thatched building" near the confluence of a pair of rivers, apparently apart from any other humans. "He loved to live there simply and at ease, away from the state and pomp of Cair Paravel, the royal city" (*LB*, ii). This statement tells us not only about the setting of the story, but also about the character of the king; one of the tale's heroes, he prefers a life of simplicity over one of pomp. Though Lewis preceded modern concepts such as *environmental footprint*, and he may not have been consciously reflecting on the fact that a life of simplicity places far fewer demands on the earth than a life of excess, it is nonetheless worth noting that time and again his heroes model the virtue of simplicity.

Lewis also continues to enchant nature in this book as in the previous six. We read, for example, that the forest near where our story takes place is in the heart of "that ancient forest—that forest where the trees of gold and of silver had once grown where a child from our world had once planted the Tree of Protection" (*LB*, ii). Thus the forest is not *merely* a forest, but a forest rooted in history, and a forest that is full of enchantment: a forest that once provided protection for all of Narnia, as readers learn in *The Magician's Nephew*. As such, the forest is more than enchanted; it is sacred. It is a forest hallowed by Aslan himself, for the purpose of protecting Narnia from the evil of the White Witch. (As noted before, to C. S. Lewis a tree is never merely a tree.) We are reminded again of Philip Sherrard's *The Rape of Man and Nature*, and the importance of seeing nature as sacred—a view that for Lewis was an implication of his Christian faith, though a view he also saw as compatible with paganism and other religions. In *The Last Battle*, Lewis demonstrates vividly what happens to nature when it is no longer seen as sacred.

We will return later to this *dis*-enchantment and *de*-sanctification of nature. For now, we observe that it is not only trees that are sacred. The plot of *The Last Battle* centers on a scheme by the ape Shift to gain power by impersonating the lion Aslan. This is accomplished by placing an old lionskin on the donkey Puzzle. When Shift first suggests his plan to Puzzle, the donkey objects, saying, "I mean, aren't all lions rather— well, rather solemn. Because of you know Who. Don't you see?" Puzzle is referring to Aslan, of course. A short time later, when Shift continues to urge him to don the skin, Puzzle repeats his objection. "I don't think it would be respectful to the Great Lion, to Aslan himself, if an ass like me went about dressed up in a lionskin" (*LB*, i). Out of respect for Aslan, the donkey is urging solemnity and respect for the skin of a dead lion. The implication is that because Aslan is holy and sacred, therefore all lions have an element of sacredness.

Lewis would carry one specific aspect of that argument into our world. Or, rather, he is illustrating in Narnia a principle he held true in our world: humans are holy to God not only because we were created in the image of God, but also because Jesus came to earth incarnate in human form. Thus it is wrong not only to murder, but even to curse other men, as James points out in his epistle. "With the tongue we praise our Lord and Father, and with it we curse men, who have been made in God's likeness. . . . My brothers, this should not be" (James 3:9–10, NIV). Even if not suggested by Puzzle's words, the idea is much broader and relates to comments made earlier about George MacDonald's view of nature: when God took on physical flesh and lived, breathed, and dwelt on earth, he gave testimony to the sacredness of the earth itself;

the earth is not only the dwelling place of humanity, but the dwelling place of God incarnate, literally God's house. As noted earlier, Jesus' first recorded miracle was changing water into wine to help celebrate a wedding. Both the fruit of the vine and the very fruitfulness of the earth, represented in the union of male and female, are sanctified in this miracle.

Now one possibly troublesome aspect of the Narnia books already mentioned earlier is that Lewis gives a special place to the Talking Beasts of Narnia, and lesser importance to other (nontalking) animals who are referred to with phrases such as "poor witless beasts." King Tirian is portrayed as both humble and heroic. Though in one instance with disastrous consequences he forsakes wisdom and acts rashly, in every other way he is a virtuous hero; he models the principles discussed in chapter 2, showing that kingship implies not rights and privileges, but responsibilities. When some of the smaller animals are in danger for trying to help him, he tells them with all sincerity, "Leave me at once, dear Beasts. I would not for all of Narnia bring any of you into danger." Their lives are more dear to him than his own. This attitude is illustrated even more poignantly later, when in anguish he cries out to Aslan, "Let *me* be killed. I ask nothing for myself. But come and save all Narnia" (*LB,* iv). As a good king and representative of humanity, he understands that *all Narnia*—a phrase suggesting the land itself as well as its other inhabitants—is his highest responsibility, and its well-being is his greatest desire.

Ah, but his desire for the Talking Beasts is greater than for the dumb ones. Tirian is upset when he sees a horse being mistreated by Calormenes, but not until he discovers it is a *talking* horse does he really get wild with anger (*LB,* ii). In Narnia, there is less moral weight attached to the treatment of common animals—such as the animals of our world—than is attached to the treatment of talking beasts. And this is a moral principle that for Lewis certainly generalizes to our world. Though Lewis gave his talking animals some traits of real animals,[3] the Talking Beasts of Narnia in many ways represent humans, or function within Narnia as moral creatures like the humans of our world. Aslan, the son of the divine Emperor-Beyond-the-Sea and the Creator of Narnia, takes incarnate form as a Beast: a great lion. The animals of Narnia are thus the image bearers of their creator, just as humans in our world are image bearers of our creator who took incarnate form as a human according to Lewis's Christian faith. And so, while it would be possible to hunt nontalking beasts of Narnia without breaking any moral law, to hunt a Talking Beast would be evil and akin to canibalism.[4]

In short, Lewis puts humans of our world and Talking Beasts of Narnia on a higher moral plane than animals (of our world) or dumb beasts (of Narnia). In Lewis's view, man is a biological being and part of nature, but not *merely* a part of nature; we are supernatural as well as natural creatures, spiritual as well as material, moral beings and not mere biological machines. We deal with one aspect of man's special role in chapter 2, addressing the rightful place of humans as kings and queens over the animals of Narnia, and in our final chapter we return in detail to the underlying question of metaphysical materialism. Now the subject surfaces again. When a cougar or a bear or a pack of wolves tears apart some "innocent" prey like a rabbit or deer, though we might not wish to watch this happen, we don't call the predator "evil" for its actions—even though many predators will begin consuming their prey while it is still alive. To call such an act "evil" in humans is to presuppose that humans are somehow above nature, at least morally, or that human nature is not completely contained within, or explained by, nature. Lynn White described one of Aldous Huxley's favorite topics as "Man's unnatural treatment of nature and its sad results."[5] But Huxley's and White's shared complaint makes no sense unless we acknowledge, as Lewis did, that humans are *not* merely a part of nature.

Indeed, though disturbing and sad, it is probably completely accurate—at least according to the past few thousands years of history—to say that polluting our world and exploiting it for our own ends, as well as killing one other, is very *much* a part of our human nature. If we accept this view that exploitation is part of human nature—what Lewis would call sinful or fallen human nature—then what we really want is for humans to rise *above* that nature and to act morally, and thus in a sense *un*naturally. In *English Literature in the Sixteenth Century,* Lewis phrases this as follows: "Christians had always held that man was a composite creature, *animal rationale,* and that it lay in his choice to be governed by his reason or his animality" (*ELISC,* 12). Readers might not agree with Lewis's worldview and its claim that humans are different from animals, but it is that very belief that allows Lewis to call humans to a higher ethical standard in our treatment of creation: in many ways (think of the wolf and the rabbit) we should not act *like* animals in our treatment *of* animals.

Lewis, whom noted scholar Clyde Kilby described not only as "an animal lover" but also as "a strong anti-vivisectionist," made this sort of argument explicitly. Though he usually turned down requests to write tracts for special interest groups, even when he agreed with their positions and principles, Lewis felt so strongly about this issue that he made an exception and agreed to help with a booklet for the National Anti-Vivisection Society of London. In the tract, Lewis argues strongly against vivisection and cruel treatment of animals. Kilby summarizes the argument, and quotes from this booklet:

> How can we formulate the human privilege for tormenting animals so that it will not equally imply the angelic privilege of tormenting men? And does not the superiority claimed for men over animals consist partly in not tormenting them? He [Lewis] agrees that there is room for honest difference of opinion on these matters, but he lays down a strict rule: "If on grounds of our real, divinely ordained, superiority a Christian pathologist thinks it right to vivisect, and does so with scrupulous care to avoid the least dram or scruple of unnecessary pain, in a trembling awe at the responsibility which he assumes, and with a vivid sense of the high mode in which human life must be lived if it is to justify the sacrifices made for it, then (whether we agree with him or no) we can respect his point of view."[6]

In short, it is the very claim that humans are higher than animals that places on our race the *moral* obligation not to "torment" animals. This includes not only cute little rodents like guinea pigs (such as Uncle Andrew's) and mice (Lewis would not use mouse traps), but also other animals, including horses (like Frank's Strawberry), bears (whose mistreatment is associated with evil in *That Hideous Strength*), and dogs and dolphins (mentioned in the next chapter). To strengthen his case, Lewis appeals to a Christian belief in angelic beings, and suggests that the same standard of good treatment we as humans would like to receive from angelic beings should be our standard for treating animals; in a sense, he takes the Golden Rule, "Do unto others as you would have them do unto you," and applies it to animals: *Do unto animals as you would have the angels do unto you.*[7] Of course it's not an exact analogy—Lewis thought it morally acceptable to eat animals—but he at least suggests we should consider the idea.

Now in humility, Lewis does acknowledge that there may be *some* hypothetical legitimate grounds for pathological experiments on animals. Perhaps, by way of our own example, the possibility of saving an entire herd or flock of some endangered species might justify an experiment on one of its members or perhaps even on a member of another species. But Lewis makes it very clear that one who carries out such an experiment must do so "with scrupulous care to avoid the least dram or scruple of unnecessary pain." The language here of "trembling awe" at our "responsibility" as moral creatures to care for creation is powerful and gives testimony to just how seriously Lewis took this issue, and the broader issue of humanity's responsibility to other creatures with whom we share the earth.

Returning then to *The Last Battle,* King Tirian unquestionably sees Talking Beasts as being of a higher order than their dumb cousins, and in fact he apparently hunts dumb beasts.[8] Yet Lewis by no means promoted the idea that *any* treatment of animals is justified for humans simply because of some hierarchical relation in which humans are higher. As noted, his view of humans as God's image bearers places on them the moral imperative to care for the earth and treat it with respect. Exploitation is never acceptable. The narrative says of Tirian that "he hated to see even a dumb horse overdriven." The reason he does not react to the Calormenes' mistreatment of horses even before he knows the horses were Talking Beasts is that at the time "he was of course thinking more about the murder of the Trees," which is what brought him away from his lodge in the first place (*LB,* ii). Though the Talking Beasts of Narnia have a special place in the mythology, all of nature is enchanted.

A final comment is in order regarding this sense of the sacredness of nature and its enchantment. Though Lewis was a Christian when he wrote all of these books, and indeed an arduous defender of the Christian faith, *The Last Battle* contains one of the strongest defenses of the virtuous pagan of any of his works. Just as an honest virtuous atheism is represented in *Prince Caspian* in the character of Trumpkin the dwarf, and believers and unbelievers among the Old Narnians are able to work together for the salvation of Narnia, in *The Last Battle* honest paganism is represented in the noble Calormene Emeth (whose name, in Hebrew, means "truth"). Emeth's fixed devotion to Tash is shown when he first passes through the stable door and finds himself in paradise. Though Aslan is king of this country, Emeth immediately goes in search of the god Tash rather than looking for Aslan. "Tash, Tash, where is Tash? I go to Tash" (*LB*, xiii). Yet it seems clear that he is as enchanted as are the followers of Aslan with nature and natural beauty represented in this Edenic setting. And when Tirian, Eustace, Jill, Lucy, and the book's great heroes meet Emeth, they see him as a friend and not a foe. Aslan himself even tells Emeth, "All the service thou hast done to Tash, I account as service done to me. . . . No service which is vile can be done for me, and none which is not vile can be done to him" (*LB*, xv).

Certainly Jewish or Christian fans of Lewis's writing ought to see the same principle at work in environmental labors: the atheist, the pagan, the Jew, and the Christian—as well as many others of different faiths—ought to be able to do "service" together even if motivated by different underlying faiths. The Jew or Christian, believing in a high calling on humans to bless the earth, may see such service as having been done to their God even if done by those who don't believe in their God. The atheist should be glad for the high moral calling of the Jew or Christian to serve the God in whose image they believe they have been created, even though the atheist herself does not believe in the same basis for that moral calling, or accept the notion of "creation."

Deforestation, Agribusiness, and Human Domination

Returning, then, to the felling of trees: as mentioned, the reason King Tirian is slow to respond to the ill treatment of the horses is his preoccupation with the horrors of the killing of his trees, which in the enchanted Narnia are sentient beings. As vile as is the sight of a cruel whip on the back of an animal, at the moment it is secondary to the other devastation he is facing. "A broad lane had already been opened. It was a hideous lane like a raw gash in the land, full of muddy ruts where felled trees had been dragged down to the river" (*LB*, ii). This is a description of a clear-cut, the start of a deforestation project in the western lands of Narnia. Tirian would have been shocked to see it. And the reader, who over the previous six books has come to love Narnia and its landscape, is also shocked. Lewis's description of it, though brief, is vivid; the scene is hideous, raw, gashed, muddy. It has also been a common scene through much of the history of our own world.

King Tirian is also shocked for another reason. When he tries to find out why the trees are being cut, and asks the water rat what he is doing, the rat responds that he is "taking logs down to sell to the Calormenes, Sire." In other words, the land is not being worked for the benefit of local inhabitants, who along with their descendants could expect to live on the land for a long time. The project is the lumbering equivalent of agribusiness (as opposed to agrarianism); the trees are being cut for commercial export, to make money for a small minority who will benefit at the expense of all who must dwell in the land for the long term—especially at the expense of the trees themselves. It is being cut much the same way that Athey Keith's Nest Egg was cut by his son-in-law Troy. As angry as Tirian is at the felling of trees, he is incredulous when he hears the reason for the deforestation. "But selling them to Calormenes! Is it possible?" (LB, ii).

For Lewis, as we mention in our introduction, this is the beginning of the end of Narnia. And as we look more closely, we see that the wanton felling of trees for commercial export is but one of many signs of human domination that mark the evil of the last days. By the end of the first chapter, even apart from the title and first line of the book, the reader knows that evil has come upon Narnia. Not only the description of the Ape Shift, but also the rhetoric of his words, speaks clearly of exploitation. We are told in the first chapter, "Puzzle was more like Shift's servant than his friend. He did all the work." Despite doing all of the labor, however, the donkey seems to have no rights or privileges. He enjoys little benefit from his labor. When he is sent to the market, "all the nicest things that Puzzle brought back were eaten by Shift" (LB, i). One might think from the description that Puzzle was part of a conquered people. But Shift has neither physical strength nor military might to enforce his will. Rather, like many modern agribusinesses, he uses manipulation to dominate Puzzle.

Nonetheless, Puzzle is completely dominated, and we could rightly replace the word *servant* with *slave*. *Slavery*? Is that too strong a word to describe Shift's treatment of Puzzle? Perhaps not. If Puzzle is not quite a slave, it is the direction that Shift hopes to move. This becomes clearer as the story progresses. The biggest reason to put on the lionskin, he tells Puzzle, is that "everyone would do whatever you told them" (LB, i).

This act of deceit is a door to power, and to the particular sort of power that will allow the ape to enforce his will on others: that is, to enslave. So readers should expect what is coming in the second chapter when the narrator describes the scene around the logging project. "There was a great crowd of people at work, and a cracking of whips, and horses tugging and straining as they dragged at the logs" (*LB*, ii). The cracking of whips and the forced labor is an unmistakable image of slavery. The brutality is savage enough that it sends the usually self-controlled Tirian into a fit of rage. Within a few chapters, we learn that Shift has sold the animals of Narnia, as well as dwarfs and other creatures, against their will into Calormene hands. Though the ape does not use the word *slavery*, others begin to use the word, and the narrator makes it clear that this is what it is.

Now not only is slavery wrong in and of itself, but it is antithetical to healthy agrarianism and the healthy sorts of communities that foster good environmental practices. As Wendell Berry explains, "people are motivated to care for land to the extent that their interest in it is direct, dependable, and permanent." Slaves have no interest in the land. Berry goes on to postulate that people "will be motivated to care for the land if they can reasonably expect to live on it as long as they live. They will be more strongly motivated if they can reasonably expect that their children and grandchildren will live on it as long as they live. In other words, there must be a mutuality of belonging: they must feel that the land belongs to them, that they belong to it, and that this belonging is a settled and unthreatened fact."[9] The felling and selling of Narnian trees by forced labor does not fit this description. And the later selling of Narnians as slaves to the land of Calormen is a clear violation of the principle both for Narnia, where the beasts have lost their interest in the land, and even for Calormen, where the work will now be done by slaves who have no interest in that land either.

We also see in the first two chapters of *The Last Battle* other hints of the replacement of agrarian culture with industrialized culture, as well as indications of the harmful attitudes that act as the motivation for industrial farming and logging. While in the first six books of the Chronicles of Narnia little is said of agriculture or about where food comes from, in *The Last Battle,* we do get our first mention of a market where Narnians can go and find food; it is in the nearby settlement of Chippingford. What kind of market, we don't know, but we suppose a sort of farmer's market, which can be a sign of healthy agrarian community. Interestingly, though, Shift sends Puzzle to the market to get bananas and oranges. These two fruits would *not* grow in the northern climate of Narnia; they are tropical or warm climate fruits that would have to be imported from Calormen or lands to the south. That Lewis was conscious of this, and made a particular choice of it, is suggested by two things: the first is that there weren't any bananas or oranges available at the market, and the second is that the other Narnian creatures aside from Shift weren't particularly interested in acquiring them (*LB*, i).

Now one of the most important ideals of agrarianism is eating locally. Food should be consumed, at least in part, by the communities who grow the food, and who have a long-term stake in the health of the land on which it is grown. A major problem in many developing nations is that lands once devoted to food for local inhabitants now are used for cash crops for commercial export—which almost always also entails a shift from crop diversity to monocrops. It is unhealthy for the land, and unhealthy for the people who live on the land. Beyond that, the cost of transporting food is tremendous. But our own country has an addiction to getting non-native produce from around the world and to having it fresh year-round. Certainly it is an enjoyable luxury. However, it may be—it almost certainly *is*—a luxury that our world can no longer afford at the present level. In an August 2006 *National Geographic* article, Bill McKibben comments on our international diet. "We've gotten used to eating across great distances. Because it's always summer somewhere, we've accustomed ourselves to a food system that delivers us fresh produce 365 days a year." Aside from the questions of community and care for the soil, the critical problem McKibben addresses is that "the energy cost is incredible." To ship fresh iceberg lettuce from California to the eastern United States requires sixteen calories of energy for each single calorie actually consumed. Though this is only one of many causes of problems facing the world today, it is a significant issue that many of us could address by a change in our lifestyles. But McKibben's motivation for such a lifestyle change is sobering: "The planet itself [is] at stake—and not from a possible scenario, like nuclear war, but from the consumption of the coal and oil and gas that power most of the actions of our lives."[10]

Now again we doubt that Lewis had much of this explicitly in mind. To the general public, global warming was an unknown problem more than fifty years ago when he was writing his stories. The term *agrarian* was in his lifetime just starting to come into use. It is unlikely he was intentionally addressing the same breadth of concerns that McKibben elucidates in his article or that Wendell Berry writes about in numerous essays. Yet as we saw earlier in his discussions and correspondence with his friends J. R. R. Tolkien and Arthur Greeves, Lewis was certainly conscious of at least some of the problems associated with an international diet, and was a defender of eating locally, and so we might guess that the association of eating exotic imported foods with the evil ape Shift was not accidental. And perhaps he was addressing something even more important: the underlying attitudes that have led to these problems. Shift has developed an unhealthy appetite for luxuries. It is bananas and oranges in the first chapter, but later it becomes nuts and other foods he extorts from squirrels even though his demands may result in their starvation. The ape is prepared to manipulate the world to satisfy his lusts. He is prepared to enslave his fellow creatures and decimate the landscape, clear-cutting the trees and even starving his neighbors, to provide himself with the luxuries he desires. And Lewis makes it clear in *The Last Battle* that the consequence of this sort of behavior, if it goes unchecked, is the destruction of the earth itself. While other connections to principles of agrarianism may be indirect—at best intuited by Lewis, or modeled because they are Christian principles—when one reads enough of Lewis it is easy to guess that this last connection is intentional on the part of the author. Furthermore, that later in the story Shift does everything he can to look like and act like a human, and even claims to *be* a human, might be a suggestion by Lewis that the ape really represents a reproachable part of humanity. In one aspect at least—his horrific and exploitive treatment of nature—Shift is already very much like the man he wishes to become.

This brings us back to the deforestation. We see now that it is *not* the beginning of the end. Those who read closely the first chapter know that the cutting of the trees is only the first *manifestation* of Shift's attitude. Like climate change, it is a *sign* or *symptom* of bad practices and harmful attitudes that have been growing for some time. Still, it is shocking when King Tirian faces it. He is sitting outside his lodge when the tree spirit approaches. "'Woe, woe, woe!' called the voice. 'Woe for my brothers and sisters! Woe for the holy trees! The woods are laid waste. The axe is loosed against us. We are being felled. Great trees are falling, falling,

falling'" (*LB*, ii). What Lewis is doing here is similar to what he does in *Prince Caspian* and in the poem "Under Sentence": he is giving voice to voiceless elements of creation that are suffering from human domination. In the passages we discuss above, it is animals to whom he gives voice. Here it is the trees. It is a powerful narrative device, and one used by many of the great nature writers of the past. His choice of "felled" and the repeated "woe, woe, woe" and later "falling, falling, falling" are reminiscent of Gerard Manley Hopkins's poem "Binsey Poplars Felled," which includes the lines, "My aspens dear, whose airy cages quelled, / Quelled or quenched in leaves the leaping sun, / All felled, felled, are all felled; / Of a fresh and following folded rank / Not spared, not one."[11] The passage gives us a sense of the violence involved in the act, as well as the "waste": the loss of something good—not merely good, but as we noted earlier, *sacred;* these are "holy trees." And if earlier resonance with aspects of agrarianism were accidental or at best intuitive, this is another choice that seems more likely to be conscious on Lewis's part— an intentional statement with environmental implications. Consider, for example, Lewis's poem "The Future of Forestry,"[12] published in 1938, more than a decade before the Narnia stories. The poem speaks of the great loss occurring when forests are cut. Don King notes with respect to this poem that "Lewis extended his social critique of contemporary life beyond the limits of the modern city; the concern in these poems is the encroachment of the modern world upon the English countryside. The poem asks, when all the trees are gone, sacrificed to roads and shops, who will tell the children what trees were."[13] The fact that Lewis worked to give voice in his poems to animals and trees suffering from human development, encroachment, and exploitation tells us that it was an important issue for him, and also suggests that his choices in the Narnia stories had more behind them than just narrative issues in telling a good story (though that, certainly, was important).

As *The Last Battle* continues, Lewis suggests yet another interesting principle through the words of one of the speaking trees. "'Justice, Lord King—' she cried. 'Come to our aid. Protect your people. They are felling us in Lantern Waste. Forty great trunks of my brothers and sisters are already on the ground'" (*LB*, ii). Not only does the sentient tree spirit lament the loss of something good, much as a human would mourn over the tragic death of a loved one due to violence, but she also calls for justice. This call for *justice* implies that there is a *moral* wrong involved in the cutting of these trees, and not merely an inconvenience, or unpleasant consequence, or aesthetic violation. Nature can be sinned against. And the humans who do these things are morally culpable for their evil.

As greedy and manipulative as Shift is, however, he is still small. His is the petty sort of greed that lacks real power, like Andrew in comparison with the Empress Jadis. As with Troy Chatham, or Lotho Sackville-Baggins in *The Lord of the Rings,* or any other small farmer who wants to become a big businessman, in order to gain power for himself Shift must invite other, bigger powers in, and rely on them. When Shift does so, it is not long before the ape becomes a tool and loses what little he once had. In this case, the bigger power is the ruler of Calormen, called the Tisroc. As the narrator tells us, "the Tisroc had always wanted to have these Northern countries for his own" (*LB,* ix). And therein lies another of the principles of agrarianism, illustrated by showing both the evil *cause* and the ill *effect* of its violation: one should own only as much land as one is able to know intimately and care for. Wendell Berry states this as follows: "It is well understood that ownership is an incentive to care. But there is a limit to how much land can be owned before an owner is unable to take proper care of it. The need for attention increases with the intensity of use. But the quality of attention decreases as acreage increases."[14] Like many agribusinesses, the Tisroc does not even want to care for Narnia and nurture it. He is not concerned for its well-being. And even if he were, it is much too large and too far away for him to pay it the "quality of attention" it needs. What the Tisroc wants is to possess Narnia: to own it, and increase his own power and wealth through that ownership.

Often Lewis's most powerful statements are among the simplest. The result of the sort of management—or, rather, *mis*-management—of the type provided by Shift, and later the Calormene officer, and eventually the Tisroc under whose authority the others acted, is bleak. It is bleak for the earth itself and for the community that dwells on it. It is much like a land and community that has been mismanaged by oppressive and exploitive land practices oft associated with agribusiness or with the powerful dictatorships of the twentieth century. As the narrator tells us, "gloom and fear reigned over Narnia" (*LB,* vi).

Technology, Exploitation, and Rhetoric

Seeing the devastating results of Shift's principles and policies, and how much those around him suffer for it, we find it reasonable to ask how one lacking in physical might and power could succeed in manipulating to his will so many fellow Narnians, beginning with the donkey Puzzle. The answer is simple, and the rhetoric probably familiar. When it comes to Puzzle, Shift accomplishes his goals with empty promises, manipulated guilt, feigned friendship, and false claims to have the donkey's and others' interests at heart.

One of the first things readers learn about Shift is that "he was the cleverest . . . Ape you can imagine." A little later we are told again that "he was a clever Ape," and that Puzzle thought that "Shift was far cleverer than himself" (*LB*, i). Though cleverness is not itself a virtue, it is certainly useful, and something that can be used for good. And though later in the story Shift becomes quite pathetic, at least at the start of the tale he shows genuine cleverness. He is not only good with his hands, but also imaginative; when the lionskin comes his way he is able to envision just what use he can make out of it. Sadly, that use is an evil one, and serves to illustrate that we can often be too clever for our own good. More specifically, Shift's particular cleverness is a sort of technical or industrial cleverness. The ape is able to take raw material, envision a final product, and create it with his hands—a very useful trait when put to good purposes.

But the abilities of the technologist may also be put to poor use, as when they are used as a means of gaining power through exploitation. This is a main concern held by Lewis, for central to technology and applied science *is* the ability to more quickly and efficiently realize our desires, and in particular the desire for control; technology provides power to adapt our surroundings to our wishes. With technology we can keep (ourselves and our food) warm in the winter and cold in the summer; we can travel and communicate across great distances; we can change the course of rivers, level mountains, and fill valleys; we can kill, and *sometimes* we can heal; we can, with great efficiency, extract resources from the earth—which often need to be consumed for the further advancement of technology. Which is why, as we have noted, C. S. Lewis and J. R. R. Tolkien (and many fantasy writers) often use magic to represent technology and the ability provided by technology for effortlessly expediting our will; magic in fantasy stories enables one to accomplish the feats that technology enables in our world.[15] In short, technology, as well as its literary cousin magic, provides a sort of control over nature. And thus it also provides a control over others—at least according to Lewis, who suggested that some of man's power of nature was really "a power exercised by some men over other men with Nature as its instrument" (*AoM*, 34).

We already cited a personal letter written in 1941, in which Lewis explicitly connects magic and science ("science" as it is known by "modern writers," which from Lewis's more polished writings we know really refers to applied science and technology); both can be techniques for attaining power.[16] What he also says in that letter is that such pursuit of power at any cost is immoral—or at least that it defies "ordinary morality." He links together Christianity, stoicism, and humanism, as being opposed to such pursuits of power, while simultaneously critiquing the negative (or dark) aspects of Platonism—at least in its Renaissance form—as being in support of occult magic. In his book *The Abolition of Man,* Lewis makes an even more telling comparison between magic and applied science, and it may get at the heart of the most important environmental concerns addressed in this book: "There is something which unites magic and applied science while separating both from the 'wisdom' of earlier ages. For the wise men of old the cardinal problem had been how to conform the soul to reality, and the solution had been knowledge, self-discipline, and virtue. For magic and applied science alike the problem is how to subdue reality to the wishes of men: the solution is a technique; and both, in the practice of this technique, are ready to do things hitherto regarded as disgusting and impious" (*AoM*, 83–84). There is an underlying question of worldviews that Lewis is addressing here. As he understands it, there are two opposing ideas. One of them acknowledges that there is some ultimate Reality in the world and asks how we as humans can know that Reality and conform to it (through virtuous practices). The other worldview seeks, by contrast, to conform (or "subdue") reality to our wishes. In writing this, Lewis could have been describing the difference between Athey Keith and Troy Chatham in Wendell Berry's novel discussed in chapter 2. When we read of Athey's philosophy that "no more land would be plowed for grain crops than could be fertilized with manure from the animals," and "no more grain would be grown than the animals could eat," we see that he is conforming his practices to the reality of the soil and water and landscape of the land he farms. This requires that he know the land, and the story certainly portrays the discipline and virtue that he practices. Then there is Troy Chatham, who, rather than adapt himself to his farm, chooses instead the "breakneck economic program" that seeks to adapt the land to his whims, as if "the farm existed to serve and enlarge him." When we express the competing worldviews in light of these examples, it is easy to see why their ecological implications might be so significant. Many of the environmental problems of today stem from our desire to subdue reality to our wishes. At the heart of sustainability is an acknowledgment of certain limitations in the nature of the world, and a willingness to submit ourselves and our practices to them. The important ecological virtue of self-discipline discussed earlier is an important part of this practice, and is explicitly mentioned in this quote. In Lewis's view, pure science could be seen as an effort to know the reality of nature—and to the extent that we then submit to that reality, science should be a vitally important aspect of the first worldview. He saw applied science and technology, by contrast, as being rooted in the second worldview; like magic, they are means to power—ways of conforming nature to our wishes.

Returning to Narnia, even in the brief description of Shift's cleverness, we see an unmistakable desire for power, and for the pleasures afforded by power. He has made power his aim, and seeks to attain it through the *technique* of his cleverness—especially through his use of cleverness to enslave others. The description of Shift is similar to that of J. R. R. Tolkien's goblins in *The Hobbit*; they "make many clever [things]," probably including "some of the machines that have since troubled the world," making use of "wheels and engines and explosions." The comparison becomes stronger when we consider Shift's manipulation of Puzzle to do his hard and unpleasant labor, and afterward his enslavement of the other creatures of Narnia. Tolkien's goblins also have the habit of "not working with their own hands more than they could help," and therefore they keep slaves who "have to work till they die for want of air and light." In hearing this description, it is difficult not to think of the oppressive factories arising in the Industrial Revolution in the nineteenth century into which both Tolkien and Lewis were born—and of sweatshops that still are in operation in various places in the world today. Shift also sold the dwarfs of Narnia into slavery to Calormen to work without air or light in the mines of the Tisroc (*LB*, vii). The judgment passed by Tolkien's narrator, who calls goblins "wicked and badhearted," applies to Shift as well, and in a very similar way.[17]

Now even the casual reader will likely see evidence of a clear distrust of modern industrialism and technology in the writings of both Tolkien and Lewis. Both writers were part of a twentieth-century romantic reaction against the ravages of industrialization of the previous century. Both writers were also certainly shaped in part by experiences serving in the bloody First World War. Some critics have used the "romanticism" label to dismiss the writings of both Lewis and Tolkien, including those aspects corresponding most closely to what we now call agrarianism. These critics see only an unrealistic and unattainable Arcadian ideal in Tolkien's depiction of the Shire, and in Lewis's references in *The Last Battle* to the "hundreds and thousands of years when peaceful King followed peaceful King till you could hardly remember their names or count their numbers" and "whole centuries in which all Narnia was so happy that notable dances and feasts, or at most tournaments, were the only things that could be remembered" (*LB*, viii). Interestingly, the same criticism has been made of the vision of the twelve southern writers whose essays constitute the classic volume *I'll Take My Stand: The South and the Agrarian Tradition*—a book originally published in 1930, about the time of Lewis's conversion to Christianity. The essays in that book also provide a critique of industrialism and of the modern vision of progress defined by economic growth. In an essay written in 1977 as an introduction to a new edition of *I'll Take My Stand*, Louis Rubin Jr. explains that "the tradition out of which they were writing was that of the pastorale; they were invoking the humane virtues of a simpler, more elemental, nonacquisitive existence, as a needed rebuke to the acquisitive, essentially materialistic compulsions of a society that from the outset was very much engaged in seeking wealth, power, and plenty on a continent whose prolific natural resources and vast acres of usable land, forests, and rivers were there for the taking."[18] Though writing from England and not the United States, and though the word *agrarian* was not in his title, one could write almost the same thing about the tradition of Lewis.

Rubin also speaks of the underlying vision of these twelve writers, "the community of individuals, the security and definition that come when men cease to wage an unrelenting war with nature and enjoy their leisure and their human dignity." Regarding the complaint that theirs was an unrealistic ideal, he says: "If never in the history of the South had that goal been fully realized, and however much it had been largely restricted to only a part of the population, it was not thereby rendered any the less desirable as a standard to be cherished. *At least it had been in men's thoughts.* At least the society had evolved that ideal out of its human circumstance. At least there was the tradition of that kind of human aspiration."[19] Likewise, even *if* Lewis had provided *only* an unrealistic ideal, it would be worthwhile. Ideals are visions to be strived for, even when they are not fully reached; without them, we often do not strive. In this regard, we may be reminded of a well-known passage in the Talmud: "The day is short, the work is great, the workmen are slothful, the reward is rich, and the Master is urgent. It is not incumbent on thee to complete the whole task, but thou art not at liberty therefore to neglect it entirely."

But Lewis's and Tolkien's critiques of the dangers of industrialization, especially its cost to the land—to wilderness, and farms, and soil, and water—as well as their exploration of the rhetoric behind industrialization, goes far beyond romanticism and provides strong impetus to resist the lure of industrialism when it come at the cost of nature.[20] They addressed real problems in the real world. Put another way, both writers at times did offer an imaginative sort of pastoral idyll, but this is a reason for praise rather than criticism, for it was precisely the sort of idyll that could inspire—and indeed has inspired—people to live lives with healthier relationships with the earth. We could use *more* imaginative and inspiring models of healthy ecologies and human lives in harmony with the earth. Those who provide such positive ideals in literature are helping to shape our imagination in healthy ways. But even in their fantasies, Lewis and Tolkien were much more realistic, and their idyllic moments are rare. More often they show us visions of evil and its effect upon the land.

What Lewis shows us in the ape Shift, for example, is that both his ends and the means toward those ends are more important to him than the well-being of those around him or of the land itself. Shift is interested in his technology and the power he can attain through it rather than in life. Thus, when he acquires the lionskin, "the Ape never looked at [Shift] or asked him how he felt. The Ape was too busy going round and round the Thing and spreading it out and patting it and smelling it." In case the reader misses the subtlety of the Ape's indifference, the narrator gives a stronger clue to Shift's character by noting the "wicked gleam" that "came into his eye." The donkey Puzzle further accentuates the attitude of Shift as a technologist by providing a sharp contrast when he wonders where the lion came from and what happened to it. "I wonder who killed the poor lion?" he asks (*LB*, i).[21] Unlike Shift, Puzzle's concern is with life.

And this brings us back to the rhetoric of the technologist, the industrialist, the agribusinessman. The ape Shift is not an especially gifted orator, but then he doesn't need to be because he is dealing with a simple and unsophisticated audience. Still, given Lewis's young audience and the genre of his tale, the author does an excellent job of revealing what that rhetoric looks like. We see it first in a simple form when Shift tries to convince Puzzle to go along with the plan. "But think of the good we could do!" the ape explains. When Puzzle suggests that things are already good and right, Shift goes on. "Everything right?—when there are no oranges or bananas?" Though he is motivated by greed and power, the ape couches his ideas in moral terms of "good." And he defines progress by the availability of commercial goods. The latter argument appeals to Puzzle, as it does to most of us living in our world today. "It would be nice if there was more sugar," the donkey admits (*LB*, i). (The rest of us can fill in our own favorite commodity. "It would be nice if there were more . . .")

By necessity, Shift's rhetoric grows slightly more sophisticated later when he must argue for his radical plans that include the commercial deforestation and the new economy including mining and slave-based agriculture in Calormen—plans that are antithetical not only to what Narnians know to be good and right, but also to what we in our world now understand are healthy environmental practices. Shift again makes claims about his superior wisdom; he should be followed because he is in the know, and others are not. He then tells the animals who are to be sold, "We'll be able, with the money you earn, to make Narnia a country worth living in. There'll be oranges and bananas pouring in—and roads and big cities and schools and offices and whips and muzzles and saddles and cages and kennels and prisons—Oh, everything" (*LB*, iii). Lewis's satire at the end of the ape's speech is perhaps too thick and obvious. It is difficult to imagine any animal thinking that whips, muzzles, cages, and kennels are good ideas for themselves. But that only serves to illustrate Lewis's point, because he ties these obviously unde-sirable outcomes together with other signs of so-called progress that *are* appealing to many. More schools may well be a good thing, as are more roads. But is all progress good? We can assume that Lewis feels the same way about many of Shift's signs of "progress" as he does about whips and muzzles, and that he is warning the reader not to be fooled by the promises. Of course big cities and offices are clear signs of a shift from agrarianism to industrialization. They are also symbols of power. Are they really symbols of the good life, as those like Shift would have us believe? Even an increase in roads may come at a cost: more roads may bring with them more prisons and whips, and they certainly bring more cars. They may be a necessary infrastructure for the growth of the economy, but they consume tremendous resources, as do the vehicles driving on them.

In his essay "Conservation and Local Economy," Wendell Berry writes: "We must see that the standardless aims of industrial commu-nism and industrial capitalism equally have failed. The aims of produc-tivity, profitability, efficiency, limitless growth, limitless wealth, limit-less power, limitless mechanization and automation can enrich and empower the few (for a while), but they will sooner or later ruin us all."[22] This is a principle well illustrated by Lewis. In the *The Last Battle*, the ape Shift is the main proponent of profitability, efficiency, and growth, and (for a time) is enriched by it, but his plans do lead to the ruin of Narnia. The most important issue for Shift, and one of the most impor-tant environmental concerns in the world today underlying so many other problems, has to do with economic growth, and with it consump-tion. Many politicians today include the promise of economic growth on their campaign platform. ("It's the economy, stupid.") Shift tells the animals that their "pay" will go directly toward the nation's treasury, to be used for "everybody's good" and for what amounts to economic growth (new roads and so on). And Shift's rhetoric also resonates with the commercialism of our modern culture. It is an appeal for increased opportunity for consumption—in Shift's case, oranges and bananas. It is a particular type of consumption earlier associated with unsustainable practices. It is also a type of consumption that is often available only to the rich, and only at the expense of the poor. Shift shows what he is really about when he says, "I want—I mean, Aslan wants—some more nuts" (*LB*, iii), and forces the squirrels to give up their winter stores and risk starvation. The cat Ginger, who is wilier than the Ape, is even clearer when she speaks to Rishda later on about the real motivation for their vision of progress: "Those who care neither for Tash nor Aslan but have only an eye to their own profit, and such reward as the Tisroc may give them when Narnia is a Calormene province, will be firm" (*LB*, vii).

Moral Responsibility and Mockery of Christian Faith

For all of the familiar effectiveness of Shift's sort of rhetoric, he likely still would have failed to sway the populace of Narnia to his agenda except for two things: he claims divine authority (and provides some phony evidence for it), and he undermines any sense of objective morality, or moral obligation. In other words, the Narnians had so many ingrained moral codes against exploitation of any kind (of trees, water, animals, humans) that the devastation wrought by Shift would have been nearly impossible to accomplish without success at these two deceits. The narrator suggests that the other crimes Shift gets away with pale in comparison with these last two evils.

The presence of some objective morality in the universe is very important to Lewis, and is at the heart of many of his essays, including a BBC radio talk he gave, titled "Right and Wrong as a Clue to the Meaning of the Universe."[23] Again, talk of objectivity and absolutes rubs many people the wrong way in modern pluralistic cultures that have adopted a philosophy of relativism as a means toward the desirable virtue of tolerance. Yet Lewis held that an objective moral system, in which exploitation (of other humans or of creation) is not merely *inconvenient* or *personally distasteful* to some people, but morally *wrong*, can be an important safeguard against exploitation. Acknowledgment of a Judeo-Christian or other objective moral system in which exploitation is understood as a moral evil doesn't mean that morality is always followed (or even *ever* completely followed), but it does provide at least a standard by which the rightness or wrongness of actions may be determined, and also a standard to strive toward (even if, as with the earlier Talmud quotation, it is never fully attained). Acceptance of a common moral system would provide a framework in a debate over policies that would allow the debate to move beyond mere personal preference of competing interests, which often degenerates into power struggle. If there is no objective moral basis for environmentalism, then why should we follow the personal preference of those who like green to those who like the conveniences provided by exploitive or otherwise nonsustainable practices? We are left only with utilitarian or pragmatic reasons, which depend on the outcomes of our actions. Even if we could predict what those outcomes might be, there would still be a matter of personal preference about which outcome is preferable. This is why Shift eventually avoids the language of good and evil. He does not want to be bound by it, especially since he has a means to power. Only briefly, when he is arguing with Puzzle, is he forced to claim that his plan is "good." For the most part, however, in dealing with Puzzle and later the other animals, he prefers to speak about efficiency and progress and satisfaction of desires rather than about what is right or wrong.[24]

Some of the characters, including the cat Ginger and the Calormene captain Rishda, have apparently long ago abandoned any thought of morality—as recently noted, they "have only an eye to their own profit"—and are able to collaborate with the ape. Sadly, by the end of the story most of the dwarfs have taken this position as well. They refuse to take sides because they don't believe in any right or wrong that would lead them to one side or another; they care only about achieving their ends, which happen to be personal autonomy and freedom from any claims (moral or otherwise) upon them. In one of the most tragic moments in the tale, the dwarfs slaughter the talking horses. And having separated themselves from moral responsibility, they are remorseless. It is Shift, Ginger, Rishda, and the dwarfs, in rejecting all moral claims, who accomplish the greatest evils in the story.

Many of the characters, however, still believe strongly in an objective moral system. Even Puzzle, though initially he takes part in Shift's plan, believes there is an objective right and wrong. He uses no uncertain terms in responding to the Ape's plan. "It would be wrong, Shift. I may be not very clever but I know that much." He even goes on to suggest the source, or definition, of morality. "What would become of us if the real Aslan turned up?" (LB, i). The ultimate arbiter of morality, according to Puzzle, is Aslan. If something is displeasing to Aslan, if it goes against his laws, it is wrong. Roonwit the Centaur gets at the same thing in his brief appearance in the tale, telling Tirian, "I drink first to Aslan and truth, Sire, and secondly to your Majesty" (LB, ii). The first allegiance must be to Aslan, which is also an allegiance to truth and—though not stated here—to goodness. This outweighs any allegiance to man (and thus is also another example of our earlier point that in Lewis's worldview human authorities, including kings, are always subject to the divine, whether they acknowledge it or not). But an allegiance to Aslan, and a desire (like Puzzle's) to please the lion, should lead to nurturing care for Aslan's creation, which is all of Narnia: its earth, waters, trees, and creatures (dumb and talking).

So how does Shift get around this allegiance? The obvious way is to mislead the creatures into thinking he is doing Aslan's will—that his vision of progress *is* good. He does this by impersonating the lion. Or, rather, by using the donkey Puzzle to impersonate the lion, and then controlling the donkey. (Even here, the donkey must take all the risks, while the ape gets all the rewards.) It is a poor impersonation. "But if someone who had never seen a lion looked at Puzzle in his lionskin, he just might mistake him for a lion, if he didn't come too close, and if the light was not good, and if Puzzle didn't let out a bray and didn't make any noise with his hoofs" (*LB*, i). This is just what happens, as Tirian finds out. "'Do you think it really is Aslan?' asked the King. 'Oh yes, yes,' said the Rabbit. 'He came out of the stable last night. We all saw him'" (*LB*, iv). Once the deceit is accomplished, and the creatures of Narnia are convinced of the lie that the lionskin-clad donkey is really the Great Lion, they obey whatever he says, or whatever Shift says he says. When Tirian questions the rat about his complicity in killing and selling the trees, the rat justifies himself by saying, "The Lion's orders, Sire. Aslan himself" (*LB*, ii).

One of the tragedies in our world today is a similar sort of deceit, in which the Christian God in whom Lewis believed is referenced in justification of actions that are antithetical to Christian teachings—as has sometimes happened in the making of policies harmful to creation. Jim Ball, in a 1998 article titled "The Use of Ecology in the Evangelical Protestant Response to the Ecological Crisis," has examined four entirely different ideas about environmental responsibility that have all been credited to or blamed upon (depending on one's perspective) Christianity. One extreme includes the so-called Wise Use movement that attempts to justify exploitation of nature with biblical appeals. Ball calls the attitude of this movement one of "extreme arrogance."[25] More to the point of this section, this attitude is also entirely at odds with Judeo-Christian teaching about environmental stewardship and care, such as we have seen in the previous two chapters—teaching that firmly denounces exploitation of all kinds, as well as hoarding and covetousness. Like the lionskin on Puzzle, if someone had never seen the actual Judeo-Christian teaching on the subject of creation care, she just *might* mistake "Wise Use" for Christian doctrine, but only if she didn't come too close, and if the light was not good. In fact, as numerous scholars and theologians through history have pointed out, trying to use Christianity to justify exploitation (of nature or of other humans) should be recognized in the same light as putting a lionskin on a donkey to impersonate Aslan. The sad thing is that many people have been fooled, just as many Narnians were fooled by Shift's schemes. One of two things usually happens to those who are deceived. Either they do evil, thinking it is good; that is, they exploit the landscape under the wrong assumption that it is God's will for them that they do so. Or they come to hate Aslan; they view Christianity as the enemy because they wrongly think it is anti-environmental.

In *The Last Battle,* the narrator makes it clear that there was little excuse for believing the ape's lies. The reason should have been clear: Shift's commands, given in the name of Aslan, are antithetical to what people know to be true about Aslan. For example, after King Tirian encounters the dreadful things that are happening, he asks the unicorn Jewel, "They all say Aslan is here. But if it were true?" Jewel's reply should be sufficient answer. "But, Sire, how *could* Aslan be commanding such dreadful things?" (*LB*, iii). Later, in a conversation with some talking mice, the king tries to get the mice to see this truth. "'What was he like?' said the King. 'Like a terrible, great Lion, to be sure,' said one of the Mice." Tirian then asks, "And you think it is really Aslan who is killing the Wood-Nymphs and making you all slaves to the King of Calormen?" (*LB*, iv). The point of Tirian's reply is obvious: Aslan would never command such evils as killing dryads or enslaving his own creatures and selling them to Calormen. As Aslan himself points out, "And if any man do a cruelty in my name, then though he says the name Aslan, it is Tash whom he serves" (*LB*, xv). Which leads to the biggest lie told by Shift, that "Tash is only another name for Aslan. All that old idea of us being right and the Calormenes wrong is silly" (*LB*, iii). It is this claim that most clearly convinces Tirian that Shift is lying. "He remembered the nonsense about Tash and Aslan being the same and knew that the whole thing must be a cheat" (*LB*, iv).

It is also this final lie that returns us to the question of morality.

Shift needs both to corrupt the Narnians' view of Aslan and to elimi-nate their moral training so that they would rape the land for profit. By associating Aslan with the pagan god Tash, Shift does both, and thus he eliminates the notion of right and wrong, calling the notion both "old" and "silly." Lewis also shows that one important step in countering this attempt to dissolve morality is for the heroes to take moral responsi-bility for their own actions. This is far more important than blaming others. It is also more difficult, as Tirian and Jewel realize after they attack the unarmed Calormenes. "Jewel," said the King. "We have done a dreadful deed." "We were sorely provoked," replied Jewel. Yet Tirian continues, "But to leap on them unawares—without defying them—while they were unarmed—faugh! We are two murderers, Jewel" (*LB*, iii). The human tendency is to look for excuses and blame others. Tirian and Jewel take responsibility; Tirian is willing to acknowledge guilt for what he has done.

This decision to acknowledge guilt is also the turning point for the donkey Puzzle, who initially seeks to excuse himself from his part in the evils by repeating the oft-used defense, "I only did what I was told" (*LB*, vi). Only later does he confess, "I see now, that I really have been a very bad donkey. I ought never to have listened to Shift. I never thought things like this would begin to happen" (*LB*, viii). The donkey uses the language of moral obligation: the language of "ought" and the label of "bad." Though Lewis does not here make the modern environmental application of this particular moral principle of personal responsibil-ity, it is a very important principle. As long as humans continue only to blame one another, or more often blame large faceless governments and industries—which, admittedly are often culpable for many abuses and crimes against the environment—nothing significant is likely to be done. Political action is a good and vital thing, but we as individuals need to change our own lifestyles as well and acknowledge our own moral responsibility for how we treat the earth.

The End of Nature

And now we can finally turn, in the context of all we have just seen, to the topic that most motivates this chapter: what Lewis makes of heaven, end times, and the end of nature. Alan Jacobs claims that "of all the Christian beliefs with which atheists disagree, the only one that seems to generate real and deep rage is the belief in eternal life—the offer of 'pie in the sky by and by'—and the corollary belief that the eternal life that some people choose is a miserable one."[26] We might disagree with Jacobs that this is the *only* belief that causes rage; the belief in real objective morality seems to cause considerable rage as well. Of course the two ideas are related, as Jacobs might well point out. In any case, the belief in a real heaven is also problematic for many on environmental grounds. In *The Great Divorce*—a short sort of fantasy story through which Lewis attempts to communicate important ideas about heaven, hell, good, and evil—the character Reginald, a saint residing in heaven, tells his sister Pam, "Didn't you know that Nature draws to an end?" (*GD*, 96). Reginald is certainly communicating a belief held by Lewis himself. Wayne Martindale summarizes this doctrine about heaven, and Lewis's view of it. "The Bible tells us plainly that we are 'sojourners and exiles here' and that 'our citizenship is in Heaven.' . . . Lewis lived in firm belief that this world is transient and that the unseen world of Heaven is permanent."[27] The implication that many see in these doctrines, put crassly but popularly, is that "it's all going to burn anyway, so what does it matter what we do with it?" One can see why those concerned with nature as it is *now* would be uneasy (at best) and even hostile to such teaching. A justification for exploitation is at the furthest extreme from the conclusion C. S. Lewis draws, however, and misses some of the most important Christian teaching on heaven. In *The Last Battle*, Lewis presents a much more helpful picture, and the implications regarding how we live on this earth are profound.

Before turning to the depiction of paradise in *The Last Battle*, we look briefly at *The Great Divorce*, in which Lewis also sets out not *literally* to depict heaven or hell, but to illustrate some *principles* about them. *The Great Divorce* begins with the idea that those in hell may take, any time they wish, a bus trip to heaven, and may stay in heaven for as long as they want, even forever. Few residents of hell, however, actually wish to take the trip, and among those who take it almost none stay in heaven. The book begins with some people getting on that bus and riding it to heaven. Most of the story then takes place at the frontier of heaven, where some of the saints come to meet those getting off the bus and welcome them to heaven. In the introduction, Lewis makes what may be the most important comment about the relationship between heaven and earth; it provides both a summary and a context for all the remaining points. "I think earth, if chosen instead of Heaven, will turn out to have been, all along, only a region in Hell: and earth, if put second to Heaven, to have been from the beginning a part of Heaven itself" (*GD*, vii). Lest there be any doubt, Lewis does again affirm the troublesome doctrine, disdained by some, that earth is secondary in importance to heaven. But in the same breath he claims that if we once understand this relationship, it doesn't devalue earth but rather adds to its value; if we make it our goal to serve heaven first and foremost, then we realize that earth is, and has been from the beginning, "a part of Heaven itself." That being the case, to serve earth is to serve heaven; to exploit the earth is to exploit heaven. Christians should need no clearer understanding than this to motivate a profound and deep concern with caring for the health of the earth.

Lewis's view about what constitutes *good* care for the earth can be seen in his contrasting portrayals of heaven and hell, and of their denizens. (There are residents of hell, but it has no citizens.) The imagined hell is a big, gray city full of "dingy lodging houses, small tobacconists, hoardings from which posters hung in rags, windowless warehouses, goods stations without trains . . ." The most important point may be that it is a city always expanding, "leaving more and more empty streets." It has no neighborhoods and no community. Each street that *might* have been a neighborhood is largely empty, having at most only one or two people (*GD*, 7–8). By contrast, heaven is green. It is a world of nature, untouched by human corruption. As the fictional bus arrives on its regular trip from hell to heaven, the first indication of the approach to heaven is a "delicious freshness" in the air. The land appears as an "emerald green stretched tight as a fiddle-string . . . a level, grassy country through which there ran a wide river" (*GD*, 15–16). The nature imagery abounds. There are also tremendous waterfalls, and an abundance of wildlife including lions and unicorns. The narrator goes on to describe it: "But very far away I could see . . . a range of mountains. Sometimes I could make out in it steep forests, far-withdrawing valleys" (*GD*, 21).

The land also has one other curious but important feature. "It was the light, the grass, the trees that were different; made of some different substance, so much solider than things in our country" (*GD*, 19). In contrast to the popular portrayals of heaven mentioned earlier, the biblical description of heaven includes, among other things, clean rivers full of fish emptying into tidal marshes (Ezekiel 47:1–12). Heaven isn't somehow *less* physical, but *more* physical. Nature doesn't become less real, but more real. This, at least, is what Lewis is trying to envision for us in *The Great Divorce* (and also, as we shall see, in *The Last Battle*). In this view, if one wants to prepare for heaven, then far from giving up a concern for nature and the physical things of this world, one should learn to become an even better steward of the things of this world.[28] The attitude toward nature and the created world, which Lewis suggests is the *proper* attitude for the Christian, is shown by contrast in *The Great Divorce* when one of the representatives from hell shares what we assume to be the opposite of Lewis's Christian attitude: "And that passion for 'real' commodities which our friend speaks of is only materialism, you know. It's retrogressive. Earth-bound! A hankering for matter. But *we* look on this spiritual city—for with all its faults it *is* spiritual—as a nursery in which the creative functions of man, now freed from the clogs of matter, begin to try their wings" (*GD*, 15). It is hell, not heaven, that is represented by the Christian writer as wanting to get rid of material reality (that is, nature, or creation).

Perhaps even more telling is the description of how some of the residents of hell have a "desire to *extend* Hell . . . into Heaven." Their ideas are "to dam the river, cut down the trees, kill the animals, build a mountain railway, smooth out the horrible grass and mass and heather with asphalt" (*GD*, 75). Again, it is hell, and not heaven, in Lewis's view, that is antinature and destructive of nature. That Lewis associates these things with hell is very suggestive of his view of Christian ecology: to be antinature is to be aligned with hell against heaven. Even more suggestive is his description of one of the saints in heaven. Of this saint's life on earth, we are told, "Every beast and bird that came near her had its place in her love. In her they became themselves. And now the abundance of life she has in Christ from the Father flows over into them" (*GD*, 110–11). Saints take care of beasts and birds; the love of God flows through them into the creatures of the earth. It is seen as a rejection of heaven to wantonly destroy animals, as well as trees, grass, and rivers. A love of heaven, Lewis says, should lead to a love of all parts of God's creation.

So let us consider again the notion that nature will one day end, as expressed in *The Last Battle*. For Narnia, that day is shown vividly in the chapter "Night Falls on Narnia," in which we read of the Dragons and Giant Lizards, who at Aslan's command "went to and fro tearing up the trees by the roots and crunching them up." When they were done, all that was left was "world of bare rock and earth" and then even that is gone leaving only "total darkness" (*LB,* xiv). In his essay "On Living in an Atomic Age," Lewis discusses the similar possibility raised by the atomic bomb: that life on earth may be blown away and cease to exist. Lewis's first point is that this is nothing new; apart from the possibility of nuclear holocaust, scientists will already tell us that:

> The whole story is going to end in NOTHING. The astrono-mers hold out no hope that this planet is going to be perma-nently inhabitable. The physicists hold out no hope that organic life is going to be a permanent possibility in any part of the material universe. Not only this earth, but the whole show, all the suns of space, are to run down. Nature is a sinking ship. Bergson talks about the élan vital, and Mr. Shaw talks about the "Life-force" as if they could surge on for ever and ever. But that comes of concentrating on biology and ignoring the other sciences. There is really no such hope. Nature does not, in the long run, favour life. If Nature is all that exists—in other words, if there is no God and no life of some quite different sort outside Nature—then all stories will end in the same way: in a universe from which all life is banished without possibility of return. It will have been an accidental flicker, and there will be no one even to remember it. (LAA, 74)

Now a point that Lewis does not explicitly make, but which follows from this, is that the materialist criticism of the Christian concept of heaven makes no sense. The materialist argues that a belief in heaven—that is, a belief that life on this earth *as we now experience it* will one day be brought to an end—will cause Christians to not care about the earth, but Lewis's argument points out that this equally applies to a materialist outlook. The materialist worldview, if true, makes it even clearer that all biological life will end one day, and adds further that it is therefore devoid of objective meaning.

So materialism is at least no better than Christianity on this count, Lewis would argue. But he goes on to claim explicitly that materialism is, in fact, much worse. For the materialist, according to Lewis, there are three possible responses to this knowledge of an undeniable ultimate end of life in the cosmos. The first is that in the face of such ultimate vanity and meaninglessness we "might commit suicide." This would help us escape the "torment" brought about by this "consciousness."[29] We will be "fooled no longer." The second approach is to live simply for pleasure, to "grab what you can," which is usually only the "coarsest sensual pleasure." The problem, unfortunately, is that it is hard to get "very serious pleasure" from love or music or anything if you know it is a "momentary and accidental pattern produced by the collision of atoms." Lewis's main point about this second option is that ultimately it is unsatisfying as "you will be forced to feel the hopeless disharmony between your own emotions and the universe in which you really live." More to the point of our book, however, environmentally the result of the second approach is sheer exploitation. If we follow this approach, we view the earth—which is seen as random and purposeless and destined for destruction—as raw material for our pleasure (LAA, 76).

The third approach for the materialist is to ignore everything she knows and "live according to human values." In short, it is to take the attitude, "let [the universe] be merciless, I will have mercy. . . . I know the universe will win in the end, but what is that to me? I will go down fighting. Amid all the wastefulness I will persevere; amid all this competition, I will make sacrifices" (LAA, 76–77). Environmentally, the third approach would be the best, and indeed the very word choices used by Lewis have great ecological connotations: it results in "sacrifice" (of personal pleasure) as opposed to "wastefulness." But Lewis argues that the third approach (if materialism is true) is a denial or ignoring of the logical implications of materialism. We may hope people live this way—and indeed, many concerned nonreligious environmentalists have done an excellent job of living this way—but according to Lewis it doesn't actually make sense or follow from any objective values. As Lewis points out, "if (as we were supposing) Nature–the space-time-matter system—is the only thing in existence, then of course there can be no other source for our standards. They must, like everything else, be the unintended and meaningless outcome of blind forces" (LAA, 77).

So what is Lewis's alternative, based on his theistic worldview that also sees nature as one day coming to an end, but not in a meaningless way? His response is a profound statement of the basis for a Christian environmentalism, as Lewis would see it.

It is our business to live . . . in private or in public life, the law of love and temperance even when they seem to be suicidal, and not the law of competition and grab, even when they seem to be necessary to our survival. For it is part of our spiritual law never to put survival first: not even the survival of our species. We must resolutely train ourselves to feel that the survival of Man on this Earth, much more of our own nation or culture or class, is not worth having unless it can be had by honourable and merciful means.

The sacrifice is not so great as it seems. Nothing is more likely to destroy a species or a nation than a determination to survive at all costs. Those who care for something else more than civilization are the only people by whom civilization is at all likely to be preserved. Those who want Heaven most have served Earth best. (LAA, 79–80)

At one level we can argue with Lewis's conclusion in the final sentence. There are plenty of examples of humans who have denied heaven and have served the earth through a very thoughtful, complete, and practical environmentalism. Many important environmentalists today hold no belief in heaven and yet have done an endless amount of commendable work. And of course there are many who claim to love heaven, who have not served earth well at all. But the point in the latter case is that their lack of service has been inconsistent with their claim to love heaven. Lewis's reasoning is consistent with Christian scripture, even if his generalizations about likelihoods are not true of all particulars. His view of heaven should lead to healthy, loving, and self-sacrificial nurturing care of the earth. He explicitly argues for a rejection of anthropocentrism, or a clinging to *immortality* of our species (or ourselves), at the cost of *morality*. We must not grab and exploit; to claim power over death of a species (or, we might add, of an individual) is to claim power over nature—and thus, Lewis would claim, to destroy *both* the species (or the individual) *and* nature.

The idea that a love of heaven, and a placing earth second, actually leads to a deeper love of the earth is also modeled in *The Last Battle*. When the heroes of the stories watch Narnia come to an end, Lucy, who is always the most perceptive of the children, says, "I am sure it is not wrong to mourn for Narnia." Tirian responds, "It would be no virtue, but great discourtesy, if we did not mourn" (*LB*, xiv). Nature was a good thing to have been, something of great value to have loved, and thus its end is worth mourning. Which is perhaps why Tirian, earlier in the story when it looked as though his doom was sure, comments, "If Aslan gave me my choice I would choose no other life than the life I have had and no other death than the one we go to" (*LB*, ix).

The Importance of Heaven

But does nature *really* end? At one point in the story, Jill wonders aloud: "*Our* world is going to have an end some day. Perhaps this one won't. Oh Jewel—wouldn't it be lovely if Narnia just went on and on—like what you said it has been?" The wise unicorn's answer is simple and direct. "Nay, sister, all worlds draw to an end; except Aslan's own country." A short time later, Farsight the eagle echoes this idea when he repeats the last words of the centaur Roonwit. "Remember that all worlds draw to an end and that noble death is a treasure which no one is too poor to buy" (*LB*, viii). Lewis is as clear on this point as on any. Nature will end.

But what does that mean? Speaking of death, the unicorn Jewel says that "it may be for us the door to Aslan's country and we shall sup at his table tonight." When the heroes, old and young alike, find themselves in Aslan's country (some having died on earth to get there), they find their bodies have been restored. Their health has returned. They are unstiffened and ageless. Tirian thinks about Jill, who had just been defeated in battle: "now she looked cool and fresh, as fresh as if she had just come from bathing. And at first he thought she looked older, but then didn't, and he could never make up his mind on that point" (*LB*, xii). Their old bodies may have passed away, but rather than being *dis*embodied, they have been *re*embodied. Thus the heroes, when they have been thrown through the door—a door representing death—and are inside the stable, find that, "in reality they stood on grass, the deep blue sky was overhead, and the air which blew gently on their faces was that of a day in early summer. Not far away from them rose a grove of trees, thickly leaved, but under every leaf there peeped out the gold or faint yellow or purple or glowing red of fruits such as no one has seen in our world." Not only are their bodies renewed, but *everything* is renewed. Nature, it seems, has passed away. But it has passed away only to be restored. "There was blue sky overhead, and grassy country spreading as far as he could see in every direction" (*LB*, xiii). As the Calormene Emeth describes it, there was "much grass and many flowers and . . . all kinds of wholesome and delectable trees" (*LB*, vx).

What the characters soon realize is that this paradise in which they find themselves, after the destruction of Narnia, is actually *still* Narnia, but a new and bigger Narnia. Here we might return to Lewis's Platonism—an appropriate return suggested by Lewis himself through the words of Lord Digory, who says, "It's all in Plato." The paradise, or heaven, pictured in *The Last Battle* could be seen as something like a Platonic ideal of which the old Narnia (now destroyed) was but an imperfect reflection. But the point is that this Platonic ideal, this heaven, as Lewis understands it is not less solid or real or physical, but more so; it is not less nature, but more nature. "You couldn't get a blue like the blue on those mountains in our world," comments Eustace. To which Lucy replies, "[The mountains here] have more colours on them and they look further away than I remembered and they're more . . . more . . . oh, I don't know . . ." And Lord Digory completes the thought, saying softly, "more like the real thing." The narrator explains "the difference between the old Narnia and the new Narnia" as follows: "The new one was a deeper country: every rock and flower and blade of grass looked as if it meant more" (*LB*, xv).

And it is not even the final Narnia, the biggest one, the most real one. "The further up and the further in you go, the bigger everything gets," announces the faun Tumnus, with whom they are reunited after crossing over the new Narnia to a walled garden in the far west above the falls. His old friend Lucy understands what he means. "This is still Narnia, and more real and more beautiful than the Narnia down below, just as *it* was more real and more beautiful than the Narnia outside the Stable door!" (*LB*, xvi). As we noted, heaven is not a place of clouds and harps. Nature grows more real and potent the deeper one goes into heaven. What of the old nature that is now destroyed? Digory (Professor Kirk) explains, "It was only a shadow or copy of the real Narnia, which has always been here and always will be here: just as our own world, England and all, is only a shadow or copy of something in Aslan's real world. You need not mourn over Narnia, Lucy. All of the old Narnia that mattered, all the dear creatures, have been drawn into the real Narnia through the Door. And of course it is different; as different as a real thing is from a shadow or as waking life is from a dream. . . . It's all in Plato, all in Plato" (*LB*, xv). There is one of the key lines: everything that matters continues. All of the goodness of the old Narnia—and it is clear from the description that this includes, and perhaps *especially* includes the goodness of nature: "forests and green slopes and sweet orchards and flashing waterfalls" (*LB*, xvi)—will remain to be valued and cherished. So when the four Pevensie children catch sight of the heavenly version of our world, Tumnus can echo Lord Digory and bring the point home. "But you are now looking at the England within England, the real England just as this is the real Narnia. And in that inner England no good thing is destroyed" (*LB*, xvi). This also emphasizes why taking good care of creation (the old Narnia) is the appropriate preparation for all eternity: heaven is just more, truer, bigger nature. One does not prepare to enjoy a thing by spending one's whole life despising its likeness.

Lewis was moved by the implications of this thinking. In a letter written in July of 1930, during the period around his conversion, Lewis discusses Traherne's *Centuries of Meditations.* "He [Traherne] has extraordinary merits. What do you think of the following;—'the world . . . is the beautiful frontispiece to Eternity'—'You never enjoy the world aright till the sea itself floweth in your veins, till you are clothed with the Heavens and crowned with the stars . . . till you can sing and rejoice and delight in God as misers do in gold'" (*L1*, 914). Pondering heaven increased rather than decreased his delight in the earth. Seeing the good things of earth as a preview of heaven is almost a necessity to Lewis in really appreciating them.

Returning to one last issue regarding the biblical view of the end of nature, Wayne Martindale provides a valuable summary of Lewis's thinking about this:

> In Genesis nature is cursed. In Revelation the curse is removed. What would be the point of removing a curse from something that was to be simply destroyed? No, there will be a new Heaven and a new earth. Here Heaven and earth mean nature—the whole creation made to order by God for his human creation. Nature will become what it was always meant to be, just as our redeemed and glorified selves will be what they were always

meant to be. Lewis says of nature, "she will be cured, but cured in character: not tamed (Heaven forbid) nor sterilized. We shall still be able to recognize our old enemy, friend, play-fellow and foster-mother, so perfected as to be not less but more, herself. And that will be a merry meeting."[30]

Chapter 5

Out of the Silent Planet
Re-imagining Ecology

What I do know is that here and now, as our only possible practical preparation for [meeting extraterrestrial beings], you and I should resolve to stand firm against all exploitation and all theological imperialism. It will not be fun. We shall be called traitors to our own species. We shall be hated of almost all men; even of some religious men. And we must not give back one single inch. We shall probably fail, but let us go down fighting for the right side. Our loyalty is due not to our species but to God. Those who are, or can become, his sons, are our real brothers even if they have shells or tusks. It is spiritual, not biological, kinship that counts.
—C. S. Lewis, "Shall We Lose God in Outer Space?"

Life in general is mobility itself; particular manifestations of life accept this mobility reluctantly, and constantly lag behind.
—Henri Bergson, *Creative Evolution*

In recent decades biologists have discovered life in some very unlikely places. Extremely hot or cold environments, such as deep-sea vents and pools under Antarctic ice, harbor an abundance of creatures. Just decades ago, conventional wisdom held that nothing could live in such places. Now we find that things do live there, things that have expanded our notions of what animals may be like. In the past, we have ruled out the possibility of life in certain places because our imaginations would not allow us to believe life could be there or because the life in those places escaped our detection. Saltwater microbes don't grow under the same conditions as freshwater microbes, and so most of the saltwater microbes we know of went undetected for centuries. It is a risky business to assume that what we have not yet seen is not there, especially since we often do not see what is right in front of our eyes because our imaginations have blind spots. This is one of the main themes of *Out of the Silent Planet*. Our imaginations have been formed by our myths; our myths have made us think our planet is either alone or under siege by hostile alien species; and so our myths have reinforced our hostility to other species. What we needed, Lewis thought, was a myth that restored some old but neglected ideas about who we are and what our world is like. We have rejected many old myths about angels and fairies because we cannot see angels or fairies. But maybe the problem was not in the old myths but in the eyes of our imaginations.

Out of the Silent Planet is a story about space travel, but its setting is decidedly pastoral and earthbound. The first novel of Lewis's Space Trilogy begins under the shelter of a tree in rural England. In the opening chapter, Cambridge professor of philology Elwin Ransom is on a walking vacation.[1] A rainstorm has just passed, and we first glimpse Ransom emerging from the branches of a large chestnut tree, where he had sought shelter. Lewis's description of the landscape calls attention to fine details, pushing the beauty of the natural environment into the foreground of our imagination: "Every tree and blade of grass was dripping, and the road shone like a river" (*OSP*, i). This thoroughly terrestrial introduction serves to inform the reader that Lewis is not interested in space travel for its own sake. Lewis held that the point of fantastic travel to other worlds ought to be to help us to see something about our own world that we could not see from our current vantage point. As Lewis wrote in *The Magician's Nephew*, "What you see and hear depends a good deal on where you are standing" (*MN*, x). For Lewis, space travel stories were an ideal vehicle to help us arrive at a new place to stand and see our own world.

Worldviews and Other Worlds

So this image at the beginning of the book is not accidentally pastoral, nor is it the last time Ransom will find sanctuary under great trees. Just as we see in Lewis's other works, trees as protectors of life are a recurrent theme in this book. In the story, Ransom will find sanctuary several times under the great trees of Mars (or Malacandra, as the Martians call it). When Ransom flies through the heavens in a spaceship he feels the rejuvenating rays of the sun, called *Arbol* in the Old Solar language spoken on Mars. Of course, *arbol* is also a Spanish word, derived from Latin, meaning "tree."[2] Finally, and perhaps most importantly, in *Out of the Silent Planet,* Lewis argues against what he considers to be a life-defeating worldview by returning to the medieval Platonist poet Bernardus Silvestris. Perhaps coincidentally, Silvestris's name means "of the forest," and is derived from the Latin word *silva,* or "forest." In *Out of the Silent Planet,* trees are indispensable refuges, both literally and figuratively. Those who would preserve the trees will find that the trees return the favor.

This natural image of trees as a source of life and refuge serves to illustrate the broader ecological issues that emerge in *Out of the Silent Planet.* In Silvestris's worldview, the whole cosmos is brimming with life, and all created things are related. For Lewis, what follows from this is that the way we treat the lower elements of creation has a direct effect on the way we treat other elements. In an article on "interrelatedness," Paul Lutz writes: "One of the most important concepts of ecology is that everything in the creation is related to everything else. *Interrelatedness* or interdependence is one of the most important ecological principles, but one that is extremely difficult to conceptualize."[3] What Lewis provides is an imaginative and compelling "conceptualization" of the sort of interrelatedness that Lutz calls us to recognize. In what follows we will show how *Out of the Silent Planet* is concerned with a conflict of worldviews. At stake in this conflict is the question of what it means to be human and how we are to relate to (and interrelate with) our environment.

The opening passage of *Out of the Silent Planet* is not intended as just a romanticized picture of nature. Lewis describes the aftermath of the thunderstorm: "a violent yellow sunset was pouring through a rift in the clouds to westward, but straight ahead over the hills the sky was the colour of dark slate" (*OSP,* i). The opening scene paints a picture of nature that is both hospitable and dynamic, not tame, nor malleable to our will. This opening scene is an important backdrop against which the rest of the book must be seen. The events that follow it provide a series of important contrasts and comparisons, and the activity that Ransom finds himself engaged in is important as well. For example, while Ransom has found shelter under the towering tree, he looks behind him at the towering spire of a town that has shown him no hospitality at all, forcing him to walk extra miles in search of a night's lodging. Nature's tower has provided him the shelter that civilization's tower has denied him.

But we must be careful not to draw this nature/city dichotomy too strongly. Ecological questions often seem to bring with them a dichotomizing, either/or perspective that places virtue only in the natural world. This is patently not the case with Lewis, however. It would be an oversimplification to assume that the essential conflict that this opening passage sets up is, therefore, the conflict between city and country, between the hostility of human environments and the paradisical hospitality of pastoral scenes. Lewis was a Christian, and quite aware of the fact that the Christian tradition he espoused does not prefer one place over another. It is, after all, a tradition of both the garden (Eden, Gethsemane) and the city (Jerusalem, Athens, Rome, and the New Jerusalem). As St. Augustine—whom Lewis admired—put it,

> The word "paradise" properly means any wooded place, but figuratively it can also be used for any spiritual region, as it were, where the soul is in a happy state. The third heaven, therefore, whatever it is (and it is, indeed, something wonderfully and singularly sublime), is Paradise; and so also a certain joy springing from a good conscience within a man himself is Paradise. Hence the church also, in the saints who live temperately and justly and devoutly, is rightly called Paradise, vigorous as it is with an abundance of graces and with pure delights. Even in the midst of tribulations she glories in her very suffering, greatly rejoicing because, according to the multitude of the sorrows in her heart, the comforts of God give joy to her soul.[4]

Etymologically, "paradise" originally meant the forest, but it has come to mean more than the mere landscape. Augustine's point, with which Lewis would agree, is that paradise must not be mistaken for the woods, or a building, or a city, but it is a spiritual region or dimension that can be found in almost any place. It is perhaps most properly understood as a kind of orientation or relationship to the landscape. The presence of God is paradise; but God is present everywhere. The question, then, is whether we are willing to acknowledge God's presence.

This is a point not to be missed: while some have argued that the Christian idea of paradise or heaven effectively saps this world of its value—a point we begin to address in the previous chapter—Augustine and Lewis both argue that it is only those whose imaginations have been charged with the idea of paradise who will see the real beauty and value of this world. This does not, of course, mean that Christians somehow see better than others. Ransom, the protagonist of *Out of the Silent Planet,* is a Christian, yet even he finds that his worldview is earthbound and disenchanted. Our worldviews can carry presuppositions that act as intellectual and spiritual blinders. Recall the dwarfs in the final scenes of *The Last Battle:* they were in a paradise they would not allow themselves to see, and were "so afraid of being taken in that they [wouldn't allow themselves to] be taken out" of their blindness. Surrounded by unimagined beauty and presented with a feast, all they allowed themselves to perceive was darkness and food gone bad.

So rather than posing a simple conflict of landscapes—country versus city, nature versus human industry and its products—*Out of the Silent Planet* poses a subtler conflict of worldviews. A worldview is a way of seeing the world, an orientation to what is there to be seen. Worldviews not only tell us what may be seen; they may also attempt to tell us what may not be seen. In a brief foreword note, Lewis hints from the very beginning that there is a worldview that he wishes to oppose. He took H. G. Wells, Henri Bergson, George Shaw, and J. B. S. Haldane to be among the chief proponents of that worldview.[5] In simple terms, it claims that human beings are the most significant achievement of nature and therefore we are justified in taking a lordly, dominating attitude toward our environment. Whatever furthers our species and its interests is justified. While this is not an explicitly ecological view, it is one with serious ecological implications. Norman Wirzba explains a fundamental prerequisite to a responsible, loving, and healthy care for the earth we live on. "The first requirement of such responsibility is that we give up the delusion that we live in a purely human world of our own making, give up the arrogant and naive belief that human ambition should be the sole measure of cultural success or failure."[6] Lewis's tale also challenges that same delusion, by manifesting it in the villains of his tale.

The scientist and sci-fi writer J. B. S. Haldane apparently recognized a caricature of himself in Weston, one of the two antagonists of *Out of the Silent Planet.* Haldane wrote a scathing review of Lewis's Space Trilogy, accusing Lewis of misunderstanding science and of libeling scientists. In his unpublished "Reply to Professor Haldane," (published posthumously in *Of Other Worlds: Essays and Stories*) Lewis wrote,

> If any of my romances [novels] could be plausibly accused of being a libel on scientists it would be *Out of the Silent Planet.* It certainly is an attack, if not on scientists, yet on something which might be called "scientism"—a certain outlook on the world which is casually connected with the popularization of the sciences, though it is much less common among real scientists than among their readers. It is, in a word, the belief that the supreme moral end is the perpetuation of our own species, and that this is to be pursued even if, in the process of being fitted for survival, our species has to be stripped of all those things for which we value it—of pity, of happiness, and of freedom. (RPH, 76–77)

In other words, Lewis wrote *Out of the Silent Planet* in order to oppose a dehumanizing worldview—and one that pitted our species in violent and pitiless conflict with others. In this chapter we will attempt to make clearer both the worldview he opposed and the one he proposed as its alternative, and we will explain the ecological significance of both.

We should of course point out that Lewis did not write *Out of the Silent Planet* as an ecological novel in the narrow sense; it is not arguing for some concrete cause such as limiting pollution or saving a particular species. This is not an environmentalist's polemic. He did, however, write it as a polemic against a way of viewing nature and our relationship to it, and Lewis did not hesitate to make plain the clear ethical and ecological ramifications of this worldview. This "romance" (as Lewis called it) uses a fictional world to provoke readers to reimagine the meaning and structure of the cosmos. This reimagination winds up raising explicit ecological themes: the treatment of other species (including hunting, vivisection, extinction, evolution, domination, and stewardship); human-land relationships (including how to assess the real value of land and natural resources, agricultural practices, recreation, and agrarianism); and economic and political issues (including human sacrifice, our debts and allegiances to other species, human nature and the fear of death as a market force that shapes human resource usage, the value of an individual compared to the value of a species, and the value of species diversity).

Re-enchantment of the World: Myth and Ecology

Over against the dehumanizing worldview, Lewis offered what we might call a re-enchantment of the world—one, we might say, in which Augustine's notion of paradise is rediscovered. Lewis's views on mythology have been written about explicitly.[7] The Space Trilogy is deeply concerned with mythology and its relevance for our lives. It is not, however, a naive or reactionary attempt to superimpose an outmoded worldview on a technological age. Rather, Lewis's attempt to reintroduce us to a mythological element in our world is a reexamination of our relationship to our world and its inhabitants.

We can say, therefore, that Lewis's ecological vision is not separable from his view of literature and myth. Myths attempt to connect us to our environment in a way quite distinct from that of the sciences. Myths do not pretend to explain everything; they do, however, provoke us to wonder. "It was in fairy-stories," J. R. R. Tolkien writes, "that I first divined the potency of the words, and the wonder of the things, such as stone, and wood, and iron; tree and grass; house and fire; bread and wine."[8] Wonder, in turn, engenders humility and curiosity, both of which have a strong ethical upshot. The world is not ours to devour, but it is ours to explore and to tend as stewards. In a mythical worldview, we find ourselves already enmeshed in a web of relationships to our environs. We can no more completely know this web than we can disentangle ourselves from it. What we know is that we are in it, and that calls for a humble epistemology, a rich and expansible metaphysics, and an ethic of mutual responsibility that extends moral agency well beyond members of our species. In less technical terms, Lewis's polemic in *Out of the Silent Planet* invites readers to reconsider our place in the cosmos, including our relationships to other species, to the land we live on, and to what we do not yet know.

In Lewis's essay "On Science Fiction," he delineates five different types of sci-fi works, and in the fifth, the kind he writes, he explains what he was up to, though there are elements of some of the others as well:

The last sub-species of science fiction represents simply an imaginative impulse as old as the human race working under the special conditions of our own time. It is not difficult to see why those who wish to visit strange regions in search of such beauty, awe, or terror as the actual world does not supply have increasingly been driven to other planets or other stars. It is the result of increasing geographical knowledge. The less known the real world is, the more plausibly your marvels can be located near at hand. As the area of knowledge spreads, you need to go farther afield. . . . It is their [that is, the strange new worlds'] wonder, or beauty, or suggestiveness that matters. (OSF, 64)

Lewis is echoing not only what other sci-fi writers say, such as what Mary Doria Russell says in *The Sparrow;*[9] Lewis is also echoing what some environmental ethicists like Aldo Leopold say.[10] Humankind craves new experiences. Lewis's favorite subgenre of science fiction was the kind that transports humans to new and fantastic environments because such places "give, like certain rare dreams, sensations we never had before, and enlarge our conception of the range of possible experience. . . . If good novels are comments on life, good stories of this sort (which are very much rarer) are actual additions to life" (OSF, 66).

Before we discuss these ecological themes and "additions to [terrestrial] life" in more detail, it may be helpful to have a quick summary of the narrative of *Out of the Silent Planet,* since there are a number of proper names to recall. Elwin Ransom continues on his walk looking for a place to stay the night. He agrees to do a favor for an old woman he meets, and this brings him—with some difficulty—to the home of Devine, a former classmate of Ransom and an ambitious social climber, and Weston, a physicist. Weston has built a spaceship capable of flight to Mars, and he and Devine are planning their second trip to Mars to extract its abundant gold. They take Ransom captive and embark on their journey. Ransom discovers en route that he is wanted as a sacrifice to be given to the *sorns* of Mars. With this news in mind, Ransom contrives to escape from Weston and Devine, running to the refuge of the Martian forests. Eventually he meets a *hross,* otterlike in appearance but rational and capable of speech. The hross, Hyoi by name, takes Ransom to his village, where Ransom (a gifted philologist) learns their language and culture. Ransom also brings them news of a *hnakra,* a sharklike creature that threatens *hrossa* children and that the hrossa hunt. Ransom is invited to join the hunt, but as the hunt is beginning, Ransom is ordered by a nearly transparent being called an *eldil* to go to Oyarsa, the governor of Mars. Both the eldils (or *eldila*) and Oyarsa appear to be spiritual beings like angels. We are told they are superior in intellect to humans and Martians, and they have subtler (though not superior) bodies than we have. Ransom and Hyoi succeed in killing the hnakra, but just then Weston and Devine catch up to Ransom. The two antagonists kill Hyoi with a distant gunshot, and Ransom is sent to Oyarsa. Ransom flees through thick woods and up a high mountain, where he meets the sorns and discovers that they are a second rational species and not at all hostile to him.

Eventually Ransom makes it to Meldilorn, the island of Oyarsa. There Ransom discovers a third rational species, the *pfifltriggi.* The three species of rational creatures—which together Lewis calls *hnau*—each inhabit a distinct environment, and each practice a distinct craft, but all interact entirely peaceably, and each respects the place and talents of the others. The island is also thick with eldila. Weston and Devine, captured by the hrossa, are brought to Meldilorn as well, and there all three humans stand trial before Oyarsa. Since Oyarsa is nearly invisible to human eyes, Weston and Devine do not believe he exists, and they direct their comments to the visible creatures on Meldilorn. Oyarsa banishes Weston and Devine from Mars and gives Ransom the choice whether he shall stay or leave. Ransom chooses to depart, and the three race back to Earth before their ship is destroyed by the eldila. The narrative of the book ends with their successful return, but there are two more chapters in which Lewis inserts himself into the story and begins to explain the rationale behind the book.

War of the Worldviews: Will the
Real Monsters Please Stand Up?

To get at some of the ecological upshot of this book, it will be helpful to take a philosophical excursus through the works of H. G. Wells and Bernardus Silvestris, whose ideas bookend Lewis's book. We can begin to see how this matters by considering the title of the book. Ransom discovers that not only Martians, but also all the other inhabitants of our solar system, call Earth *Thulcandra,* or "the silent land." This is a little surprising, since from our perspective it is all the other planets that are silent; ours is never really silent, but no sound arrives across the vacuum of space to our planetary home. Here Lewis is trying to give us that alternative vantage point from which to view our own world. How would people living on other planets view our world? Two possibilities dominated our imaginative landscape in the middle of the twentieth century. One view was the view offered by the Soviet cosmonaut Yuri Gagarin. Gagarin claimed he had been to heaven and had seen no God.[11] Gagarin's point was, of course, that we are alone on this planet. The other view was offered by science fiction writers such as H. G. Wells, who suggested that the cosmos was inhabited by other species, all of whom harbor sinister intentions toward us. Ransom's cosmos turns out to be richly inhabited by intelligent species, but only one species is intentionally and habitually hostile to other species: humans.

Early in his visit to Mars, Ransom asks Hyoi why the Old Solar name for Earth is Thulcandra, the silent land. Hyoi has no answer for him, and we are left to speculate about this. One answer we might give is that by the end of the book, it is fairly clear that Earth is a cosmic loner, intentionally out of touch with the other planets. This alienation finds expression in several ways. One spiritual explanation is offered, for instance. Each planet, we learn, has an *Oyarsa,* or "tutelary spirit," and the spirit of our planet has become hostile to all the other Oyarsas of the solar system. Another explanation for our loner status has to do with the fact that our planet has only one species of hnau,[12] so humans have no one but ourselves to talk to. The result, it is suggested, is that we become more hostile to other species, arrogantly assuming that if we alone have speech, then we alone are valuable.[13] At one point in the novel, Ransom is interviewed by the sorns (the Malacandrian hnau who are most concerned with science and scholarship). Ransom later recalls that interview like this: "Two things about our world particularly stuck in their minds. One was the extraordinary degree to which problems of lifting and carrying things absorbed our energy. The other was the fact that we had only one kind of hnau: they thought this must have far-reaching effects in the narrowing of sympathies and even of thought. 'Your thought must be at the mercy of your blood,' said the old sorn. 'For you cannot compare it with thought that floats on a different blood'" (*OSP,* xvii). To the rest of the cosmos, we are the monstrous aliens: we live in alienation from other species that might otherwise be able to broaden our minds and our hearts alike. One more explanation may be added to these: Lewis understands our planet as silent inasmuch as modern humans have come to believe that we are alone in the cosmos. We do not converse with the cosmos because we have come to believe that there is nothing there to converse with.

This is perhaps the best place to begin to understand the conflict of worldviews that Lewis is engaging in. Lewis gives the context for this conflict in his brief preface and in his final chapters, bookending, as it were, the narrative with references to the ideas and worldviews in question. The first "bookend" concerns H. G. Wells. Lewis's preface to *Out of the Silent Planet* consists of a single brief "note" that reads: "Certain slighting references to earlier stories of this type which will be found in the following pages have been put there for purely dramatic purposes. The author would be sorry if any reader supposed he was too stupid to have enjoyed Mr. H. G. Wells's fantasies or too ungrateful to acknowledge his debt to them. C.S.L." Lewis was in fact an admirer of Wells's stories, but, despite this disclaimer, he was also a strong critic of two facets of Wells's worldview. First, Lewis connects Wells with what he calls the "great myth" of inevitable human progress. Lewis also calls this myth "Evolutionism,"[14] "Developmentalism," "Emergence," and "Wellsianity." Its chief philosophical proponent was the French philosopher Henri Bergson, whose book *Creative Evolution* was so influential in Lewis's thinking after the First World War. Later, however, Lewis argued against Bergson and Wells.

Bergson held that life emerged through the action of the élan vital, or life force, that impersonally brought it into being from inert matter. What this means, in a sense, is that life is self-begotten. Though Bergson occasionally denied that the upshot of his philosophy was "finalism," or the view that humanity was the highest form of life, Lewis and others of Bergson's critics were not convinced. As Bergson wrote in *Creative Evolution*, "Life in general is mobility itself; particular manifestations of life accept this mobility reluctantly, and constantly lag behind."[15] Bergson's implication seems sometimes to be that those forms of life that "accept this mobility reluctantly" are rightly left behind. Of course, just as Darwin's biological theory was appropriated by social theorists, so was Bergson's. Regardless of whether this is what Bergson intended, it nevertheless described what many people seemed to believe and to be acting on. Lewis argued that their view of moral progress could lead to the dangerous beliefs that whatever humans *can* do we *may* do, and that humans are the universe's highest achievement and therefore its natural lords.

Second, and connected to the first point, Lewis criticizes Wells and writers like Wells who portray humanity as good and alien species as irredeemably malicious. Lewis criticized this view because it had ramifications both for meeting aliens (which Lewis took to be an unlikely event) and for the way we treat one another and other species on earth. In his essay "The Seeing Eye," Lewis responded to Yuri Gagarin's claim that he had been to heaven and had not seen God. In his response, Lewis was not so much interested in proving that there was a God as in examining the ethical consequences of an atheism that, by emptying the universe of deity higher than humanity, makes humanity the highest and most important form of life, thereby opening the door to human tyranny over other species. Lewis wrote:

> To be frank, I have no pleasure in looking forward to a meeting between humanity and any alien rational species. I observe how the white man has hitherto treated the black, and how, even among civilized men, the stronger have treated the weaker. If we encounter in the depth of space a race, however innocent and amiable, which is technologically weaker than ourselves, I do not doubt that the same revolting story will be repeated. We shall enslave, deceive, exploit or exterminate; at the very least we shall corrupt it with our vices and infect it with our diseases. We are not yet fit to visit other worlds. We have filled our own with massacre, torture, syphilis, famine, dust bowls and all that is hideous to ear or eye. Must we go on to infect new realms? . . . It was in part these reflections that first moved me to make my own small contributions to science fiction. *In those days writers in the genre almost automatically represented the inhabitants of other worlds as monsters and the terrestrial invaders as good.* . . . The same problem, by the way, is beginning to threaten us as regards the dolphins. I don't think it has yet been proved that they are rational. But if they are, we have no more right to enslave them than to enslave our fellow-men. And some of us will continue to say this, but we shall be mocked.[16]

In a similar vein, Lewis opposed Bergson's apparent atheism, and feared the social consequences of Bergsonism that Wells and others seemed to be expressing. The atheism describes an ontologically lonely universe, one in which there is nothing higher than human life. The social applications of Bergsonism seemed to be twofold: first, that humans who resist "progress" (whatever that may be taken to mean) are recalcitrants and should be dealt with accordingly; second, that other species that hinder human "progress" (again, an ambiguous term) may be treated as bothersome and unnecessary roadblocks. Lewis's *Out of the Silent Planet* is, then, a literary polemic against Wells's Bergsonian philosophy.

So, what are these "slighting references" to Wells? Probably the most important reference is indirect and may be found in the scene in which Ransom is being interviewed by Oyarsa. Ransom explains why he was afraid of everyone he met on Mars, saying that "the tellers of tales in our world make us think that if there is any life beyond our own air it is evil" (*OSP*, xviii). This is plainly a reference to Wells and others like him, since earlier in the book Lewis wrote of Ransom that "his mind, like so many minds of his generation, was richly furnished with bogies. He had read his H. G. Wells and others. His universe was peopled with horrors such as ancient and medieval mythology could hardly rival. No insect-like, vermiculate or crustacean Abominable, no twitching feelers, rasping wings, slimy coils, curling tentacles, no monstrous union of superhuman intelligence and insatiable cruelty seemed to him anything but likely on an alien world" (*OSP*, v). In other words, our contemporary mythologies have made a common practice of assuming that other rational species will greet us with violence and hostility. Our collective literary imagination has already prepared us to assume that any aliens we meet will be malicious. Our planet's "silence" is born out of this ignorant and defensive posture; our myths have made us hostile.

Lewis takes this attitude to be pandemic. Even Ransom, a devout Christian and a professor at Cambridge, holds it. This is not merely an uneducated view of the cosmos but one that Lewis thinks has its roots in contemporary academia, and education alone is not sufficient to unseat this bias, which has its roots in our literature and the mythologies it engenders. We read that Ransom's "whole imaginative training," which has, of course, taken place through other science fiction stories, "somehow encouraged him to associate superhuman intelligence with monstrosity of form and ruthlessness of will" (*OSP*, x). When Ransom finally meets the sorns, he is surprised to find that "they were quite unlike the horrors his imagination had conjured up, and for that reason had taken him off guard. They appealed away from the Wellsian fantasies to an earlier, almost infantile complex of fears" (*OSP*, viii). Ransom finds that he is totally unprepared to meet alien species on anything less than hostile terms; the literature of his day has engendered a worldview and a view of the cosmos that is really ignorance masquerading as wisdom. When the Malacandrians ask him about his own planet, he is humiliated by the constant discoveries he makes "of his own ignorance about his native planet" and by his own unwillingness to divulge too much information about his planet. This unwillingness makes Ransom look like a prisoner of war who fears that what he discloses will be used to harm his friends: "He did not want to tell them too much of our human wars and industrialisms. He remembered how H. G. Wells's Cavor met his end on the Moon . . ." (*OSP*, xi).

Hostility or Hospitality? Interspecies Relations

In this last passage we may begin to see that this attitude is entirely relevant to our terrestrial relationships with one another and with other species. The quotation is not merely about how we might meet putative aliens; it is rather about a fearful and self-interested attitude toward others in our own world.

Weston's character represents Bergsonism, and his worldview may be summed up as the *human natural right to domination*. The key word here is *domination*, from the Latin *dominus*, "lord." Weston sees himself as the emissary of his species and his species as the bearers of the natural right to act as absolute sovereign lords over nature. Nature, for its part, calls for domination because it contains natural impediments to human progress. Since there can be no higher goal than human progress, nature merits hostility from its human lords.

This attitude of domination and the hostility that results from it is illustrated early on in the text: Ransom is denied the hospitality of the towns he walks through because the innkeeper does not want to be inconvenienced. When he tries to enter the property of Weston and Devine, he finds the gate locked and the property surrounded by a defensive hedge. Once he struggles through the hedge, he discovers Weston and Devine attempting to force a mentally challenged man into a spaceship so they can use him as a sacrifice with which to get gold from Mars. When Ransom succeeds in freeing the young man, Ransom himself is taken captive in his stead. We learn that Weston and Devine have also carried out experiments on their dog, resulting in the dog's death. Upon their arrival on Mars, Weston and Devine shoot wantonly at an animal they think might endanger them (the hnakra), when in fact it would have sufficed for them to get out of the water to avoid it. Later they shoot a hross without provocation and without risk to themselves. When they are finally brought before Oyarsa to give an account of their actions, Weston claims that he has the natural and unquestionable right not only to kill individuals but also to destroy entire species that get in his way. He further claims that nothing can rightfully stand in the way of the human drive toward self-preservation, even if that means killing native species on other planets to make room for human migration from a planet that loses its ability to host human life.

Ransom's sojourn on Malacandra acquaints him with the contrasting worldview of the hnau of Mars, which may be characterized by the single word *hospitality*. When Ransom arrives in the hross village, he is shown immediate hospitality without being asked to pay for it. Mars is a world without money and without locks, keys, or fences. Ransom is given a bed and meals for as long as he wishes to stay. It does not even occur to the hrossa to treat him otherwise. Nor would it occur to them to make a sacrifice of another creature for their own well-being. The hrossa only know self-sacrifice and very little killing of animals: the only animal the hrossa hunt is the sharklike hnakra,[17] which they kill in order to protect their own young, risking their own lives in the process. The hrossa are aware that their planet is losing its atmosphere and cooling off, and that one day they will all die. Nevertheless they do not contemplate leaving their planet for the safety of another, choosing rather to enjoy the days and the world allotted to them.

Taken on its own, this Martian worldview seems, well, outlandish. But Lewis's second "bookend" shows not only that he takes it seriously, but that he thinks he has good reason for doing so. This reason has to do with the related themes of *plenitude, relationship,* and *stewardship.*

The second bookend is formed by the last two chapters. Here Lewis enters the story in his own voice and informs us that this is a book with an agenda. "At this point, if I were guided by purely literary considerations, my story would end, but it is time to remove the mask and to acquaint the reader with the real and practical purpose for which this book has been written" (*OSP,* xxii). Lewis writes that he learned Ransom's story when Lewis wrote to Ransom to ask him about a Latin translation. His letter reads as follows:

> I am now working at the Platonists of the twelfth century and incidentally discovering that they wrote damnably difficult Latin. In one of them, Bernardus Silvestris, there is a word I should particularly like your views on—the word *Oyarses.* It occurs in the description of a voyage through the heavens, and an *Oyarses* seems to be the "intelligence" or tutelary spirit of a heavenly sphere, i.e. in our language, of a planet. I asked C.J. about it and he says it ought to be *Ousiarches.* That, of course, would make sense, but I do not feel quite satisfied. Have you by any chance ever come across a word like *Oyarses,* or can you hazard a guess as to what language it may be? (*OSP,* xxii)

Of course, Ransom responds to this letter by letting Lewis in on his adventure. Fiction aside, this is no irrelevant literary bauble; it is, in fact, a brief statement of Lewis's own view of nature, for which he owes a significant debt to Bernardus Silvestris. Bernardus is remembered for his philosophical poem *Cosmographia,* in which he gives a medieval Platonist's view of nature.

Though Bernardus is mentioned only briefly here, nevertheless these brief statements act as footnotes pointing to Lewis's other works. Lewis ended up writing about the worldview of Bernardus Silvestris in nearly every one of his literary works. For instance, his reference to "C.J." is almost certainly a reference to Appendix I of Lewis's *Allegory of Love,* in which he devotes several pages to Bernardus Silvestris's word *Oyarses* and to Professor C. C. J. Webb, who was known to his friends as "C.J." Lewis writes there, "The name *Oyarses,* as Professor C. C. J. Webb has pointed out to me, must be a corruption of *ousiarches . . .*" (*AoL,* 362). The word *ousiarches* refers to one of the ranks of angels in medieval angelology, and points to Bernardus's (and Lewis's) insistence that all space—the whole cosmos—is ontologically full, whether Yuri Gagarin sees it or not.

As David Downing has pointed out in his book *Planets in Peril,* Lewis is "at once being perfectly candid and perfectly crafty."[18] That is, he is introducing as fiction what he actually holds to be true of the cosmos, knowing that his view of nature would be ignored or mocked were it introduced in a straightforward fashion. Lewis writes, "It was Dr. Ransom who first saw that our only chance was to publish in the form of *fiction* what would certainly not be listened to as fact." What Lewis hoped people would listen to in this fictionalized account is the idea of *plenitude,* that is, that the cosmos is not empty but full. One way of getting at this idea is to give an imaginative picture of space not as a void but as a region even more full of life than our world. So Lewis wrote at the end of this chapter: "What we need for the moment is not so much a body of belief as a body of people familiarized with certain ideas. If we could even effect in one per cent of our readers a change-over from the conception of Space to the conception of Heaven we should have made a beginning" (*OSP,* xxii).

According to much of medieval cosmology, the universe must be full since it is made by God. If any part were empty, it was thought that this would imply an imperfection. Why would God make a space then fail to give it a purpose and inhabitants? Similarly, according to some medieval physics, there can be no action at a distance. If one thing moves another, then the mover and the moved must be in contact with each other. These two ideas came together in what has long been called the Great Chain of Being. In Bernardus's book the reader is taken on a journey through the cosmos, past level after level of being, from the highest empyrean heavens to the lowest forms of life on earth.

Lewis regarded Bernardus as the headmaster of a philosophical "school" of writers who took this idea of plenitude seriously. For instance, writing about the "Romance of the Rose," Lewis said that "what has impressed the poet—no doubt through the pages of Bernardus—is a vivid sense of the ageless fecundity, the endless and multiform going on, of life" (*AoL,* 150).

What Lewis lauds about this view is not its physics or even its metaphysics but its emphasis on relation. There is no corner of the universe in which there is not some good, and it has all been created by the same God; everything has some relationship to everything else; and therefore we may rightly feel both love for the whole of creation and a grounded and serious sense of responsibility for the well-being of everything. Thus the notion of interrelatedness—which is something stronger than simply saying that "everyone lives downstream," since in the relationships Lewis describes, the "stream" flows in both directions—really is central to Lewis's writing. The sensory and ideal beauty of the cosmos is intimately connected to an ecological ethic in which nothing is left out as irrelevant. In an essay on the poetry of Spenser, Lewis lamented the loss of this kind of view. He wrote, "There has been no delight (of that sort) in 'nature' since the old cosmology was rejected. No one can respond in just that way to the Einsteinian, or even the Newtonian, universe. To excite and satisfy such love the model must be clearly finite yet unimaginably large; patterned and hierarchical; moved in the last resort by love."[19]

When Ransom first leaves Earth's atmosphere he is able to escape the limitations of a terrestrial worldview. He feels for the first time the unfiltered rays of the sun fall on him through the spaceship's window. The narrator describes Ransom as being like "a second Danae . . . almost he felt, wholly he imagined, 'sweet influence' pouring or even stabbing into his surrendered body" (*OSP*, v). As he travels through space, he feels constantly invigorated by the sunlight. Lewis was not attempting what we often think of as "science fiction" here. Lewis readily admitted that he was not a scientist or a mathematician, and throughout his Space Trilogy one may find places where, scientifically speaking, Lewis betrays his ignorance of physics. We mustn't misunderstand Lewis's intention. He is not trying to make a scientific point about solar radiation. In fact, when Weston attempts to explain it only in terms of natural science, Ransom finds this explanation inadequate. What is really of concern to Lewis is the idea not of escaping Earth's literal gravity into literal solar radiation, but escaping the grave errors that our mythologies of Bergsonism and scientism have given us, and imagining the sunshine of another possible worldview enlightening us. As the narrator recounts,

but Ransom, as time wore on, became aware of another and more spiritual cause for his progressive lightening and exultation of heart. A nightmare, long engendered in the modern mind by the mythology that follows in the wake of science, was falling off him. He had read of "Space": at the back of his thinking for years had lurked the dismal fancy of the cold, black vacuity, the utter deadness, which was supposed to separate the worlds. He had not known how much it affected him till now— now that the very name "Space" seemed a blasphemous libel for this empyrean ocean of radiance in which they swam. . . . He had thought it barren: he saw now it was the womb of worlds. . . . No: Space was the wrong name.[20] Older thinkers had been wiser when they named it simply the heavens. (OSP, v)

Here we have one of the fullest statements of the modern, Wellsian nightmare-myth—that the universe is empty and we are alone and free to do as we will. And likewise here we have a clear statement of Lewis's imaginative rejoinder to this myth—what if we are mistaken and the universe turns out to be full?

But why should we adopt Lewis's point of view? Lewis gives two main reasons, each of which counters his main objections to Wells. The first reason is aesthetic: it is more beautiful than the Wellsian nightmare that finds us all alone in a cold universe. The second reason is ethical: unless we adopt something like Bernardus's view, we will wind up staking out the whole universe as our own to dominate. If, on the other hand, we remain humbly open to learning that there are others who rightfully share this place with us, we will be in a position to recognize our moral obligations to one another and so to live as we ought to live—to give up, as Wirzba calls us to, the arrogance and naiveté of anthropocentrism. Alone, neither reason is adequate. We should be cautious about adopting the first alone, lest it become a wish fulfillment,[21] and we should be cautious about the second, lest we become merely consequentialist in our thinking, preferring useful outcomes to the best outcomes. Still, together they begin to make a compelling argument that appeals both to our aesthetic judgment and to our moral faculty.

So our planet is silent because we have recently made up a myth about it in which we are all alone in an empty universe, with no one else to talk to and no one to relate to. We call it "space" as though our world floated in a vacuum; but why not call it "heaven" and recognize that there may in fact be life everywhere, if only we had eyes to see it?

In the long passage cited above Lewis suggests that our planet is overwhelmed by mythologies like those of Wells and Bergson. Just as our atmosphere does not admit the "sweet influence" of the sun's rays, so the predominant worldview does not allow us easily to imagine a world like the one Bernardus describes. The planet of Malacandra, then, becomes Lewis's imaginative laboratory where he can show us what it might look like to choose to live according to Bernardus's worldview.

The hospitality the hrossa show to Ransom is entirely natural to them, and it turns out to be the same hospitality they show to one another. There is some commercial trade but if any need food they are simply given it. All the fields of the hrossa are "worked communally" and the food is shared communally (*OSP*, xi). This hospitality extends beyond the one species to all the hnau of Malacandra. The sorns are shepherds and scholars; the hrossa are poets, vegetable farmers, and occasional fishermen; the pfifltriggi work in stone and metal. Each species gives to the others what it produces in exchange for what the others produce. Even though Ransom discovers that Malacandra is full of gold, there is no coin or currency, and no hoarding. As hoarding, and its cousin covetousness, are among the most ecologically damaging vices, Lewis is providing an important imaginative model that goes against this modern anti-ecological trend—a trend described by Richard Foster, who claims that "we must clearly understand that the lust for affluence in contemporary society is psychotic. It is psychotic because it has completely lost touch with reality. We crave things we neither need nor enjoy.... Covetousness we call ambition. Hoarding we call prudence. Greed we call industry."[22] If there is a system of private ownership, it is muted in the text. In all this Lewis is not arguing for communism—far from it! He was adamantly opposed to communism. Rather, Lewis is arguing for a life lived with concern for others that is at least as great as one's concern for one's self. The hrossa's communal life is more reminiscent of the ideal held by early Christianity than that of twentieth-century communism.[23] Each regards the portion of nature allotted to him not as his private possession but as something entrusted to him for the common good. Scott Sanders writes: "[Aldo Leopold] recognized that we have to make a living from the land, that we all need shelter and clothes and food. But he also realized that we need a great deal more if we are to lead sane and honorable lives: we need beauty, community, and purpose; we need 'spiritual relationships to things of the land.'"[24]

Lewis subtly argues that this is an ideal of common life that we all quietly and instinctively long for. The illustration of this is in pet ownership on earth. Ransom writes to Lewis in the final chapter that the Malacandrians need no pets, because "each of them is to the others *both* what a man is to us *and* what an animal is to us.... Some instinct starved in us, which we try to soothe by treating irrational creatures almost as if they were rational, is really satisfied in Malacandra. They don't need pets."[25]

This doesn't mean that the Malacandrians therefore regard all other animals as their equals. The sorns keep animals that are somewhat like our sheep, and the hrossa eat an oysterlike shellfish (*OSP*, xi). It is the hierarchy of nature that allows them to do this. At the same time, the sorns and hrossa do not consider themselves the absolute lords over the other animals. As we will see in the next chapter, the privilege of hierarchy is mitigated by the responsibility of higher creatures to improve the lower creatures.

The Ethics of Hunting

In all the Narnia stories, the only professed vegetarians are Eustace's modern and ridiculous parents. Even the beavers eat ham (as well as trout). On Malacandra, vegetarianism seems to be more the rule than the exception, but even there it is not a hard-and-fast rule. What may we conclude about the ethics of killing other animals from *Out of the Silent Planet?* Very little is said about the pfifltriggi and their ways, and not much more is said about the sorns. Presumably the sorns use the "wool" of their "sheep" for textiles, but we do not know if they also eat the meat of their animals. Since Ransom spends most of his time with the hrossa, we will have to confine our examination to that species.

The hrossa appear to get most of their food from plants, chiefly of their own growing, but they are not vegetarians. In chapter 11 there is a long passage describing the hross culture, with many references to their diet and food production. We are told there that the hrossa are fishermen, and we also learn later that the hrossa hunt the hnakra, although they do not eat the meat. At the beginning of this chapter Ransom describes the hrossa culture:

> His first diagnosis of their culture was what he called "old stone age." The few cutting instruments they possessed were made of stone. They seemed to have no pottery but a few clumsy vessels used for boiling, and boiling was the only cookery they attempted. Their common drink vessel, dish and ladle all in one, was the oyster-like shell in which he had first tasted hross hospitality; the fish which it contained was their only animal

food. Vegetable fare they had in great plenty and variety, some of it delicious. . . . He discovered their agriculture in the first week. About a mile down the *handramit* [valley, or lowland] one came to broad roads free of forest and clothed for many miles together in low pulpy vegetation in which yellow, orange and blue predominated. Later on, there were lettuce-like plants about the height of a terrestrial birch-tree. . . . These food-producing areas were worked communally by the surrounding villages, and division of labor had been carried to a higher point than he had expected. (*OSP*, xi)

We will return to the issue of land use and agriculture briefly at the end of this chapter, but first let us consider the use and killing of animals on Malacandra. As in Narnia, on Malacandra there appears to be a sharp distinction between the killing of rational animals and the killing of nonrational animals.[26] Oyarsa and the hrossa are troubled to learn that Weston and Devine have killed three hrossa, although, as we will see, the deaths of two of them are not as troubling as the death of the third. On the other hand, the deaths of the oysters and of hnakra are not troubling, and are even causes for delight.

Two chapters later we are presented with two juxtaposed and contrasting examples of killing. These two examples offer insights into how Lewis regarded the issue of hunting. In the first instance, Ransom, Hyoi, and their companion Whin together achieve one of the highest honors hrossa confer on one another: they kill a hnakra with harpoons in close combat and so earn the title *hnakrapunti*, or hnakra killers. "'So,' said Hyoi, 'we are hnakrapunti. This is what I have wanted all my life.'" The second instance comes immediately after this hunt. Just after Ransom and the hrossa pull their boat onto the shore, they hear "the crack of an English rifle" (*OSP*, xiii). Hyoi drops to the ground, slain by Weston and Devine. These juxtaposed scenes have strikingly different effects on Ransom. The slaying of the hnakra causes them great joy; the slaying of the hross plunges Ransom into grief and self-condemnation for having led his pursuers into the land of his new friends.

What makes these scenes different? For Weston and Devine, the answer is simple: they are not. Every species has the right to destroy the lower things that resist it. Later, in his trial before Oyarsa, Weston claims that the natural life-force that brought about humanity justifies such killing: "'Life is greater than any system of morality. . . . It is in her right,' said Weston, 'the right, or, if you will, the might of life herself, that I am prepared without flinching to plant the flag of man on the soil of Malacandra: to march on, step by step, superseding, where necessary, the lower forms of life that we find, claiming planet after planet, system after system, till our posterity . . . dwell in the universe wherever the universe is habitable'" (*OSP,* xx). Of course there are echoes of Machiavellian "might-makes-right" thinking here, but there are even stronger parallels to the Evolutionism of Bergson. During Weston's defense speech, Lewis has Ransom translate Weston's words into Malacandrian. This is Lewis at his philosophical cleverest—translating high-sounding speeches into simple terms to expose what he takes to be their true meanings. Here's how Ransom translates Weston's speech above: "'He says,' translated Ransom, 'that because of this it would *not* be a bent action—or else it *would* be a possible action—for him to kill you all and bring us here. He says he would feel no pity. He is saying again that perhaps they would be able to keep moving from one world to another and wherever they came they would kill everyone'" (*OSP,* xx). Ransom finds it nearly impossible to translate Weston's speech into the Malacandrian language because the Malacandrians don't think as we do, and so they lack the vocabulary of hostility. They do have a word for "kill," though, because they have a language for hunting.

Both of the killing scenes in chapter 13 look, to an outside observer, like hunting. In each case, a hunter from one species uses a weapon to kill a creature of another species. In neither case is there any evidence that the body of the dead animal will be put to use by the hunter. Both scenes strongly resemble various kinds of hunts enacted in our world: the hnakra hunt is not unlike a traditional whale hunt with harpoons and a small boat, and the killing of the hross resembles big-game hunting with a rifle at a long distance. In each case, the killer justifies the killing as a defensive act. In one way, the killing of the hross seems more defensible, since it is not premeditated and is done as an act of defense rather than as sport.

The hnakra hunt is a surprising event, in fact. What makes a nearly vegetarian and pacificist race engage in this bloody chase? When Ransom reports to the hrossa that he has seen a hnakra in their valley, "they were intensely excited. There had not been a hnakra in the valley for many years. The youth of the hrossa got out their weapons—primitive harpoons with points of bone—and the very cubs began playing at hnakra-hunting in the shallows. Some of the mothers showed signs of anxiety and wanted the cubs to be kept out of the water, but in general the news of the hnakra seemed to be immensely popular" (*OSP,* xi). Ransom discusses this with the hrossa, asking why they regard this as such a good thing. If hnakra are so dangerous, why are the hrossa glad to find one is in the river in which they all swim and seek their food? Hyoi replies that it is in the nature of the hross and of the hnakra alike to seek out this conflict. The killing that will ensue from their encounter is a good and a noble thing, if it is carried out honorably.

Moreover, the hnakra and the hrossa are bound together not only in a kind of enmity, but, paradoxically, also in love. Hyoi replies to Ransom,

> I long to kill this hnakra as he also longs to kill me. I hope that my ship will be the first and I first in my ship with my straight spear when the black jaws snap. And if he kills me, my people will mourn and my brothers will desire still more to kill him. But they will not wish that there were no *hnéraki* [the plural of *hnakra*]; nor do I. How can I make you understand, when you do not understand the poets? The hnakra is our enemy, but he is also our beloved. We feel in our hearts his joy as he looks down from the mountain of water in the north where he was born; we leap with him when he jumps the falls; and when winter comes, and the lake smokes higher than our heads, it is with his eyes that we see it and know that his roaming time is come. We hang images of him in our houses, and the sign of all the hrossa is a hnakra. In him the spirit of the valley lives; and our young play at being hnéraki as soon as they can splash in the shallows. (*OSP,* xii)

Ransom then asks if the reason for this hunt is that the hnéraki have already killed many hrossa. Hyoi replies that this is not the case: "The hrossa would be bent hrossa if they let him get so near. Long before he had come down so far we should have sought him out" (*OSP,* xii). According to Hyoi, it is the ethical obligation of hrossa to kill hnéraki, just as it is in the instinct of the hnéraki to hunt the hrossa. It is easy to see how this is so, since all rational creatures may be said to have an obligation to defend the defenseless. But when Hyoi says "how can I make you understand, when you do not understand the poets?" he indicates that there are subtle aesthetic reasons to engage in the hunt. The argument in favor of the hunt is like the argument that may be said to be in a poem; it is not just understood analytically, but also felt. There is poetry in the hunt, the poetry of the body and of a dance between species. This dance has solemn steps and, like a waltz, it cannot happen without strong sympathy between the partners. If the hrossa were to eliminate the threat of hnéraki from their lives (by avoiding the waters, for instance, or by exterminating all the hnéraki), the lives of the hrossa would become much less rich. The hnakra helps the hrossa to see their world through fresh eyes: "when winter comes, and the lake smokes higher than our heads, it is with his eyes that we see it." In this way, the hnakra is to the hross what a good science fiction story is to Lewis: it allows one to see one's own world through new eyes. Every good hunter knows the importance of seeing habitat through the eyes of the prey. This may be an often overlooked benefit of having hunters roaming the woods, and it is a decided difference between hunting and hiking.[27] The hiker usually sees through human eyes; the hunter is intentional about trying to see what can only be seen when one sympathizes with the prey, and only the hunter who loves the prey can fully do this: "The hnakra is our enemy, but he is also our beloved. We feel in our hearts his joy." The hrossa identify with the hnakra so much that they have made him their sign. In embracing their greatest foe they have embraced life. Hyoi recounts climbing to the pool where the hnéraki originate and drinking from its waters: "There I drank life because death was in the pool. That was the best of drinks save one" (*OSP*, xii). The only better drink, he says, is the drink of death itself the day he goes to "Maleldil."[28]

Seen in light of Hyoi's speeches, the killing of the three hrossa by Weston and Devine stands in sharp contrast to the killing of the hnakra. In capturing Weston and Devine, two other hrossa were killed. Hyoi's brother explains to Oyarsa, "For the death of these two, Oyarsa, I do not so much complain, for when we fell upon the [humans] by night they were in terror. You may say it was as a hunt and these two were killed as they might have been by a *hnakra*. But Hyoi they hit from afar with a coward's weapon when he had done nothing to frighten them" (*OSP*, xix).

Four times, Oyarsa asks Weston and Devine, "Why have you

killed my hnau?" The first three times, Weston avoids the question and attempts to intimidate Oyarsa. The fourth time Weston replies in his broken Malacandrian, sounding like a parody of the Western conqueror bearing the white man's burden to the far-flung savages: "We kill him. . . . show what we can do. Every one who no do all we say—pouff! Bang!—kill him same as that one. You do all we say and we give you much pretty things." All the gathered assembly laugh at the absurdity of Weston's suggestion, and Oyarsa asks a fifth time. This time, Weston replies, "We run after [Ransom]. See big black one [that is, Hyoi], think he kill us, we kill him. Pouff! Bang!"

Weston attempts to explain that the killing was done out of fear, and in self-defense. While superficially this seems like a good reason to kill, Oyarsa does not accept it. Fear may be of different sorts. It is reasonable to fear a crocodile in a river or a polar bear on pack ice, since both are known to kill humans. In this regard, when Weston and Devine shoot at the hnakra that attacks them early in the book, this is a somewhat justifiable action. The hnakra is plainly hostile. And even though the hrossa who capture them in the night do not intend to kill them, the hrossa do not complain about the two hrossa whom Weston and Devine kill then, because they see that it was reasonable for the humans to think that they were threatened. But when they kill Hyoi, they do so preemptively, with no knowledge of their prey, and therefore without any sympathy. The hross is not their beloved; they do not feel his joy; they do not realize they could speak with him. They have only contempt for his life, and so they throw it away.

Life, Death, and the Worth of Good Land

So far in this chapter we focus chiefly on what Lewis has to say about relationships between species. *Out of the Silent Planet* also has a good deal to say about land use as well. We won't belabor any of the points here because much of what we could say has already been said in the Narnia chapters, but we want to briefly draw attention to several points Lewis makes in this book.

When Ransom, the philologist, is learning the Malacandrian language, he notices a number of words that use the sound *andra*. Among them are *handramit, harandra, Malacandra,* and *Thulcandra*. The root *andra*, he learns, means "land." The fact that it shows up so often as a root in the Malacandrian language is significant; the fact that it shows up so often in the book is even more so. Lewis gives only a small number of Malacandrian words, but this is one of the most important ones, because the land is so important to the inhabitants of Malacandra. When Ransom first meets Hyoi, soil is the third thing Hyoi uses to teach Ransom their language, after they teach each other the names of their respective species. In doing so, Hyoi underscores that though they are different species, each one may be assumed to have an interest in and connection to the same land. In fact, each of the three rational species on Malacandra has an important connection to the soil. The pfifltriggi live underground and work in the metals they mine, and the hrossa are farmers. The *seroni* are shepherds who live off the land, and they are also stargazers who love to learn of other lands.

Although the hrossa love the land, all the Malacandrians also know that their land will not last forever. In *Out of the Silent Planet* Lewis offers a subtler picture of death and extinction than in *The Last Battle*. In *Out of the Silent Planet,* we learn that Mars is in its last habitable years. Moreover, we learn that it has already gone through a great extinction and loss of atmosphere. Life on Mars is limited to deep valleys that, we learn, have been artificially created to contain the last bits of water and air that sustain life on Mars. The highlands are littered with the bones and stems of extinct species.

From this it is evident that Lewis would not argue for a strict hands-off policy of preservationism. When Mars went through its ecological crisis, some species could not be saved, and Mars was refashioned to save what could be saved. While this is sad to the Malacandrians, it is not devastatingly so. All living things pass away, and the Malacandrians accept this as part of the gift of life. As Hyoi says, "it is not a few deaths roving the world around him that make a hnau miserable. It is a bent hnau that would blacken the world. And I say also this. I do not think the forest would be so bright, nor the water so warm, nor love so sweet, if there were no danger in the lakes" (*OSP,* xii). Hyoi does not mind growing old, or dying, or the fact that his world will one day die. Why should he try to stop these things, when they are part of the life of a world? Hyoi tells Ransom that "a pleasure is full grown only when it is remembered. . . . When you and I met, the meeting was over very shortly, it was nothing. Now it is growing something as we remember it. But we still know very little about it. What it will be when I remember it as I lie down to die, what it makes me in all my days till then—that is the real meeting. The other is only the beginning of it. You say you have poets in your world. Do they not teach you this?" (*OSP,* xii). Ransom, faced with such questions on Malacandra, is frequently ashamed to tell the Malacandrians what our contemporary mythmakers and poets are in fact telling us. "If a thing is a pleasure, a [human] wants it again," Ransom tells Hyoi. Humans sometimes make the mistake of thinking that good things, like pleasures, are better if they last longer. It is not only Christians who make the mistake of displacing value to eternity; the drive to preservationism might be tempted to take itself too far and assume that the best thing is to make all things last. Paradoxically, strict preservationism thus makes the good eternally inaccessible by claiming that the only good is for nothing to end. Hyoi argues that the best thing is to preserve what one can (for example, defending one's children from dangers, tending one's farm, and living harmoniously with other species—even with hnéraki), to embrace life by acknowledging mortality, and not to forget what has been given.

This does not mean Lewis is throwing in the towel and saying that environmental degradation and mass extinctions are to be welcomed. We have already quoted Lewis as saying that we are unfit to travel to new worlds because of the harm we have done to our own. "We have filled our own with massacre, torture, syphilis, famine, dust bowls and all that is hideous to ear or eye." Lewis is rather attempting to avoid two extreme errors: on the one extreme, the Wellsian/Bergsonian error of assuming that whatever serves our species' immediate need for more resources is acceptable at any price to other species; on the other extreme, the assumption of some deep ecologists, for example, that a thing is good only if it is preserved forever, and any price to humans is acceptable. The one error is hostility toward other species; the other error amounts to hostility toward our own. The way between them lies in an obdurate hospitality toward all, and in a recognition of the finitude of all as well.

Perhaps what it boils down to is this: the wrong worldview leads us to view ourselves wrongly, and to make us willing to sacrifice other creatures for our own good. Lewis was writing against the backdrop of the Second World War and of the memory of his own experiences in the First World War, to be sure, but also against the backdrop of his own experience as a walker. This brings us back to the beginning of this chapter—Lewis knew the importance of walking, of experiencing the hospitality and diversity of the natural world for its own sake. In the trial before Oyarsa, it becomes plain that the driving force behind all three humans is fear. Lewis's Christian worldview rejects this as a legitimate motivation or principle for guiding our relationships with other species. Or rather, it argues for fearing only that which truly deserves to be feared.

All of this flows out of Lewis's Christian belief. As we said earlier, Lewis does not claim special privilege for Christians, as though only Christians truly appreciated the world. But Lewis does cherish a part of the Christian tradition in which all of creation is, by virtue of its being *creation,* valuable and lovely. He also takes the Christian idea of sin seriously, and believes it was demonstrated in human history: we kill and enslave one another, we kill and enslave other species, and we lay waste to the land in search of wealth we want but do not need. This idea is one without which any ecological vision will be incomplete, because it will thereby omit one of the most devastating factors. Other science fiction writers had already prepared our imaginations for hostile invasions from space; another mythology had prepared us to imagine that the cosmos was empty. What was still missing was a mythology that would prepare us to meet a species that did not share our predilection for violence. Lewis argued that such a meeting would be dangerous for the other species, and that it is the obligation of Christians and all who cherish charity, hospitality, and stewardship to prepare to do whatever we can to protect that new species from dangerous humans.

> What I do know is that here and now, as our only possible practical preparation for such a meeting you and I should resolve to stand firm against all exploitation and all theological imperialism. It will not be fun. We shall be called traitors to our own species. We shall be hated of almost all men; even of some religious men. And we must not give back one single inch. We shall probably fail, but let us go down fighting for the right side. Our loyalty is due not to our species but to God. Those who are, or can become, his sons, are our real brothers even if they have shells or tusks. It is spiritual, not biological, kinship that counts.[29]

Of course, in this passage he is talking about extraterrestrials. But he has already argued in *Out of the Silent Planet* that the cosmos might be brimming with life in places we haven't thought to look, or having bodies we have no eyes to see. In other words, those other species that need our hospitality might already be sharing our planet. We are dangerous, but we might learn, by a re-enchantment of our worldview, to be hospitable as well.

Chapter 6

Perelandra

Creation and Conscience

We murder to dissect.
—C. S. Lewis, *The Four Loves*

In what belongs to the deeper meanings of nature and her mediation between us and God, the appearances of nature are the truths of nature, far deeper than any scientific discoveries in and concerning them. The show of things is that for which God cares *most,* for their show is the face of far deeper things than they. . . . It is through their show, not through their analysis, that we enter into their deepest truths.
—George MacDonald, in Lewis's *George MacDonald:*
  An Anthology

In 1960 a young girl named Meredith wrote to Lewis and asked him which of his books he thought was most "representational." Lewis replied, "Do you mean simply which do I like the best? Now, the answer w[oul]d be *Till We Have Faces* and *Perelandra*."[1] For the last few decades of his life, Lewis considered *Perelandra* (written in 1941–1942) one of his best works.

Most of *Perelandra* takes place on Venus, which is called Perelandra by its inhabitants. This second book in the Space Trilogy is quite different from the other two novels. Nearly all of its dialogue is among three characters, each of whom is, if not "representational," at least representative or archetypal. This book, perhaps more than any other of Lewis's, reads like a Platonic dialogue. In the central chapters of the book there is very little action and much dialogue concerning ethics, metaphysics, and the best life. At the end of *Out of the Silent Planet,* Lewis claimed to be "removing the mask," and revealing directly some of the theological purpose of that book. In *Perelandra* that mask remains off.[2] In *Perelandra,* more than in the other two novels in the trilogy, issues of practical theology rise to the surface and remain there for close scrutiny. David Downing, in his *Planets in Peril,* notes, "Lewis commented that he wrote *Perelandra* for his 'co-religionists' . . . —that is, fellow Christians. The theology in the second book of the trilogy is thus not smuggled in but carried in through the front door. *Perelandra* is the story of 'Paradise Retained,' of an Eve who is able to resist the tempter long enough for Ransom to destroy him. In fulfilling his quest, Ransom too learns a great deal about the reality of myth and how ordinary mortals may be called upon to engage in mythic labors."[3] Downing is right: *Perelandra* lends itself readily to discussions about Lewis's theology and his views of myth. For that reason, one might think that *Perelandra* is not perhaps very pertinent to a discussion of Lewis's ecology. Of course, we do not want to "murder to dissect" Lewis's writing, nor attempt to make this out to be a more ecologically interested novel than it is. Nevertheless, this apparently abstract and dialogic novel is rich with ecological significance. We encounter Perelandra, if not exactly at the moment of its creation, then at the moment of its creation as an ethically inhabited world.

Old Worlds and Deep Ecologies

Perhaps Lewis liked this book so much because it was so different from other books he had written. Its distinct style and setting offer a unique perspective on several features of Lewis's ecological vision. In this chapter we will examine two such features: first, the unique setting of an old world recently populated. This is different from what we saw in *The Magician's Nephew,* in which the world was created anew. Perelandra is a world with animal life and even possibly ancient subterranean civilizations, but recently populated with rational creatures on its surface. This allows Lewis to explore a different notion of creation: creation is not merely the making of a physical world, but also the discovery and acceptance within that world, by its inhabitants, of their place within it—which, in fact, *is* a central question of human ecology. Lewis's philosophy of nature involves, if not a hierarchy of beings, then at least a continuum of beings, in which there are real rational and ontological differences. This entails distinct ethical roles for each kind of being, but two similarities: all rational beings participate in creation by affirming their place in creation, and all beings have natures that long to grow into perfection. *The Magician's Nephew* showed us the creation of a new world and talked explicitly about the care of it. *Perelandra* examines a world that was *created* long ago, but only recently *morally inhabited*. The emphasis, then, is not on the particular forms of life of that world (which are, nevertheless, fascinating) but on what it means for creatures capable of ethical reflection and action to dwell in such a world. It is the obligation of such creatures to care for other creatures and to help them to grow to perfection. This is a mutual effort; in helping other creatures grow, we ourselves grow. This growth includes a growing knowledge of what "perfection" means; this requires us to be humble as we seek to help others to grow, since we cannot see what the end or *telos* of each creature may be.

Second, *Perelandra* remains relevant as a critique of at least certain forms of contemporary *deep ecology*. Deep ecology is, as David Landis Barnhill and Roger S. Gottlieb have noted, a term that is "multivalent and in dispute."[4] In general, deep ecologies are deep because they are not just concerned with surface issues like particular ecological problems, but with an examination of worldviews and philosophies of nature that underlie ecological thinking. In that regard, much of what we have been pointing to in Lewis's fiction more closely resembles deep ecology than ecology more narrowly construed as principles of activism, for instance. Barnhill and Gottlieb and others, like Bill Devall,[5] have nonetheless articulated some general principles common to deep ecologies.[6] Some of these elements look very much like what we have so far identified in Lewis's ecological vision, for instance, "an emphasis on the intrinsic value of nature." Especially if we see this as opposed to an instrumentalist view of nature, wherein all things exist for human use, this closely approximates Lewis's view. Barnhill and Gottlieb also add "an emphasis on interrelationships" and "a humility toward nature, in regards to our place in the natural world, our knowledge of it, and our ability to manipulate nature in a responsible way." As we have already seen, these are principles Lewis's fiction strongly affirms.

On the other hand, deep ecologies tend to endorse certain ecological principles to which Lewis explicitly objects. For instance, Barnhill and Gottlieb mention "a tendency to value all things in nature equally

(biocentric egalitarianism)," "an affirmation that humans are not separate from the natural world (there is no 'ontological gap' between
humans and the natural world)," and "an identification of the self with
the natural world."[7] There are reasons to suppose that these points are
not wholly opposed to Lewis's view, but as we will see in this chapter,
Lewis would argue against each of them and especially against the last.
Lewis's chief concern appears to be that each of these latter principles
can actually undermine human moral responsibility. This, then, is
related to the point we make directly above: creation is not just a place;
it is a place quickened by real relationships and real ethical responsibility. As we will see shortly, one of the hinge pins on which the *Perelandra*
narrative turns is the moment at which the Queen of Perelandra makes
an ethical decision that affirms her place in nature. She does nothing
physically, but she speaks from her heart, and Lewis offers this to the
reader as tantamount to a moment of creation. Similarly, the culmi-
nation of the novel occurs in a moment of praise—a "moment" that
lasts for many months. The passage of time in that moment goes virtually unmarked by the three people who are offering their praise. Their
praise is directed specifically toward God as creator and sustainer of
life. It is worth remarking that the passage of time leaves the protagonist
Ransom apparently younger and surprisingly more robust. In praising
their creator, the three humans affirm their intermediate place in the
cosmos, and the result is a transcendent moment in which they experience heaven and earth at once.

So Lewis's narrative is deeply theological, which means it is deeply
concerned with the place and meaning of human life in the world and
in light of the divine. This, however indirectly, makes *Perelandra* a text
about worldview and the philosophy of nature. Perhaps this is why Lewis
loved it so. But perhaps he loved it simply because it is beautiful. The
unique picture of life on Perelandra is something that may be enjoyed
for its own sake, and not without profit. This is one of the functions
of myth. The plants and animals of Perelandra, simply enjoyed by the
reader, may matter all by themselves, even if we draw no deeper conclusions from them. Lewis gives reason to believe that the unique creatures
we encounter on Perelandra may be instructive to us, but he also argues
that the use we may make of animals is not the whole of their value.
As we say in our opening chapter, Lewis attempted to weld together
his beliefs into a consistent whole. His view of nature is, of course, tied

to his theological view of creation. In one of his books, Lewis collects 365 readings from George MacDonald. In one of these readings, which Lewis evidently approves, MacDonald says, "In what belongs to the deeper meanings of nature and her mediation between us and God, the appearances of nature are the truths of nature, far deeper than any scientific discoveries in and concerning them. . . . It is through their show, not through their analysis, that we enter into their deepest truths. What they say to the childlike soul is the truest thing to be gathered of them. . . . By an infinite decomposition we should know nothing more of what a thing really is, for, the moment we decompose it, it ceases to be, and all its meaning is vanished."[8] With this caveat in mind, we will nevertheless attempt to do some analysis, though we hope without decomposing that which Lewis felt he had so beautifully composed.

Life without Stars: Finding God in Nature

While he was writing *Perelandra,* Lewis explained to his friend Arthur Greeves what he was attempting to do. "I'm engaged on a sequel to *The Silent Planet* in wh[ich] the same man goes to Venus. The idea is that Venus is at the Adam-Eve stage: i.e. the first two rational creatures have just appeared and are still innocent. My hero arrives in time to prevent their 'falling' as *our* first pair did" (*L2*, 504). The Oyarsa of Malacandra sends Ransom this time to Perelandra without telling him why he must go. Ransom is transported to Perelandra in a sort of flying coffin that lands in a vast ocean. Ransom emerges to find several peculiar features to this planet. For instance, there are only two people on the planet besides Ransom, and they dwell on floating islands of dense vegetation. Ransom also finds that there is a constant high-altitude cloud cover on Perelandra that wholly obscures the stars each night.

The passage cited above from George MacDonald goes on to reflect on how much we learn from stargazing.

> Infinitely more than astronomy even, which destroys nothing, can do for us, is done by the mere aspect and changes of the vault over our heads. Think for a moment what would be our idea of greatness, of God, of infinitude, of aspiration, if, instead of a blue, far withdrawn, light-spangled firmament, we were born and reared under a flat white ceiling! I would not be supposed

to depreciate the labors of science, but I say its discoveries are unspeakably less precious than the merest gifts of Nature, those which, from morning to night, we take unthinking from her hands. One day, I trust, we shall be able to enter into their secrets from within them—by natural contact.[9]

In his essay "On Science Fiction," Lewis suggests that observing the night sky can at least serve to awaken in us humility and an awareness of our place in the cosmos: "those who . . . stare long at the night sky are less likely than others to be ardent or orthodox partisans" (OSF, 63). But what if this were not a possibility? *Perelandra* attempts to see how much it is possible to "enter into [Nature's] secrets . . . by natural contact." If the Perelandrans are to discover divine virtue, they must do it without having their thoughts drawn upward by their view of the night sky. Their encounters with the divine in nature will take place entirely at a tangible level. This is part of why we say that *Perelandra* has some relevance for thinking about contemporary ecology, since so much of contemporary ecology does precisely this. One caricature of the difference between natural philosophy and science, on the one hand, and theology, on the other hand, is that theology begins with knowledge of heaven and tries to relate it to life on earth, while science and philosophy begin with the world before us and attempt to discover within it that which belongs to heaven. "That which belongs to heaven" may mean the unseen but real physical principles and laws of nature, or it may mean something more like what contemporary eco-pagans mean by finding the divine in nature. Both are examples of what is not seen prima facie, but only by close examination. For MacDonald and Lewis, the principles of nature and the divine are not unrelated to each other: an orderly creator begets an orderly creation in which principles may be discovered. Lewis takes this inquiry to Venus, rather than enacting it on Earth, because there he may ask to what degree our extant worldviews, affected by time, culture, and sin, have obscured nature's "secrets."

Perelandra differs from our world in another way as well. In addition to being cut off from the heavens, the inhabitants are also cut off from whatever lies beneath the ground. For most of the book, Ransom is in contact with only one Perelandran, whom he calls the Green Lady or the Queen. She turns out to be the first woman on Perelandra, and she has become separated from the only man, her husband the King.

Their dwelling is in the sea, on floating mats of vegetation, and they have been prohibited by Maleldil from spending the night on any solid ground. They dwell entirely on the surface, and what lies far below is as unknown to them as what lies beyond the clouds.

Shortly after his arrival, Ransom and the Green Lady see something fall into the sea. It is Weston, the antagonist from *Out of the Silent Planet,* who has also been sent to Perelandra on a mission. Weston believes his mission to be somehow scientific, but he is plainly under the influence of ideas and beings he does not understand. His mission is, in a sense, to persuade the Queen that there is no "ontological gap" between herself and nature. That is, he wants to convince her that there is no God above her and no reason to view the world below her as different from herself. He wants her to identify herself, not only partly, but *entirely* with nature, and so to use nature however she wishes. If she accepts this, the only way to assert her individuality will be through some act of violence.

Though Ransom has not known why he is on Perelandra, when he sees Weston, he takes it as his mission to prevent Weston from doing harm to Perelandra and especially to the Queen. This is not a minor point: in this way, Ransom is very much like us. We also may have a sense that we should "do something," yet have no idea what that something may be. Like us, Ransom does not know whether his actions will be the best thing or if they will wind up doing harm. In the end, he chooses to do what he can in the face of potential disaster. He is no hero; he is only a man who offers himself to do the best he can.

Weston is a peculiarly diabolical missionary, one who attempts to convert individuals to the belief that the notion of an "individual" is misguided. He preaches the identification of the human being with nature and the erasure of all ontological and ethical differences (much as Frost does in *That Hideous Strength*). The tragedy for Weston is that he receives his wish: in attempting to persuade others, he is himself converted and thus loses himself. He is left with no place in the world, no ability to participate morally in nature and, therefore, no relationship to nature. His worldview entails first his moral, then his intellectual, then finally his physical death.

Do Individuals Matter? The Un-Man

Weston's identification of himself and the world has not diminished

Weston's self-estimation as one might expect; it has instead diminished the world to nothing. He is not curious, he is not enchanted by the strangeness of this new world, and he does not see the point of knowledge if it cannot be put immediately to use. That is, Weston does not care about science, but only about the uses of scientific knowledge as a means to power. He cares only about applied science, or technology. He tells Ransom, "The false humanist ideal of knowledge as an end in itself never appealed to me. I always wanted to know in order to achieve utility. At first, that utility naturally appeared to me in a personal form—I wanted scholarships, an income, and that generally recognized position in the world without which a man has no leverage. When those were attained, I began to look farther: to the utility of the human race!" (*Per,* vii). Shortly after, Weston describes in more detail this change and its later development:

> "I began to see that my own exclusive devotion to human utility was really based on an unconscious dualism."
> "What do you mean?"
> "I mean that all my life I had been making a wholly unscientific dichotomy or antithesis between Man and Nature—had conceived myself fighting *for* Man against his non-human environment. . . . Hitherto, as a physicist, I had been content to regard Life as a subject outside my scope. The conflicting views of those who drew a sharp line between the organic and the inorganic and those who held that what we call Life was inherent in matter from the very beginning had not interested me. Now it did. I saw almost at once that I could admit no break, no discontinuity, in the unfolding of the cosmic process. I became a convinced believer in emergent evolution. All is one. The stuff of mind, the unconsciously purposive dynamism, is present from the very beginning." (*Per,* vii)

One advantage of Lewis pulling off the mask in *Perelandra* is that he frequently states more baldly what his philosophical point is. *Perelandra* comes close, at times, to reading like a Socratic dialogue. Weston explains the upshot of his belief like this:

> The majestic spectacle of this blind, inarticulate purposive-

ness thrusting its way upward and ever upward in an endless unity of differentiated achievements towards an ever-increasing complexity of organization, towards spontaneity and spirituality, swept away all my old conception of a duty to Man as such. Man in himself is nothing. The forward movement of Life—the growing spirituality—is everything. I say to you quite freely, Ransom, that I should have been wrong in liquidating the Malacandrians. It was a mere prejudice that made me prefer our own race to theirs. To spread spirituality, not to spread the human race, is henceforth my mission. This sets the coping-stone on my career. I worked first for myself; then for science; then for humanity; but now at last for Spirit itself—I might say, borrowing language which will be more familiar to you, the Holy Spirit. (*Per*, vii)

Ransom objects that this is not in fact familiar usage, but a distorted usage. It is what Lewis would call a "verbicide," the killing of a useful word by trying to make it do too much. "I'm a Christian," replies Ransom, " and what we mean by the Holy Ghost is *not* a blind, inarticulate purposiveness." Now this is certainly a theological objection, but it is not *just* a theological objection, since the topic at hand is not primarily theology. Interestingly, it is Weston who insists on discussing this in theological terms. The problem is that Weston, in trying to eliminate all categorical distinctions (for example, human versus nature, organic versus inorganic, species distinctions) winds up eliminating the possibility of meaningful conversation. It is entirely safe for him to bring up theological language at this point because he has effectively stripped it of its usefulness. "Nothing divides you and me except a few outworn theological technicalities with which organized religion has unhappily allowed itself to get incrusted. But I have penetrated that crust." Weston finally states it flatly: "There is no possible distinction in concrete thought between me and the universe" (*Per*, vii). All ontological difference has been erased in his thinking.

This view has several alarming consequences. One of them is that along with the disappearance of ontological difference, relationships are also blurred, and therefore ethics become for Weston obsolete. Ransom asks Weston if ever his allegiance to the universe compelled him to kill Ransom, or to "sell England to the Germans," or to "print lies as serious research," would he do it? Weston immediately replies to each question that he would.

Another disturbing consequence of Weston's worldview is that all places are alike to him. By ignoring the apparent differences in things, the things themselves vanish from his horizon, and Weston displays scant curiosity about his surroundings. The uniqueness and beauty of the world he has just entered have no effect on him. When he first encounters Ransom, "Ransom could hardly help admiring the massive egoism which enabled this man in the very moment of his arrival on an unknown world to stand there unmoved in all his authoritative vulgarity, his arms akimbo, his face scowling, and his feet planted as solidly on that unearthly soil as if he had been standing with his back to the fire in his own study." Ransom observes later that Weston is "like an actor who cannot think of anything but his celebrity, or a lover who can think of nothing but his mistress" (*Per*, vii). Perelandra does not matter to Weston. In fact, Weston's view of the world is almost wholly anaesthetic. Shortly after his arrival Weston has a seizure. Ransom offers the panting Weston some brandy, and Weston bites clean through the bottle, swallowing broken glass. Ransom is sure Weston will die from this, but Weston is incapable even of feeling the pain.

The explanation Lewis offers is that Weston has become the willing host to a diabolic eldil, a sort of possession. Occasionally, Weston cries out in fear, as though his soul were trapped in a body nearly taken over by demonic forces. "Ransom! Ransom! For Christ's sake don't let them—" (*Per*, vii) and then he is cut off by his seizure. But Lewis is not writing gothic horror; this "possession" is not a random event but the consequence of Weston's playing host to a diabolical worldview. The theologians tell us that the Devil hates God's works and longs to destroy them. If that is so, then there is more than one way to destroy them. Weston becomes an example of this. Weston's denial of the intrinsic value of individual things and of the reality of ontological difference is tantamount to the destruction of Weston *by* Weston. Little by little Weston's personality vanishes and what is left is Weston's body, steered by a demon or a demonic ideology that is bent on destruction. The narrator begins to refer to Weston as "the Un-Man."

This happens roughly halfway through the book. After a long conversation in which Weston tries to persuade the Lady to live where she has been forbidden to live, the Lady goes to sleep. Ransom sits watch over her, fearing what the Un-Man might do to her while she sleeps. Instead of harming her, the Un-Man tortures Ransom by saying Ransom's name over and over until Ransom explodes "What?" "Nothing," the Un-Man replies, and then begins to say "Ransom" again. "What kept him steady, long after all possibility of thinking about something else had disappeared, was the decision that if he must hear either the word Ransom or the word Nothing a million times, he would prefer the word Ransom" (*Per,* ix). As Weston is slipping into the oblivion and erasure of ontological difference his worldview calls for, Ransom makes the opposite choice. This illustrates a point about Lewis's view of individuals:[10] we feel our difference from one another and from our world, and that feeling is instructive. We are different, and in that difference our ethical obligations to one another are exposed.

But this is unsteady ground, and Ransom feels that as well. Can feeling alone be the substance of ethics? The Un-Man speaks with real rhetorical force, and Ransom asks himself how he can know that he is right and the Un-Man wrong. Ransom clings to his Christian personalism, that is, his belief that persons are of irreducible importance. He will not worship an abstract idea, especially if that idea winds up demanding the sacrifice of individual living beings. Earlier in the narrative, Weston asks Ransom, "Don't you worship [God] because He is pure spirit?" Ransom retorts, "Good heavens, no! We worship Him because He is wise and good. There's nothing specially fine about simply being a spirit. The Devil is a spirit." Weston objects to this distinction between God and the Devil, because he holds that abstractions in general are higher than material things, and that they are without distinction: "In my view no real dualism in the universe is admissible" (*Per,* vii). God and the Devil, good and evil, all are one. The essential distinction for Weston has become the class distinction between those enlightened enough to see that all other distinctions are irrelevant, and those who are not. For Ransom it is the ethical distinction between right and wrong action, right and wrong belief.

But how can Ransom know that he is right? Weston's position is no straw man, and it has advocates, as we see in *Out of the Silent Planet,* in Bergson's various disciples. In the end, Ransom makes a pragmatic decision: he would rather hear himself named as an individual than as a personless part of the whole. Weston is the embodied illustration of the consequences of the belief that all is indistinguishably and ultimately one: he loses his humanity and his personality, often in painful episodes. Ransom, urged on by nothing clearer and firmer than his conscience, his fellow feeling and his Christian tradition, insists that actual lives, not Life as an abstraction, are what matter. Earlier in the book, prior to Weston's arrival on Perelandra, Ransom reflects on the views Weston had espoused on Malacandra:

> Professor Weston . . . was a man obsessed with the idea which is at this moment circulating all over our planet in obscure works of "scientifiction," in little Interplanetary Societies and Rocketry Clubs, and between the covers of monstrous magazines, ignored or mocked by the intellectuals, but ready, if ever the power is put into its hands, to open a new chapter of misery for the universe. It is the idea that humanity, having now sufficiently corrupted the planet where it arose, must at all costs contrive to seed itself over a larger area: that the vast astronomical distances which are God's quarantine regulations, must somehow be overcome. This for a start. But beyond this lies the sweet poison of the false infinite—the wild dream that planet after planet, system after system, in the end galaxy after galaxy, can be forced to sustain, everywhere and for ever, the sort of life which is contained in the loins of our own species—a dream begotten by the hatred of death upon the fear of true immortality, fondled in secret by thousands of ignorant men and hundreds who are not ignorant. The destruction or enslavement of other species in the universe, if such there are, is to these minds a welcome corollary. (*Per,* vi)

Of course the first obvious implication of Ransom's reflection is that "destruction or enslavement of other species" is associated with evil, but there is something else significant, though less obvious, going on. On Perelandra, Ransom sees that Weston's ideas have evolved even further. Once again, Lewis is suggesting that when we begin with contempt for one part of creation, our contempt will wind up spreading to encompass all of creation. Weston's description of his upward progress—"I worked first for myself; then for science; then for humanity; but now at last for Spirit itself"—sounds good until we consider what he does not say directly: each of these upward steps on the ladder of progress has amounted to a rejection of what lies on the lower rungs. The individual, the pursuit of knowledge for its own sake, love of one's fellow humans—all are good, but Weston has rejected them all in his worship of the abstraction *Life*.

What we must not miss here is the ecological upshot of this: Weston has attempted to level the playing field for all life, to regard all things as identical. He has effectively eliminated the possibility of all hierarchy and of all difference, hauling God down and earth up until they meet and become one. The result he aimed at, no doubt, was the divinization of the cosmos, but the effect is quite the opposite. He says, "In so far as I am the conductor of the central forward pressure of the universe, I am it. Do you see, you timid, scruple-mongering fool? I *am* the Universe. I, Weston, am our God and your Devil" (*Per*, vii). With nothing left below him, there is nothing to care for. With nothing left above him there is nothing else to worship but himself, and no transcendent basis for ecological ethics. He ends this speech in a spasm that leaves him unconscious—symbolic of the way his philosophy of nature has stripped him of his curiosity, his rationality, and his concern for creation.

Being the Stone: Engaging in Moral Conflict

Lewis makes it plain that he is also writing against the backdrop of another moral conflict, and it is significant that the conflict on Perelandra is not just among Perelandrans. It is significant that there are two humans from earth there. Walter Hooper, like Downing, has remarked that this book probably grew out of Lewis's long experience in teaching *Paradise Lost*.[11] Certainly this is likely, but *Perelandra* could have been written about Venutians without including human characters. This book is not just an interesting speculation, then, about what an unfallen world might be like. It is also concerned with how humans might behave in such a world, and what humans might bring back from such a world. To put it differently, Lewis is asking, how should we regard the creation? Lewis considers three possible answers:

One is Weston, who, as we have seen, becomes the Un-Man as the result of his ethical decisions.

The second is Ransom's vain hope: leave it alone and God will take care of it all. When he is engaged in his disputes with Weston, Ransom tires and is tempted to give up. "Terrible follies came into his mind. He would fail to obey the Voice, but it would be all right because he would repent later on, when he was back on Earth." Lewis agrees: we can, as Christians, choose this option, and we may do so with confidence that God will make all things right. But then he asks, is it worth the price? How terrible a price did God pay for our sin already? Do we really intend to ask for even more? What if we ruin another world? Is that gratitude? Can it legitimately be considered piety? Ransom knows the answer to these questions: "The small external evil which Satan had done in Malacandra [blighting the planet] was only as a line: the deeper evil he had done in Earth was as a square: if Venus fell, her evil would be a cube—her Redemption beyond conceiving" (*Per*, xi). Christians are often (and often correctly) accused of not caring for creation because of the Christian belief that one day history will end and God will set all things right. *The Last Battle* answers part of this charge; here we go further. Lewis's Ransom is an enacted answer to that belief: if we fail to care, God may set things right, but we will have acted with impiety.

The third option is the only one left, and it is the one Ransom chooses: do something. Act. Fight against evil. Are you guaranteed to win? No. Are you guaranteed comfort? No. As Lewis wrote in *The Four Loves,* "we find thus by experience that there is no good applying to Heaven for earthly comfort. Heaven can give heavenly comfort; no other kind. And earth cannot give earthly comfort either. There is no earthly comfort in the long run" (*FL*, 190). Ransom argues with Weston until he realizes that Weston, the Un-Man, will be relentless in his destructive drive. He must be stopped for the sake of this young world. Ransom feels inadequate to the task, but, remembering the war that is going on back at home, he takes up his fists and battles Weston. Both men are badly beaten, and they wind up first in the sea, then in a sea-cave, before Ransom finally succeeds in killing his enemy. In the process, Ransom is badly hurt with a wound that never heals. He is frightened out of his wits. He is lost in a cave, underground, for days. This battle winds up being very costly to him. Many fighting the battle in our world for a healthier ecology may feel the same way. The result, however, is the safety of a whole world, and Ransom considers it worth the cost.

This is a peculiar incident, and Lewis does not seem to be advocating violence on earth. Rather, Lewis describes this battle as a mythic battle and one that could not have been done ethically on earth. The killing of Weston is not murder but rather symbolic of a battle against a vicious idea that negates life: "Ages ago it had been a Person: but the ruins of personality now survived in [the Un-Man] only as weapons at the disposal of a furious self-exiled negation" (*Per,* xii). The Un-Man has shown its true colors in telling the Lady, "I have come that you may have Death in abundance" (*Per,* ix). In another chapter we witness him maiming frogs for no reason at all. He takes animals apart not just to see what he can learn but for his own pleasure. Later, when he is fleeing from Ransom, the Un-Man straddles a fish and tortures it into giving him a ride, much like Jadis did with Strawberry in London.

This choice is not an easy one for Ransom, and he struggles for a long time looking for some other way out. As a Christian who has been sent to Perelandra by angels, he has some right to expect miraculous intervention on behalf of the planet, but none is apparent. "Why did no miracle come? Or rather, why no miracle on the right side? . . . He did not understand why Maleldil should remain absent when the Enemy was there in person." His expectation is that he is brought to this world as a mere observer. It slowly dawns on him that his place in this world is to contend for what is right. His very being is, in a sense, a miracle. "The answer which came back to him . . . seemed Blasphemous. . . . That miracle on the right side, which he had demanded, had in fact occurred. He himself was the miracle." Over against Weston's insistence that humans are identical with the universe, Lewis argues that it is precisely in our differences that the possibility of moral conduct emerges. We are miracles—part of the Creator's work in redeeming creation. And in embracing the necessity of making ethical decisions on behalf of those others to whom we are related, we affirm our place in the world and participate most fully in the world's creation. "Thus and not otherwise the world was made. Either something or nothing must depend on individual choices. And if something, who could set bounds to it? A stone may determine the course of a river. He was that stone at this horrible moment" (*Per,* xi).

The Animals of Perelandra

We say in the chapter on *The Magician's Nephew* that we will return to the imperative to improve animals. Perhaps because Lewis himself always kept animals, he frequently used human relationships with animals to illustrate other points. In *Perelandra* this theme receives one of its fullest literary treatments. We must decide what animals are here for.

Are they, as Uncle Andrew and Jadis argued, here for our arbitrary use? Or are they here so that we might care for them? There is no third possibility. If we ignore them, we act as though they were part of the landscape and make the decision of the builders of Babel (which we discuss in the next chapter). Even in our loves for them we must decide in what way we are loving them. If we love them to satisfy some need in us, we wind up harming them. If we love them with affection in order to see them flourish, we are serving them. Lewis discusses this in the section of *The Four Loves* on "Affection," where he says,

> to learn that someone is "fond of animals" tells us very little until we know in what way. For there are two ways. On the one hand the higher and domesticated animal is, so to speak, a "bridge" between us and the rest of nature. We all at times feel somewhat painfully our human isolation from the sub-human world—the atrophy of instinct which our intelligence entails, our excessive self-consciousness, the innumerable complexities of our situation, our inability to live in the present. If only we could shuffle it all off! We must not—and incidentally we can't—become beasts. But we can be *with* a beast. It is personal enough to give the word *with* a real meaning; yet it remains very largely an unconscious little bundle of biological impulses. . . . Man with dog closes a gap in the universe. But of course animals are often used in a worse fashion. If you need to be needed and if your family, very properly, decline to need you, a pet is the obvious substitute. You can keep it all its life in need of you. You can keep it permanently infantile, reduce it to permanent invalidism, cut it off from all genuine animal well-being, and compensate for this by creating needs for countless little indulgences which only you can grant. The unfortunate creature thus becomes very useful to the rest of the household; it acts as a sump or drain—you are too busy spoiling a dog's life to spoil theirs. . . . probably it cannot fully realise the wrong you have done it. Better still, you would never know if it did. The most down-trodden human, driven too far, may one day turn and blurt out a terrible truth. Animals can't speak. (*FL*, 79)

For Ransom, Weston and the Green Lady represent the two possible and opposite consequences of this basic decision. As we have noted above, the choice we face is not whether we will think of ourselves as kings over some piece of creation; the choice is what *kind* of royalty we will choose to be. Weston, as we have said, attempts to erase the differences between himself and the world, so the animals become unimportant until he has use for one. Then, when he has use for one, he considers himself its rightful lord, free to kill it at whim. His notion of kingship is one of absolute sovereignty, with no ethical obligation to his subjects.

The Lady, by contrast, loves the animals for their own sake. She does not caress them simply to enjoy them, though she obviously does delight in them. She caresses them and cares for them because it is both her right and her responsibility to do so. The way Lewis describes this is, at first, off-putting: "There was in her face an authority, in her caresses a condescension, which by taking seriously the inferiority of her adorers made them somehow less inferior—raised them from the status of pets to that of slaves." The words *condescension* and *slaves* are not attractive to our ears; the one sounds like sneering mockery from a superior, the other like a state of torturous bondage. We must gloss this, then. In *The Magician's Nephew* we see that slavery was too mean a state for animals. So on Perelandra. These "slaves" are not abused but elevated. We must not let our distaste for the word *slave* get in the way of our noticing that Lewis considers "slave" a higher status than "pet." We must also not fail to notice that the Lady takes the animals seriously as inferiors. The alternative to this is to pretend that they are not inferior; but such pretense immediately eliminates the possibility of improving the lives of the animals. We cannot elevate our absolute peers. Finally, we should notice the effect of the Lady's attention: she makes them less inferior. Her task is not to enslave the animals (which would ensure their perpetual degradation) but to improve them. *Slavery* may be an apt term for their current state, but it is not their *telos,* not the end for which they were created.

The Lady is therefore not their slaver but their tutor. Ransom observes her communion with the animals and remarks, "The beasts in your world seem almost rational." "We make them older [that is, wiser] every day," she answers. "Is not that what it means to be a beast?" (*Per,* v). Later the King echoes her words, saying, "We will know this world to the centre. We will make the nobler of the beasts so wise that they will become hnau and speak: their lives shall awake to a new life in us as we awake in Maleldil" (*Per,* xvii). In *The Magician's Nephew* we see this in a compressed form when Aslan breathes rationality into certain animals and then enjoins them to safeguard that rationality. In *Perelandra* Lewis shows what it might look like for humans to attempt the same. This is not the same as "training" an animal to obey commands. Toward the close of the book, when the Queen and the King meet the Oyarsa of Perelandra, Oyarsa says to them, "Give names to all the creatures, guide all natures to perfection. Strengthen the feebler, lighten the darker, love all" (*Per,* xvii).

This passage could be Lewis's gloss on Genesis 1.26ff and 2.15–20a, in which Adam is given charge over Eden and its animals, and in which he names all the animals. Genesis 1:26 is the primary source of many ecological complaints about the Judeo-Christian worldview, including what Aldo Leopold calls the "Abrahamic" domination of the earth. However this is only part of the divine calling for humans. Calvin DeWitt makes a very important observation about the specific words used in the later passage.

> Genesis 2:15 expects human people and their descendants to *serve* and *keep* the garden. The word "keep" is the Hebrew word "*shamar,*" which means a loving, caring, sustaining kind of keeping. This word is used in the Aaronic blessing, "The lord bless you and *keep* you" (Num. 6:24). When we invoke God to keep *us,* it is not that God would keep us in a kind of preserved, inactive state. Instead it is that God would keep us in all of our vitality, energy and beauty. . . . It is the kind of rich and full keeping that we should bring to God's garden, his creatures and all of Creation. As God keeps his people, so should people keep Creation.[12]

In other words, our understanding of the original Hebrew words used in the instructions to Adam must be considered in our understanding of human dominion; our dominion is to be a blessing—it should keep the world, much as we would desire God to keep us. Bouma-Prediger makes the same point about Genesis 1 and 2. "Yes, we are called to exercise dominion, but we are also called to service. For example Genesis 2:5 speaks of humans serving the earth . . . and Genesis 2:15 . . . defines the human calling in terms of service: we are to serve (*abad*) and protect (*samar*)."[13] As we see, Lewis's gloss also understands *domination* in the context of *care* and *tutelage*. In Lewis's worldview, all "natures," or species, have a *telos* or perfection toward which they want to grow. It is the task of the King and Queen—and their offspring—to help the animals to become what they should be. By accepting this task, the King and Queen participate in the creation of their world. It is also the way they themselves grow into the perfection of *their* nature.

When she is arguing with Weston, the Green Lady sees for the first time that her offspring might one day be greater than she is. Though Weston had intended to tempt her to become envious of them, instead she rejoices at the thought that the effect of her life might be to contribute to the improvement of the lives of others. For Lewis, this is both good theology and healthy ecology.

When the Queen and King have affirmed their place in the creation, something is revealed to them that Ransom already knows: their world is brimming with more life than they had imagined. Even at the beginning, the Queen knows nothing of eldila or of life on other planets. Some of these things are revealed to her mystically, by direct communion with God. Through Ransom's eyes we see signs of abundant life throughout Perelandra. Deep below the sea are mer-folk, whose rationality, if it exists at all, is wholly unlike Ransom's.[14] He describes them as having "faces in which humanity slept while some other life, neither bestial nor diabolic, but merely elvish, out of our orbit, was irrelevantly awake" (*Per*, viii). He goes on to speculate that the Queen and King may have evolved from these mer-folk, which suggests what the task of perfecting the nature of the mer-folk may be like: the Queen and King are to elevate the mer-folk, to awaken in them latent rationality, and to live in harmony with them. But again, this can only come about as a result of the Queen and King affirming their place in creation. Prior to this affirmation, Ransom encounters the mer-folk a second time, and he reflects that "it is significant that it never occurred to him to try to establish contact with these beings, as he had done with every other animal on Perelandra, nor did they try to establish any with him. They did not seem to be the natural subjects of man as the other creatures were. He got the impression that they simply shared a planet with him as sheep and horses share a field, each species ignoring each other" (*Per*, xiii). It is only after the Queen and King have ascended to the throne of their responsibility that they learn that "the others under the waves whom yet you know not; all these Maleldil puts into your hand from this day forth" (*Per,* xvii).

Similarly, when Ransom is in the cave, he sees and hears evidence of at least one culture far underground. He sees great thrones in a huge throne room, apparently made for giants; he peers over an underground cliff and sees charioteers far below; and he sees stonework he takes to be the work of dwarfs. When he looks down on the charioteer, "upright, unshaken . . . a mantled form, huge and still and slender," he is aware of intruding into the realm of another creature (*Per,* xv). The normal human impulse is to think of other creatures as beneath us. Weston, for instance, protests that he has not "murdered" Hyoi the hross on Malacandra, because, after all, "the creature killed was not a human being" (*Per,* vii). For Ransom, the effect of seeing this charioteer is the opposite. He becomes aware that the cosmos is brimming with life, no corner of it unimportant or empty. Space, Ransom reminds himself, is a misnomer for "Heaven, tingling with a fullness of life for which infinity itself was not one cubic inch too large" (*Per,* xiii). In this cave Ransom is not the rightful occupant; he is the intruder. "Assuredly the inside of this world was not for man. But it was for something. And it appeared to Ransom that there might, if a man could find it, be some way to renew the old Pagan practice of propitiating the local gods of unknown places in such fashion that it was no offence to God himself but only a prudent and courteous apology for trespass. That thing, that swathed form in its chariot, was no doubt his fellow creature. It did not follow that they were equals or had an equal right in the under-land" (*Per,* xv). This is an important passage, one that affirms some of the impulses of contemporary Paganism and eco-paganism and what Michael Zimmerman calls "Spiritually-oriented Deep Ecologies": "Many spiritually-oriented deep ecologists (SDEs) explain the ecological crisis as the failure of modern people to revere the sacredness of nature. The West in particular is said to be governed by an arrogant anthropocentrism, subject-object or humanity-nature dualism, and a consumerist mentality, which act in concert to disclose nature as nothing but raw material for human ends."[15] The problem with this approach is that many SDEs want to reject modernity and its "arrogant anthropocentrism, subject-object or humanity-nature dualism, and a consumerist mentality" by the same move Weston makes: the sacralizing of the earth and the assertion of the identity or sameness of all being. Zimmerman calls this a "Flatland ontology," in which all being is brought to the same level and the divine is placed in the ground, so to speak. Ransom's experience in the ground offers a different way of answering the sins of modernity by reaffirming a rich ontology and recognizing that humanity occupies only a small place in that great continuum of being.

It is rational, if there are such beings as the charioteer, to suppose that they might be as offended by trespass as we are. But what significance does this mythical notion have for us? Without pretending to be exhaustive, we can make several suggestions: first, regardless of whether such beings exist or not, our knowledge of the natural world is limited. There may be wisdom in walking lightly and not causing harm where no harm is necessary. Second, the old notion of making ritual sacrifices may be outdated, but it may be quite reasonable to continue to make sacrifices for the sake of other beings around us: sacrificing excessive consumption and arrogant anthropocentrism may be good places to start.

But this entails a risk with no obvious payoff. How do we know that our attempts to show elevating care for those creatures below us and respect for all creatures—including those we have not yet discovered, some of which may be above us—will actually benefit those creatures? We do know that there will be a cost.[16] Do we know that there will be a benefit?

Lewis does not offer a direct answer to this in *Perelandra*. The answer he offers is indirect, through the story itself, and we doubt that an analysis of it can equal the argument of reading the story and being caught by it. His appeal is, to some degree, to our experience. The cost of sacrifice is economically plain, and Ransom, as we have observed, returns from Perelandra with a wound that will never heal. The benefit is one that Ransom experiences, but then has great difficulty explaining to his friends. His experiences in harmonious nature on Perelandra can find no strict analogues in English. He says, "It is words that are vague. The reason why the thing can't be expressed is that it's too *definite* for language." So he must, for instance, describe tastes by saying things like "it was like the discovery of a totally new *genus* of pleasures" (*Per*, iii).

The story itself is nevertheless an invitation to examine our own experiences to see if we have not been drawn in by beauty and wonder to the point where we have seen that there is in nature that which demands our pious care and attention and that may even demand sacrifice on our part.

This pertains even to those creatures for which we can imagine no possible use. The last creature Ransom observes is a very shy "singing beast" that stands alone in the woods and sings beautifully when she thinks she is not being watched. If she is seen, she grows silent and retreats. Ransom asks the Oyarsa of Perelandra about this creature, and the Oyarsa explains some of its biology:

> "The beasts of that kind have no milk and always what they bring forth is suckled by the she-beast of another kind. She is great and beautiful and dumb, and until the young singing beast is weaned it is among her whelps and is subject to her. But when it is grown it becomes the most delicate and glorious of all beasts and goes from her. And she wonders at its song."
>
> "Why has Maleldil made such a thing?" said Ransom.
>
> "That is to ask why Maleldil has made me," said Perelandra. "But now it is enough to say that from the habits of these two beasts much wisdom will come into the minds of my King and my Queen and their children." (*Per*, xvi)

Is it worth the cost of maintaining such creatures if they stand in the way of progress? We can only answer that question if we attend to it, aware that Maleldil "has immeasurable use for each thing that is made" and that "We also have need beyond measure of all that He has made" (*Per*, xvii). The answer to the question "Is it worth the cost of maintaining such creatures?" is that we cannot afford not to care for them. We are bound together with them.

Sharp, Sweet, Wild, and Holy

Lewis insists that humans have a natural and appropriate place within creation. As we see in *Out of the Silent Planet*, one way we wind up rejecting our place in creation is to divorce ourselves from the creation and to insist that we may legitimately do to created things whatever suits and pleases us. As we have seen in this chapter, another way we reject our place in creation is to attempt to blur the distinctions between us and creation. Weston's insistence that he and the cosmos are one effectively distances him from any obligations toward the cosmos. If all is indivisibly and indistinguishably one, then there can be no question of relationships; and without relationships there can be no ownership, relative status, or obligation. If the universe and I are one, then it follows that whatever I desire the universe desires. The universe ceases to exist as *other* and therefore there can be no claim that I have wronged another. The first of these views must deny the sense that we belong in the cosmos; it makes humans into absolute aliens and, as we saw in the previous chapter, the real monsters. The other view denies our sense of being different from the cosmos; it blurs the distinctions and must dismiss them as illusory.

We may affirm both of these senses, however, if we have a natural place in the cosmos. When Ransom travels by night from the solid land to the floating islands, he cannot see where he is going, but he can smell the aroma of the islands. This single sense of smell is enough to affirm for him that he has a place in the created order.

> He knew well what it was. He would know it henceforward out of the whole universe—the night-breath of a floating island in the star Venus. It was strange to be filled with homesickness for places where his sojourn had been so brief and which were, by any objective standard, so alien to all our race. Or were they? The cord of longing which drew him to the invisible isle seemed to him at that moment to have been fastened long, long before his coming to Perelandra, long before the earliest times that memory could recover in his childhood, before birth, before the birth of man himself, before the origins of time. It was *sharp, sweet, wild, and holy,* all in one, and in any world where men's nerves have ceased to obey their central desires would doubtless have been aphrodisiac too, but not in Perelandra. (*Per,* viii; emphasis added)

This passage is striking: Ransom has spent only a few nights on one of these islands, but he has the uncanny sense of homesickness for it. The aroma of this place is both wild and holy. How can an aroma be holy? His recognition of the aroma points back to something built into him. Already before time his olfactory sense and this aroma of a welcoming place for humans to live were made for each other. The suitability of person and place predates time and hints at a divine intention.

Praise and Moral Creation

In ending this chapter let us return to a brief but important event that occurs right in the middle of the narrative. Ransom, lying awake in the darkness, has just overheard a conversation between Weston and the Green Lady. At the conclusion of the conversation, Ransom "was conscious of a sense of triumph. But it was not he who was triumphant. The whole darkness about him rang with victory. . . . It was as if Perelandra had that moment been created—and perhaps in some sense it had" (*Per*, viii).

Immediately before this point, Weston has been badgering the Lady about moving to the nearby solid land. She protests that Maleldil has forbidden her to spend the night on that land. Weston insists that Maleldil has forbidden it so that she might choose to do it on her own, and so assert her independence from a moral code that originates outside her. He tells her that she would think differently if she could see women from our world. "Their minds run ahead of what Maleldil has told them. They do not need to wait for him to tell them what is good, but they know for themselves as He does. They are, as it were, little Maleldils." She replies that it would be wonderful to see them, and she praises the Creator for having made them and for the possibility that her children might be greater and know greater things than she. She concludes her praise by saying that both curiosity and joy grow like trees. "I see it is not only questions and thoughts that grow out wider and wider like branches. Joy also widens out and comes where we had never thought" (*Per*, viii). Weston's response to this unexpected praise is to fall suddenly asleep.

Since Weston in this book has become a symbolic character, we may surmise Lewis's point. In praising creation and its creator, the Lady acknowledges who she is in the cosmos. She is only one woman of one generation, a queen, but one bound to do what is good. She humbly acknowledges that nature will be for later generations and not just for hers. Even though she is Queen of Perelandra, her own world presents her with mysteries, the depths of which she cannot yet plumb.

Her praise amounts to the rejection of Weston's diabolical insistence that she view herself as wiser than the Creator. This has an ecological upshot, of course: his insistence is both an urging to reject the command she has received from God and an urging to choose to live by her own rules, in a place that is, frankly, not suitable for her life. Weston obviously plays the role of the serpent in Lewis's Edenic narrative. What is interesting about the temptation he offers her is its ecological nature. Though the world is hers, she knows that her royal status does not legitimate any misuse of her world. Weston's aim as tempter is to entice her to do this one thing, then: to force unsuitable land to be a home for her, to live outside of her element, to bend the land beyond its nature in order to suit her whim. He tries to tempt her to arrogate to herself the right to exploitation as a natural corollary of her royalty. This is, of course, a response to those who hold that since Adam's race is granted dominion over the earth, we therefore have a right to dominate it how we will. For Lewis, this is absurd. If we agree that God has given us this place, then we also agree that God is its rightful owner and we are just the stewards. We furthermore implicitly agree that the one who establishes standards of conduct is God, not us. We may not behave however we will with impunity. Abuse of that which we are supposed to steward is disobedience and an attempt to divorce ourselves from our rightful position in the cosmos. It is effectively a rejection of creation.

So when the Queen responds with praise rather than with arrogance, she effectively reaffirms her place in the great chain of being: not at its top, but as a responsible steward in the middle.

This, then, is the context in which Ransom senses triumph. It is not *his* triumph, nor even hers. It is the triumph of the world Perelandra, which "in some sense" has just been created. The creation of a world is not a static event; it entails, at least in part, human ethical decisions to affirm our place in the world. The creation of Perelandra is not just the calling together of its constituent parts to create a physical mass, nor the organization of that mass into geography, flora, and fauna. It is, ultimately, the establishment of a set of relationships between the world and its inhabitants and their creator. The triumph occurs when those who are made for those relationships affirm their rightful place within them. Weston, praising himself, hopes to erase the distinction between heaven and earth. In doing so, he loses heaven and earth alike.

The Green Lady affirms the distinction in the act of giving praise, which is echoed in her acceptance of her being in the world, and in her stewardship of what is given to her care. In doing so, she enriches the world with the presence of heaven.

Chapter 7

That Hideous Strength

Assault on the Soil and Soul of England

Instead of making the world safer for humankind, the foolish tinkering with the powers of life and death by the occidental scientist-engineer-ruler puts the whole planet on the brink of degradation.
—Gary Snyder, "The Etiquette of Freedom"

The grip of the N.I.C.E. on Edgestow was tightening. The river itself which had once been brownish green and amber and smooth-skinned silver, tugging at the reeds and playing with the red roots, now flowed opaque, thick with mud, sailed on by endless fleets of empty tins, sheets of paper, cigarette ends and fragments of wood, sometimes varied by rainbow patches of oil. . . . Twenty-four hours later the N.I.C.E. boarded over the doomed Wynd and converted the terrace into a dump.
—C. S. Lewis, *Out of the Silent Planet*

In *The Lord of the Rings,* J. R. R. Tolkien provides a threefold glimpse of the destructive ecological impact of evil. After portraying environmental devastation in its most extreme form in the faraway landscape of Mordor, and also in the ravaged land of Isengard, he brings the battle back to the Shire, the homeland of the Hobbits. For many readers, this third and final portrayal of devastation—the destruction of the soil, water, and air of the Shire—is the saddest and most deeply moving of the three ravaged landscapes, even though it is the least extreme. Tolkien modeled the Shire in part after the late nineteenth-century English countryside of his youth. So it is reminiscent of our world, closer to our time. English readers especially have good cause to feel about the devastation of the Shire the same way Sam does, that it is "worse than Mordor! Much worse in a way. It comes home to you, as they say."[1]

C. S. Lewis does something similar in the third book of his space trilogy.[2] After setting two novels on other planets, he brings the battle to his own home soil, and more or less to his own time.[3] We might say it is a battle *for* his home soil, both literally and metaphorically: literally, because the very health of England's soil and all that depends upon it is at stake, and metaphorically, because the struggle is a battle for England's soul as well as its soil.

Deforestation in Edgestow and Belbury

At the start of this book, we observe that the final volumes of both of Lewis's two fantasy series, the Chronicles of Narnia and the Space Trilogy, begin with a deforestation project. Though not the *cause* of all the troubles to come, this deforestation is at least the first visible *symptom* of these troubles and the first ground over which the battle is fought (and lost). In *That Hideous Strength,* the deforestation begins with the ancient Bragdon Wood, located in the fictional English academic town of Edgestow on the campus of Bracton College. In the opening chapter, readers learn that some of the wood is to be sold and cut to make room for development, namely, the new headquarters for the N.I.C.E., the National Institute for Coordinated Experiments.[4] Now Bragdon Wood is only about one quarter square mile in size, or 160 acres, and not all of it is supposed to be cut; thus "deforestation" may seem at first to be too strong a word. Nonetheless, even this small-scale deforestation is significant for several reasons. One is that Bragdon is a very important and symbolic wood, and thus its destruction is a symbolic destruction, with implications beyond the mere felling of local timber; the fate of the symbolic wood symbolizes the worldview of those responsible for that fate. Another is that the *means* by which permission is obtained for the cutting of the woods is through deceit and manipulation, and is representative of the rhetoric of so-called industrial progress, giving considerable insight into the evil represented by the N.I.C.E. and its hostile view toward nature.[5]

One of the first things the narrator mentions about the town of Edgestow is how beautiful it is—more beautiful than either Oxford or

Cambridge. "For one thing it is so small. No maker of cars or sausages or marmalades has yet come to industrialise the country town" (*THS*, 1.2). In other words, the Edgestow area still belongs to and is symbolic of the older and more agrarian English landscape prevalent in the previous century before industrialization. The Wood itself is mysterious, even holy. "Very few people were allowed into Bragdon Wood. . . . A high wall enclosed [it, and] if you came in from the street and went through the College to reach it, the sense of the gradual penetration into a holy of holies was very strong. . . . When a thing is enclosed, the mind does not willingly regard it as common." The narrator even puts himself into the story and describes a previous (fictitious) visit there, thus further personalizing the significance of the Wood. "As I went forward over the quiet turf I had the sense of being received. The trees were just so wide apart that one saw uninterrupted foliage in the distance but the place where one stood seemed always to be a clearing; surrounded by a world of shadows, one walked in mild sunshine" (*THS*, 1.3). The imagery is both rich in life and light, and also very personal: the sense of the trees receiving visitors implies a collective consciousness and awareness on their part, not unlike the dryad-haunted woods of Narnia, Digory's experience in the "LeFay Fragment," Ransom's frequent refuge under trees in *Out of the Silent Planet*, or Tolkien's Ent-inhabited Fangorn Forest. Lewis's repeated use of the indefinite pronoun "one"—which refers to any and all persons, and not just to the narrator—suggests that this is an archetypal wood. We learn later that it has stood there since the time of Merlin. It is a sanctuary and a remnant of ancient times, walled up as a sacred place. As such, it acts as a symbol of all such ancient woods.

However, none of this matters to the majority of those who vote to sell the Wood. The fact that the N.I.C.E. "wanted a site for the building which would worthily house this remarkable organization" is sufficient reason for most members of the college to vote to sell. Having the N.I.C.E. in Edgestow, rather than in the competing Oxford or Cambridge, is perceived as a coup for the university that will enhance its status—its power, prestige, and ultimately its wealth. This is where Lewis explicitly presents the rhetoric of progress. Any consideration of value of Bragdon Wood other than utilitarian value—any consideration of its beauty, or its historical value, or simply its value as a wood, a place of peace and sanctuary, where birds, sheep, and men are nurtured—is

dismissed as mere sentiment. The ancient Wood is reduced to an economic commodity: not even a measurement of board feet of lumber,
but simply a development site. "Three years ago, if Mark Studdock had
come to a College Meeting at which such a question was to be decided,
he would have expected to hear the claims of sentiment against progress
and beauty against utility openly debated. Today, as he took his seat . . . he
expected no such matter. He knew now that that was not the way things
are done" (*THS*, 1.4). Once the so-called Progressive Element is able to
associate selling the Wood with progress (regardless of the cost of this
progress), then any opposition is viewed as backward.

Not surprisingly, Lewis connects some of the success of this view
of progress with deceit. In our discussion of the ape Shift in chapter 4,
we cite Norman Wirzba's comments about the rhetoric of agribusiness.
David Orr also writes about those who promote progress at the expense
of the health of the land: "That they wish to bamboozle should astonish
no one; that they get away with it, however, depends on a high level of
public drowsiness and gullibility. But that is an altogether more compli-
cated thing—a kind of co-conspiracy involving a combination of ignorance and apathy on one side and a desire to mislead on the other, all
disguised by a language unhinged from reality."[6] This is much the sort
of bamboozling that Lewis illustrates in the manipulations used by the
Progressive Element to sell the Wood. The narrator first tells us that "the
Progressive Element managed its business really very well. Most of the
Fellows did not know when they came . . . that there was any question of
selling the Wood." Thus some manipulation comes through a deceitful
hiding of the real agenda. But some comes from a basic appeal to greed:
through promises that those who support this sort of progress will reap
financial benefits. In the case of Bragdon Wood, it is the junior fellows
at the university who should expect (they are told) to see their stipends
increase, because the college will not only lose the burden of the upkeep
of the Wood, but will also get a large sum of money for its sale. "When,
at quarter to two, the Fellows came surging out . . . for lunch, hungry
and headachy and ravenous for tobacco, every junior had it fixed in his
mind that a new wall for the Wood and a rise in his own stipend were
strictly exclusive alternatives. 'That darn Wood has been in our way all
morning,' said one. 'We're not out of it yet,' answered another." Thus the
junior fellows become, in the language of David Orr, *co-conspirators*. In

fact, the reader is given enough insights into the successful workings of the Progressive Element right from the start that it is a foregone conclusion that the Wood will be sold. "The few real 'Die-hards' present, to whom Bragdon Wood was almost a basic assumption of life . . . were maneuvered into the position of appearing as the party who passionately desired to see Bragdon surrounded with barbed wire" (*THS*, 1.4).

The reader only later learns that what is proposed as the loss of a small part of one ancient wood turns out to be a massive project involving the widespread destruction of trees all around Edgestow and—given the national and even international power of the N.I.C.E.—perhaps all over England and the world. About Bragdon Wood, for example, Cosser, who works for the N.I.C.E., explains to the protagonist Mark, "You see, all that land at Bragdon Wood is going to be little better than a swamp once they get to work. Why the hell we wanted to go there I don't know. Anyway, the latest plan is to divert the Wynd [River]: block up the old channel through Edgestow altogether" (*THS*, 4.6). Cosser's knowledge of these plans makes it clear that the N.I.C.E. had conspired from the very beginning to cut far more than they were telling; considerable deceit was involved in the manipulation of Bracton College to sell the land. Once the N.I.C.E. takes over Edgestow, the organization begins evicting people from their homes and cutting down trees left and right. We see this through the eyes of the other protagonist, Jane, the wife of Mark. Mrs. Dimble (one of the evictees) tells Jane: "By that time, the big beech that you used to be so fond of had been cut down, and all the plum trees . . . great lorries and traction engines roaring past all the time, and a crane on a thing like a railway truck" (*THS*, 4.1). It is a bleak picture. Beech trees and plum trees are out; the machines of industrialization are in. Humans and trees both fall victim to progress.

The most telling scene, however, may be at Belbury, where the N.I.C.E. is headquartered. In addition to Wither and Frost, Filostrato is one of two characters (the other being Straik) closest to the inner workings and power structure of the N.I.C.E. Filostrato argues that the cutting of trees is not merely a means (perhaps regrettable, perhaps not) to some other end, but that the destruction of trees is an end in itself. He gives orders for "the cutting down of some fine beech trees in the grounds" of Belbury for no other reason than to get rid of them. When another member of the N.I.C.E. complains, Filostrato defends his order.

The forest tree is a weed. But I tell you I have seen the civilised tree in Persia. It was a French *attaché* who had it because he was in a place where trees do not grow. It was made of metal. A poor, crude thing. But how if it were perfected? Light, made of aluminum. So natural, it would even deceive. . . . Consider the advantages! You get tired of him in one place: two workmen carry him somewhere else; wherever you please. It never dies. No leaves to fall, no twigs, no birds building nests, no mulch and mess. . . . Why one or two? At present, I allow, we must have forests, for the atmosphere. Presently we find a chemical substitute. And then, why *any* natural trees? I foresee nothing but the *art* tree all over the earth. In fact, we *clean* the planet. (*THS*, 8.2)

We will return to this passage later in the chapter, but for now we note that the cutting of Bragdon Wood is not partial (as originally promised) but complete, and also that it is only a first step in deforesting the whole landscape of England. As we have seen, trees soon begin to fall *en masse* all around the town of Edgestow, as well as in the nearby Belbury (where the N.I.C.E. is currently headquartered), and presumably also in the agricultural community of Cure Hardy,[7] since it is to be entirely flooded by a new dam. So "deforestation" is not too strong of a word; if the plans of Filostrato (and thus of the N.I.C.E.) are realized, it will be a worldwide deforestation.

The N.I.C.E. Rejection of Nature

All of this leads to the question, Just what are the plans of the N.I.C.E.? This turns out to be more complex than one might guess, and the answer depends very much on to whom one speaks at Belbury. Frost, Wither, Straik, and Filostrato, the four most important figures at the N.I.C.E., seem to have not only very different means to their end, but also different motives. In many ways, Frost and Wither represent opposite extremes of evil. Yet Lewis gives one tantalizing hint that they are also almost interchangeable: two sides, but two sides of the same coin. Both desire power and are willing to do whatever it takes to gain that power.

An exploration of these characters and their means toward power is beyond the scope of this book and has already been undertaken in the critical literature.[8] As regards the subjects of ecology and nature, however, a more interesting question pertains to the *perceived* plans and objectives of the N.I.C.E. and the work at Belbury: the objectives given by the N.I.C.E. propagandists to the public at large—and accepted by the public—as justification for their actions. Busby, one of the influential members of the Progressive Element at Bracton who helps promote the sale of Bragdon Wood to the N.I.C.E., in a conversation with Lord Feverstone (the character known as Dick Devine in *Out of the Silent Planet*), gives a good overview of the public's general perception: "I should have thought the objects of the N.I.C.E. were pretty clear. It's the first attempt to take applied science seriously from the national point of view. The difference in scale between it and anything we've had before amounts to a difference in kind. The buildings alone, the apparatus alone—! Think what it has done already for industry. Think how it is going to mobilize all the talent of the country: and not only scientific talent in the narrower sense. Fifteen departmental directors at fifteen thousand a year each! Its own legal staff! Its own police, I'm told!" (*THS*, 2.1). Lewis's tone here is quite satirical. Busby is one of the villains of the novel, albeit a minor one, and what he promotes should be understood as very different from C. S. Lewis's perspective of the direction his country should be taking. Busby—like the ape Shift—is enamored of the outward signs of technological progress: big buildings, apparatus, industry, and things done at a large scale. (We can assume without too much risk that he would argue for the superiority of large-scale technologically driven agribusiness over the agrarianism of the small farm.) There is little doubt in his mind that this sort of progress is what the N.I.C.E. stands for—and to the extent that the N.I.C.E. stands for anything other than power itself, he is correct. That the N.I.C.E. advertises its own police force as well as its own legal staff suggests that the desire for power is not far below the surface.

Now for some of Lewis's readers, the mention of science in a negative context is troublesome, and we are brought back yet again to this sticky issue already explored in our treatment of *Out of the Silent Planet* and *Perelandra* and even the Narnia stories. Since *That Hideous Strength* sheds yet more light on Lewis's view of technology and applied science, it is worth one more look. At most colleges and universities, environmental studies is heavily based in the sciences. We ask again whether Lewis is associating the evil of the N.I.C.E. with science, and if he is thus anti-science. As a close look at the book makes clear, the answer to both parts of this question is no. First, we see even in Busby's words that the villainous N.I.C.E. is not especially interested in science itself or in what we might call "pure science"; it is interested only in "applied science," which is the *use* of scientific knowledge for the sake of gaining technological power. Even Busby mentions pure science as being the "narrower sense" of talent—"narrow" being a pejorative here, as in "narrow-minded." The N.I.C.E. is full of pseudoscientists and has as its figurehead a science-fiction writer. The only real scientist we meet in Belbury, however, is a chemist named Bill Hingest. Hingest, it turns out, speaks of the institute with disdain; when we meet him he is in the process of leaving it. "I came here," he says, "because I thought it had something to do with science. Now that I find it's something more like a political conspiracy, I shall go home." This one real scientist in the story turns out to be a person of considerable integrity. He even tries (in vain) to talk Mark out of joining the N.I.C.E., and adds that he'd rather give up chemistry altogether than see it corrupted. As a scientist, he is committed to truth. "There are a dozen views about everything," he comments, "until you know the answer. Then there's never more than one" (*THS*, 3.4). Unfortunately, the institute is the sort of place one does not leave. Hingest is killed and becomes something of a martyred hero in the story. So Lewis's view of real scientists who care about science as a means of learning the truth of the universe and its workings, and not merely as a means to some other end (technological or political power), can be seen to be quite high; the N.I.C.E. is explicitly disassociated from real science.

Now the point here is not to defend Lewis's view of science. Lewis has already given his own defense; the points made above are made explicitly by C. S. Lewis in various places, most notably in his article "A Reply to Professor Haldane," cited earlier in this book. In an article in *The Modern Quarterly*, Haldane had attacked Lewis as being anti-science, in large part because of *That Hideous Strength* and passages such as Busby's explanation cited above. But in looking at Lewis's answer—that is, at his criticisms of the applied scientist as opposed to the "real scientist," both in his essay and in his novel—we learn something important about Lewis's view of nature. In his reply to Haldane, Lewis distinguishes between "science" and "scientism": the latter being "the belief that the supreme moral end is the perpetuation of our own species, and that this is to be pursued even if, in the process of being fitted for survival, our species has to be stripped of all those things for which we value it—of pity, of happiness, and of freedom" (RPH, 76–77). It is of this *scientism*, as a worldview (to which some scientists happen to be devoted, but which itself is by no means scientific), that Lewis is critical. Specifically, he is criticizing a sort of species-ism among humans: a view that values only human life (or survival) and does not take into consideration human interaction with the rest of the earth. Survival of our species, Lewis writes, should not come at the cost of the oppression of other life; that would be immoral, and if stripped of moral virtue, our species is not deserving of survival—a point he also makes in his essay "On Living in an Atomic Age," as we note earlier.

There is one other important comment to be made about applied science and technology, and it can be seen in Filostrato's speech cited at the end of the previous section. Filostrato says of the artificial tree, "Consider the advantages! You get tired of him in one place: two workmen carry him somewhere else; wherever you please." The underlying assumption of Filostrato is that humans should conform nature (the world, reality) to our own personal tastes and preferences rather than seeking to conform ourselves to nature. It is the same sort of species-ism, or anthropocentrism, stemming from the false beliefs that *only* humans matter; if nature doesn't fit our wishes, we rearrange nature. As we mention earlier, Lewis explicitly addresses this issue in his book *The Abolition of Man*. Many of his ideas are rooted in one very important contrast: "For the wise men of old the cardinal problem had been how to conform the soul to reality, and the solution had been knowledge, self-discipline, and virtue. For magic and applied science alike the problem is how to subdue reality to the wishes of men" (AOM, 77). This is why the N.I.C.E. is as interested in getting hold of Merlin and his magic as they are in technological power: they assume (wrongly, as it turns out) that Merlin will use his magic to provide them with exploitive power over nature. Lewis's writings suggest that the correct human approach should be very different: that there is an order and pattern and purpose to creation, and it is our responsibility to see how and where we fit in. What Lewis would see as the positive goal of the real scientist is to study nature with a goal of understanding it, thus providing us with the knowledge to conform *our* practices to *its* patterns. Lewis criticizes the applied scientist and the technologist who seek only to understand enough about nature to conform it to our wishes; if we can't just move a tree whenever it's convenient, Filostrato suggests, we create an artificial one that can be manipulated.

What the N.I.C.E. seeks is this technologist who can manipulate nature and humans alike. That is why, as the institute gains power, it is not only trees, but all biological life, that comes under attack. When Filostrato defends his deforestation program, a minor character named Gould asks him, "Do you mean that we are to have no vegetation at all?" Filostrato responds, "Exactly. You shave your face: even in the English fashion, you shave him every day. One day we shave the planet. . . . I would not have any birds either" (*THS*, 8.2).

Even before Filostrato is introduced, Lord Feverstone (Dick Devine) works from the same sort of anthropocentric assumptions and makes similar arguments for the wiping out of organic life. He explains to Mark the sorts of "problems" he thinks the N.I.C.E. needs to solve: "The second problem is our rivals on this planet. I don't mean only insects and bacteria. There's far too much life of every kind about, animal and vegetable. We haven't really cleared the place yet. First we couldn't; and then we had aesthetic and humanitarian scruples; and we still haven't short-circuited the question of the balance of nature. All that is to be gone into. The third problem is man himself" (*THS*, 2.1). The villain Feverstone is explicitly arguing for clearing the planet of all nonhuman life: animal as well as vegetable. He makes mention of the "balance of nature," but it is only lip service; he doesn't argue for preserving the balance of nature for the sake of nature itself, but only insofar as it meets human purposes. According to the antagonists, "aesthetic and humanitarian scruples"—what Lewis would call beauty and goodness—are obstacles to be overcome. Of course this suggests that Lewis's notions of beauty and goodness should fall on the side of those who really do care about nature, the balance of nature, and preserving animal and vegetable life.

Lewis also expresses these ideas in his poem "Iron Will Eat the World's Old Beauty Up"—a poem that criticizes sensationalist journalism as well as the destruction of nature in the name of progress. Don King gives an astute summary of the poem's main themes: "'Iron Will Eat the World's Old Beauty Up' is a direct commentary on the modern world as Lewis sees it . . . echoing his distrust of human progress when it occurs at the expense of beauty and truth. He imagines the industrial revolution, particularly the new machines of his own day, involved in the destruction of Nature; as the new cities and buildings emerge (the 'iron forests'), they will block out Nature so there will be 'no green or growth.'"[9] In both the poem and the novel, we see that it is not human progress or even industrial machines per se that are the problem, but human progress *at the expense of* beauty, truth, and green growth; the problem is industrialism *resulting in* the destruction of nature. We also see again that this sort of ecological thinking runs through Lewis's large body of work, including essays and poems as well as stories, and for that reason we must assume that it is not merely accidental in or incidental to the fiction.

Moreover, Lewis doesn't merely represent as abstract ideas these sorts of arguments he finds appalling. In *That Hideous Strength,* he shows us what they look like when they are put into practice; his imaginative story makes the ideas concrete. Even before the devastation at Edgestow becomes too severe, Mark has the opportunity to see firsthand the treatment of animals at the Institute.

> This time he wandered round to the back parts of the house where the newer and lower buildings joined it. Here he was surprised by a stable-like smell and a medley of growls, grunts and whimpers—all the signs, in fact, of a considerable zoo. At first he did not understand, but presently he remembered that an immense programme of vivisection, freed at last from Red Tape and from niggling economy, was one of the plans of the N.I.C.E. He had not been particularly interested and had thought vaguely of rats, rabbits, and an occasional dog. The confused noises from within suggested something very different. As he stood there a loud melancholy howl arose and then, as if it had set the key, all manner of trumpetings, bayings, screams, laughter even, which shuddered and protested for a moment and then died away into mutterings and whines. Mark had no scruples about vivisection. What the noise meant to him was the greatness and grandiosity of the whole undertaking from which, apparently, he had been excluded. (*THS,* 5.1)

Now Mark, who has been taken in by all of the rhetoric of the N.I.C.E., doesn't (yet) see anything wrong with what is happening. Indeed, as a journalist for multiple newspapers, he has become one of the chief rhetoricians for manipulating the English population into accepting the N.I.C.E. agenda. (Lewis had as low of an opinion of journalists who told the populace what to think about various issues or public figures as he did of sensationalist journalism.)[10] But Lewis's own view of the atrocities of the N.I.C.E. come through in the narrative, despite Mark's selfish disregard for the sufferings of these animals. Mixed with the description of Mark's dispassionate observation is enough description of suffering that all but the most calloused readers of the book should be horrified. If nothing else, the very fact that this treatment of animals happens at the institute is enough to associate it with evil.

Perhaps one more account of the treatment of nature under the authority of the N.I.C.E. suffices to illustrate Lewis's portrayal of evil as it relates to ecology and nature. Not many days after the sale of Bragdon Wood, we read: "The grip of the N.I.C.E. on Edgestow was tightening. The river itself which had once been brownish green and amber and smooth-skinned silver, tugging at the reeds and playing with the red roots, now flowed opaque, thick with mud, sailed on by endless fleets of empty tins, sheets of paper, cigarette ends and fragments of wood, sometimes varied by rainbow patches of oil. . . . Twenty-four hours later the N.I.C.E. boarded over the doomed Wynd and converted the terrace into a dump" (*THS*, 6.2). Returning to "The Scouring of the Shire" in Tolkien's *The Lord of the Rings*, we see that Lewis's description of Edgestow under the grip of the N.I.C.E. is very similar to Tolkien's depiction of the Shire under the grip of Saruman. Both authors had seen firsthand (and lamented) the industrialization and subsequent degradation of their beloved English countryside.

We could continue with more of these descriptions from Lewis's novel, but we would be seeing only more of the same. Thomas Howard, who wrote a fine treatment of Lewis's fiction, summarizes the position of Filostrato and Belbury. Filostrato's "entire goal in life is to fumigate the earth . . . to sterilize the world from all the weeds and trees and leaves and eggs—all this fecundity." He goes on to draw the interesting conclusion that Filostrato's "punishment not only fits the crime, but . . . is simply the crime itself turned back on the perpetrator. If you will reject and violate Nature—Nature in all of its manifestations . . . then Nature will spring back upon you and destroy you, which is what happens with the unleashing of animals at Belbury."[11]

What the N.I.C.E. has done, as both Filostrato and Feverstone make clear, is more than just exploit nature for the sake of power and selfish gain. They have rejected nature altogether. They have rejected it as significant and as valuable. Many members of the N.I.C.E. have the unhealthy view that nature is a commodity to be exploited. But at the core of the N.I.C.E. is the fatal view that nature is an enemy to be defeated. In holding this view, they must deny that they themselves are a part of nature; they must wholly separate humanity from nature. Lewis seems to be suggesting in his novel that these three things all go hand in hand: though exploiters of nature—those who view it merely as a resource—may not readily acknowledge this, to exploit nature is to make it an enemy; to make it an enemy is to treat ourselves as something entirely other. Thomas Howard summarizes what Lewis, in *That Hideous Strength*, shows to be the result of that thinking: "If you tinker about with things the way Frost does . . . treating them as mere data, deracinating them, and introducing a fissure between head and body (that is, form and content, or mind and matter, or theory and plain actuality)—if you do that, which Gnosticism does, you may awaken and unloose things that you hadn't quite anticipated. . . . We pillage the earth and find ourselves without fuel; we wrench the finely-tuned ecological balance that seems to obtain in Nature, and find ourselves poisoned, polluted, starved."[12]

The Unbodying of Man

This leads us to the last and most gruesome aspect of the N.I.C.E. attacks on nature: their attempted fissure between head and body. Our human bodies are, it is difficult to deny, made up of the stuff of nature. Lewis sees the obvious connection: if we make nature our enemy, then eventually we must view our bodies as the enemy. For all of the aspects of Platonism to which Lewis was attracted, there was one Platonistic doctrine he could not accept after his conversion to Christianity. It is the doctrine that the mind, or the world of ideas, is all that matters, and that our bodies are our enemies to be defeated or at least escaped from.[13]

At the heart of the agenda at Belbury is the effort to separate persons from their biology, represented in the literal effort to separate a head (and all its functionality of thought processes) from its body. As the protagonist, Mark, gets closer to the inner circle of power at the

N.I.C.E., he begins to realize this. Try as he does to be "progressive" and to go along with whatever those in the elusive inner circles of power are saying, Mark can't help but find this agenda disturbing. "It sounds," he comments at one point, "like abolishing pretty well all organic life." Filostrato's answer leaves no doubts. "I grant it. That is the point. In us organic life has produced Mind. It has done its work. After that we want no more of it. We do not want the world any longer furred over with organic life, like what you call this blue mould—all sprouting and budding and breeding and decaying. We must get rid of it" (*THS,* 8.3). It is evident from Filostrato's speech that he (and his superiors at the N.I.C.E.) believe that Mind is what really matters. Mind is good. Organic life, by contrast, is something to be disposed of now that it has finished its important work of producing Mind. Filostrato does not want any more organic life, and as soon as he can sustain his mind inorganically, he is eager to do so.

Now by this point in the story, these developments should not be surprising either to Mark or to the readers. Ridding the human mind of its biology is not much different from deforesting, or "shaving" the planet—that is, saving it from its biology. And here it may be worth making a digression in order to consider a fragment of verse Lewis uses as an epigraph for *That Hideous Strength:* "The Shadow of that Hyddeous Strength / Sax Myle and More It Is of Length." These lines come from the poem "Ane Dialog," by Sir David Lyndsay.[14] It is a poem describing the Tower of Babel. The biblical account of the Tower of Babel is given in the eleventh chapter of Genesis. In that story, men gather together and decide to build a great city with a tower reaching toward heaven, "so that we can make a name for ourselves and not be scattered over the face of the whole earth" (Genesis 11:4, NIV). Lewis's epigraph offers a hint that some of the ideas in his book can be understood in relation to the Tower of Babel tale. That the schemes of the N.I.C.E. end, like Babel, in the mayhem of lost language and confusion, is highly suggestive that Lewis connects Belbury with the city of Babel in Genesis 11. There are additional clues as well. For example, in the first mention of the N.I.C.E., the narrator notes that "the building proposed for it was one which would make a quite noticeable addition to the skyline of New York" (*THS,* 1.4). Another hint may be seen in the similarity of the names "Babel" and "Belbury"; Belbury is a modern-day Babel. The construction of the first Babel and the construction of Belbury share several essential features: both of them are towering monuments to human arrogance, and both of them represent a rejection of the earth in favor of some putative but ultimately self-defeating lofty goal.

So what does the tale of Babel have to do with *That Hideous Strength?* There are probably many good answers to this question, as Lewis's novel is rich in meanings. One of these answers seems particularly pertinent to our discussion. The Tower of Babel was an attempt to reach heaven. Why? Part of the answer usually given (and one suggested in Genesis 11:7) is that men were trying to become like gods. But another possible aspect of this is that Babel was an attempt to escape the earth (using the latest technologies). In that sense, it is not so much where men were *going* that was important, but where they were *leaving;* the Tower of Babel is a rejection of *this* world. This certainly makes sense both metaphorically and literally; a tower reaching all the way to heaven would be an escape *from nature.* That the construction of this tower happens in the city—or, more specifically, that the building of the tower corresponds with the building of a city and a movement away from structures of nature and into the edifices of man—certainly coincides with this understanding.

In any case, whether the biblical account or the poem of David Lyndsay had in mind the Tower of Babel as an escape from earth, Lewis seems to have been making this connection. In Filostrato's speech about shaving the planet and the abolition of organic life, we have Lewis portraying not just the attempt to conquer heaven, but also an abandonment of everything representing life on this physical world.[15] The body and the organic are to be replaced by ideas. First Feverstone, and then Filostrato, and eventually Frost, all attempt to sell Mark Studdock on the advantage of rejecting the body and finally being free from nature. Indeed, they want not only to gain heaven and escape the earth, but also to destroy Earth in the process of escape.

By the end of the novel, this agenda for first controlling and then destroying the body, in favor of having only mind, becomes the central aspect of the story. As Mark discovers, the technologists at the N.I.C.E. have found a way of keeping a severed head artificially breathing, under the illusion that the mind within it is somehow still alive. But long before Mark sees this monstrosity, from as early as the second chapter of the book, he might have guessed what was coming. The severed head is another natural outcome of the propaganda that Feverstone is feeding to Mark from their first meeting at Belbury: "It sounds rather in Busby's style to say that Humanity is at the cross-roads. But it is the main question at the moment: which side one's on—obscurantism or Order. It does really look as if we now had the power to dig ourselves in as a species for a pretty staggering period, to take control of our own destiny. If Science is really given a free hand it can now take over the human race and re-condition it: make man a really efficient animal. If it doesn't—well, we're done" (*THS*, 2.1). Note that Feverstone has said nothing about a severed head. Readers don't see the head until much later in the story. What Feverstone has said, rightly, is that humanity is at a crossroads and that it matters which side one is on. Both sides—Belbury as well as St. Anne's—would agree to this. Feverstone associates his own side, the side of the N.I.C.E., with Order. Again, the community at St. Anne's, which opposes the N.I.C.E., would also see order as a good thing. However, what Feverstone means by "Order," it becomes clear, is the ability of a select few in power to impose their order on others—that is, to have the power to order others. "'Man has got to take charge of Man,' he goes on to say. 'That means, remember, that some men have got to take charge of the rest—which is another reason for cashing in on it as soon as one can. You and I want to be the people who do the taking charge, not the ones who are taken charge of'" (*THS*, 2.1). Filostrato makes this even clearer later on, repeating a principle that Lewis himself has written in various essays, but with a different application: "All that talk about the power of Man over Nature—Man in the abstract—is only for the [common people]. You know as well as I do that Man's power over Nature means the power of some men over other men with Nature as the instrument. There is no such thing as Man—it is a word. There are only men. No! It is not Man who will be omnipotent, it is some one man, some immortal man" (*THS*, 8.3). Not surprisingly, Feverstone explicitly advocates as a means for the few (or one) to control the many: forced sterilization, genocide, selective breeding, and mandatory psychological and biochemical conditioning (*THS*, 2.1). These are means to power, to control the masses—to force most humans to fit the pattern chosen by the few. And again we get the suggestion that Feverstone only cares about the human species. He wants the human species to dig itself in at the expense of all other life. Or, rather, what he really cares about is the human mind; the human as a biological species isn't really important.

When Mark later meets the Head—the severed head of the criminal, kept artificially "alive"—he is seeing the result of Feverstone's philosophy and its doctrine that holds that nature and the biological body are evil and mind is good. Filostrato takes up the defense of this philosophy where Feverstone leaves off. He argues, for example, that humans should be "learning how to reproduce ourselves without copulation." When Mark wonders if that would take all the fun out of reproduction, Filostrato says, "What are the things that most offend the dignity of man? Birth and breeding and death. How if we are about to discover that man can live without any of the three?" Filostrato then speaks of the real leaders of the N.I.C.E., the so-called *Macrobes*[16] who are his models for a bodiless existence: "[The Masters] do not need to be born and breed and die; only their common people . . . do that. The Masters live on. They retain their intelligence: they can keep it artificially alive after the organic body has been dispensed with—a miracle of applied biochemistry. They do not need organic food. You understand? They are almost free of Nature, attached to her only by the thinnest, finest cord" (*THS*, 8.3). To be free of nature, like the Macrobes, or Masters as they are called earlier in the tale, is the ultimate goal of the highest officials at the N.I.C.E., the next obvious step from the stated agenda. The purpose of following these Masters, Filostrato explains, "is for the conquest of death: or for the conquest of organic life, if you prefer. They are the same." Filostrato believes that by following the Macrobes, they are seeking for "the man who will not die, the artificial man, free from Nature. Nature is the ladder we have climbed up by, now we have kicked her away" (*THS*, 8.3)—and we are back again at the idea that the fight against death also inevitably ends up as a fight against nature.

It is no wonder, then, that Wither, the deputy director of the N.I.C.E., has worked so hard to separate himself from his body. He has eventually reached a state where "he [has] learned to withdraw most of his consciousness from the task of living" so that while "colours, tastes, smells, and tactual sensations no doubt bombarded his physical senses in the normal matter: they did not now reach his ego" (*THS*, 12.2). As the narrator later tells us about the Macrobes, however—and as Lewis seeks to make clear to his readers—"these creatures . . . breathed death on the human race and on all joy" and were part of a "movement opposite to Nature" (*THS*, 12.7). To follow this agenda of disregarding the body and the earth, Lewis believed, was a path toward death; indeed, to be opposed to nature, or "opposite to nature" as the narrator says, *is* death.

Interestingly enough, Jane must also learn this. At the start of the book, we learn that she is writing a doctoral thesis on the writings of the poet Donne and his "triumphant vindication of the body." Like the reference to Lyndsay's poem, this is a significant hint about the central ideas of the story. Thomas Howard notes, "Donne's poetry and prose *Devotions* are, of course, shot through with the lively awareness that the flesh is the very mediator of meaning to us mortals, and Jane apparently finds this intriguing." Lewis certainly agrees with Donne on this point, as we note repeatedly throughout our book, and this view of the importance of our bodies is an important aspect of Lewis's healthy ecology. But Jane has also been influenced by the prevailing ideas that have captivated Mark and that permeate the N.I.C.E., that only the mind is important. So, as Howard notes, "what she really wants is to be thought of as an intellectual. She would like the dignity of being a *mind*." This desire is harmless enough on its own, and is certainly one shared by much of humanity—the desire to have our ideas, our minds, appreciated. But when it leads to a complete disregard of the importance of body, then it is dangerous, which as Howard then concludes is a central idea to *That Hideous Strength*: "The drama in this tale happens to disclose for us the diabolical horrors that stand at the far end of the disjunction of mind and body—of Gnosticism, say. That very old and popular and persistent idea that the division between spirit and flesh is a division between worthy and worthless. . . . You cannot, in the interest of pure intellect, disavow the body, for all of its plumbing and embarrassing fleshliness. In our human and mortal realm here, words without meaning, idea without action, mind without body, all turn out to be chaos."[17]

Now for some readers, the rhetoric and agenda of the N.I.C.E. may seem far-fetched—a gross exaggeration of various ideas that Lewis may or may not actually have encountered. But they are not unimaginable. Ideas espoused by Lewis's villains at the N.I.C.E. were put forward by well-known and well-respected scientists in Lewis's day and have continued to be put forward into the next century.[18] Consider, for example, Feverstone's comment that "some men have got to take charge of the rest" and his suggestion of forced sterilization, selective breeding, and so on, as means of accomplishing this. In March 1971, about a quarter-century after *That Hideous Strength* was published, Dr. Francis Crick, co-unraveler (with Dr. James Watson) of DNA, presented a lecture in St. Louis in which he argued that "some group of people should decide some people should have more children and some should have fewer. . . . You have to decide who is to be born. . . . I think it will turn out that thinking along these lines will have to take place, and if you don't do it in this country, it will start in another country."[19] We may disagree with how Lewis connects Feverstone's (and Crick's) agenda to other ecological ideas about nature, but it is clear that he did not simply fabricate Feverstone's arguments.

Regarding the idea of separating head from body, or severing our thinking process from our biology, an even more interesting example is the brilliant and well-known inventor and "futurist" Ray Kurzweil. Kurzweil is known not only for his innovative work in such areas as sound synthesizers and speech recognition and artificial intelligence— he has won numerous awards and honors such as the 1988 M.I.T. Inventor of the Year—but has also written several books about the future of humanity. Many of his ideas can be found in his book *The Age of Spiritual Machines: When Computers Exceed Human Intelligence*,[20] written just over half a century after *That Hideous Strength*. Consider what Kurzweil writes about mortality, for example.

> Actually there won't be mortality by the end of the twenty-first century. Not in the sense that we have known it. Not if you take advantage of the twenty-first century's brain-porting technology. Up until now, our mortality was tied to the longevity of our *hardware*. When the hardware crashed, that was it. For many of our forebears, the hardware gradually deteriorated before it disintegrated. Yeats lamented our dependence on a physical self that was "but a paltry thing, a tattered coat upon a stick." As we cross the divide to instantiate ourselves into our computational technology, our identity will be based on our evolving mind file. *We will be software, not hardware.*[21]

The agenda suggested by Kurzweil's prediction is stunningly similar to that proposed by the N.I.C.E.: a sort of immortality of the mind achieved by an abandonment of the body. But our main point actually regards the worldview that underlies this agenda: that mind (our *software*) is all that matters, and that we will be better off when we can abandon the body (our *hardware*). This idea runs through his book. A few pages later, for example, Kurzweil acknowledges vaguely that bodies are important, but suggests that the importance is probably only psychological; having bodies keeps us from "quickly get[ting] depressed." Even the significant fact that being bodiless might make us depressed is disregarded with a dismissive comment that the resulting depression would come only because our current body is "the body we're used to."[22] The implication is that once we are used to being disembodied—or to having only virtual bodies—then we won't be bothered any more. He then quickly suggests that the bodies we do have will and should become more synthetic, more efficient, and less biological. He lists all the artificial joints, skin, and even heart valves that already exist and are in use, and proposes a continued movement in that direction toward the completely engineered body—eventually toward nano-technology as a replacement for our current bodies, a move away from biology and toward engineered synthetic bodies.[23] The goal is efficiency. "Our twenty-first-century physical technology," he predicts, "will also greatly exceed the capabilities of the amino acid–based nanotechnology of the natural world."[24]

Again, running through Kurzweil's entire discussion is the underlying concept that the mind is what is important; the goal of the body is just to support the mind, or provide a vehicle for the mind. He goes on to write, "There is no obvious place to stop this progression until the human race has largely replaced the brains and bodies that evolution first provided." This will become possible because "we don't always need real bodies. If we happen to be in a virtual environment, then a virtual body will do just fine."[25] Eventually, he claims, we will have virtual sex, which, among other things, will free us from the last constraints of monogamy. "Drawing clear lines [about the freedom in a 'relationship' to experiment sexually with multiple people] will become difficult with the level of privacy that this future technology affords. It is likely that society will accept practice and activities in the virtual arena that it frowns upon in the physical world, as the consequences of virtual activities are often (although not always) easier to undo." Indeed, virtual lives will also free us from all constraints and limitations of living in a physical world, as he goes on to illustrate with examples from the realm of virtual sex and romance. "In addition to direct sensual and sexual contact, virtual reality will be a great place for romance in general. Stroll with your lover along a virtual Champs-Élysées, take a walk along a virtual Cancún beach. . . . Your whole relationship can be in Cyberland."[26] Like the denizens of Babel, and the leaders of Belbury, the popular Kurzweil seeks to escape nature. In his view, mind is what matters—and the more powerful we can make our minds, the better.

Now earlier we commented that if we make nature our enemy then eventually we must view our bodies as the enemy. This is the progression we see in *That Hideous Strength*. But we might say this the other way around. Indeed, it is the other direction that is particularly important, and in our present culture troublesome: if we make our bodies the enemy—if we believe that all that matters is mind—then we will eventually make all of nature into our enemy. Body is what connects us to the earth. Our bodies depend on food and water and air. They live and walk and drink and breathe. Healthy earth nourishes our body. Pollution and toxins in the air and soil and water make our bodies sick.[27] If we deny the body, then everything physical and bodily—all bodies and not just our own—are to be jettisoned. Wendell Berry has made astute observations about this. In his essay "The Body and the Earth," he writes: "By dividing body and soul, we divide both from all else. We thus condemn ourselves to a loneliness for which the only compensation is violence— against other creatures, against the earth, against ourselves. . . . The willingness to abuse other bodies is the willingness to abuse our own. To damage the earth is to damage your children. To despise the ground is to despise its fruit; to despise the fruit is to despise its eaters. The wholeness of the earth is broken by despite."[28] He goes on to comment on the visible evidence of this damaging worldview: "And it is clear to anyone who looks carefully at any crowd that we are wasting our bodies exactly as we are wasting our land. . . . Our bodies have become marginal; they are growing useless like our 'marginal' land because we have less and less use for them. After the games and idle flourishes of modern youth, we use them only as shipping cartons to transport our brains and our few employable muscles back and forth to work."[29] Berry could well have been commenting on *That Hideous Strength* when he wrote that essay—or, more accurately, both Berry and Lewis were observing the same thing.

Norman Wirzba, in his essay "Placing the Soul: An Agrarian Philosophical Principle," has also observed the same general ecological principle: "To put the point more practically, can we *properly* engage the world if we despise the bodies in terms of which such engagement occurs, or despise the natural bodies upon which our own lives so clearly depend? One of the lasting contributions of *The Unsettling of America* was to show that on both counts the answer is a resounding *No!* Though we might dream of ourselves as disembodied, immortal souls, or as complex computers that will finally shed all biological and physiological limitations, the fact remains that we live necessarily through our bodies."[30] If Lewis, Berry, and Wirzba are right, then we should be appalled at the ideas and corresponding agenda put forward by those like Kurzweil, if on no other grounds than on the ecological consequences of these ideas.

The Theories of Mark Studdock (and Recalcitrant Agrarians)

There is yet another way in which Lewis explores the relationship between ideas and consequences, between theories and realities; it is through Mark Studdock's academic profession as a sociologist. The work Mark does for the N.I.C.E.—propaganda in the guise of sociology and journalism—brings his academic theories into conflict with reality. What Lewis shows in this conflict are the damaging consequences of holding false ideas. Interestingly, he does this in relation to issues of agrarianism—specifically in the context of the contrast between agrarians and technologists.

As readers learn—though Mark, in his naiveté or arrogance, seemingly does not—the interest of Belbury in recruiting the protagonist seems to be twofold. One intention is for Mark to help them get his wife, Jane. We learn almost at the start of the book that Jane is having supernatural dreams or visions showing her what the authorities at the N.I.C.E. are doing. These dreams provide valuable information that could be (and eventually is) used by the leaders at St. Anne's to help them thwart Belbury. The N.I.C.E. becomes aware of Jane's supernatural gift and tries to get to her through Mark. For the highest leaders of the N.I.C.E., this is almost certainly the most important of the two reasons—Jane is much more important to either side than is Mark.

There is also a secondary reason for Belbury's interest in Mark: he is an academic sociologist who not only believes in the stated agenda of the N.I.C.E. (or at least he is willing to accept any agenda associated with "progress" in order to rise in the ranks of academic prestige and power), but is also an excellent propagandist. He knows how to write about abstract theories for all sorts of audiences in order to sway the populace. As Lord Feverstone tells him early on, in a little exercise of flattery that is probably obvious to everybody but Mark, "you are what we need: a trained sociologist with a radically realistic outlook, not afraid of responsibility. Also, a sociologist who can write" (*THS*, 2.1). One important aspect of this sociological agenda is to convince the public that agrarian ways are backward, that progress lies in increased use of technology, and that the destruction of the old agrarian ways is necessary to make way for development.[31]

That these old agrarian ways are in fact far healthier than the technological progress promised by Belbury is not only suggested in the name "Cure Hardy" (see note 7) but comes out most clearly in the protagonist's visit to the agricultural town early in the story. Cosser, initially Mark's supervisor, takes Mark on a trip out to Cure Hardy so that they can make a token effort of studying the town before submitting articles they have already essentially written criticizing its old agrarian ways. Mark, who is not as completely convinced as Cosser that agrarianism is evil, comments, "The small *rentier* is a bad element, I agree. I suppose the agricultural labourer is more controversial." By this Mark likely means that he thinks agriculture laborers are actually important to society, and are not "bad elements," although he is not willing to say this explicitly, in case it is not the correct progressive view he is supposed to hold. Cosser responds with the official position of the N.I.C.E. "The Institute doesn't approve of him [the agricultural laborer]. He's a very recalcitrant element in a planned community, and he's always backward. We're not going in for English agricultural. So you see, all we have to do is to verify a few facts. Otherwise, the report writes itself" (*THS*, 4.6). Cosser's basic assumption—and one he knows Mark will agree with—is that anything that is not part of progress is backward and anything backward is bad. He therefore needs only to apply the "backward" label to English agriculture and immediately it becomes the enemy. Again, remember that in all essential regards, Lewis represents in the N.I.C.E. the opposite of what he believes to be a true and healthy worldview. That the N.I.C.E. wants to destroy "English agriculture" in order to pave the way for development such as planned suburban communities is a sure sign that Lewis thought that the old English agriculture was in fact superior. Ed Chapman, in his article on Lewis's ecology, draws the same conclusion. After quoting from *A God Within* by Rene Dubos about the dangerous idea of "the conquest of nature," Chapman notes that "this line of thought would support the superiority of Cure Hardy, rich in its traditions and relationship to nature, to whatever kind of experimental village the N.I.C.E. or any other technocratic 'think tank' might devise."[32]

An even surer sign that Lewis associates Cosser's (and later Mark's) view with evil is that this view is put forward by Frost himself. When Mark suggests that the purpose of the N.I.C.E. (with which he agrees to the extent that he understands it) includes not only the "scientific reconstruction of the human race" but also "a fuller exploitation of nature," Frost responds not that Mark has gone too far but that he hasn't gone far enough. While Mark wants to preserve "a pretty large population for the full exploitation of Nature, if for nothing else," Frost is all for killing off (through some sort of scientific war) the sort of humans he finds to be not useful in his vision for the future. This includes primarily those humans most closely in contact with the earth. "A large agricultural population *was* essential; and war destroyed types which were *then* still useful," Frost admits (emphasis added). But then he goes on to say, "But every advance in industry and agriculture reduces the number of work-people who are required." The value of humans, in this view, is reduced (like nature) to just their economic value in a prescribed system of exchange with limited membership; they become simply "work-people." In the present day, he argues, getting rid of "superstitious peasants" and "low-grade . . . agricultural workers" would actually be beneficial. "The effect of modern war is to eliminate retrogressive types, while sparing the technocracy and increasing its hold upon public affairs"[33] (*THS*, 12.4). This, then, is near the heart of the deeper agenda of the N.I.C.E.: get rid of the agrarians (who are retrogressive and no longer useful) and replace them with a ruling party of technologists.

It is also important to note that Cosser and Mark aren't even really interested in discovering the truth. They are merely "verifying" what they have already assumed to be true; without observing whether there is anything valuable in these agricultural communities that are to be destroyed, they have already concluded the report—it needs only to "write itself." Nonetheless, Lewis gives the reader a glimpse, through the eyes of Mark, of just how wrong the conclusions of the report are: "It did not quite escape him that the face of the backward labourer was rather more interesting than Cosser's and his voice a great deal more pleasing to the ear. . . . All this did not in the least influence his sociological convictions . . . for his education had had the curious effect of making things that he read and wrote more real to him than things he saw. Statistics about agricultural labourers were the substance; any real ditcher, ploughman, or farmer's boy was the shadow" (*THS*, 4.6). Again Lewis is showing how our ideas have consequences. The N.I.C.E., which wants to sever the head from the body, has preached that mind is what matters, and that the body is to be despised. So, of course, ideas (like statistics) are more real to Mark than the actual physical flesh-and-blood farmer standing in front of him. But the narrator also makes it clear how deceived Mark is, and so the most obvious conclusion Lewis means his readers to draw is precisely the opposite of what Mark believes; for Lewis, the agricultural laborers, ditcher, ploughman, and farmer's boy are the substance, and the ideas about them—the statistics—are the shadows. Put another way, the real flesh and blood is more real than the academic concepts. Lewis also seems to be suggesting not only that agricultural laborers are more real, but that people who are in touch with the earth, the members of these farming families, are more likely to *know* what really is substantive—the body, the land, the crops—than the progressive techno-idolaters like Cosser who worship an invisible ideal that rejects this world. It is the educated Cosser and Mark Studdock and not the simplistic farmer's boy who has bought into Gnostic Platonism.

Unfortunately, Mark proves to be an excellent propagandist, and his writing succeeds in convincing the English populace to go along with the destruction of agricultural communities like Cure Hardy, with their "recalcitrant" agricultural workers. Either the public agrees that these communities are bad, or at least they accept that the results being sought by the N.I.C.E. under the name of "progress" are inevitable and that resistance is futile.[34] Even if Mark isn't completely taken in by his own writing, his readers are. And if his conscience is bothered by the deceit he is putting forth, he defends his actions to himself, in part by thinking that it is all part of progress, and that progress is inevitable. "It wasn't as if he were taken in by the articles himself. He was writing with his tongue in his cheek—a phrase that somehow comforted him by making the whole thing appear like a practical joke. And anyway, if he didn't do it, somebody else would" (*THS*, 6.4).

An Alternative at St. Anne's

Even if all that Lewis showed us were the ideas behind an unhealthy ecology and the impact of those ideas—that is, if the book *only* showed us Belbury—then *That Hideous Strength* still might be praised for its contributions to ecology. Exploitation, progress at the expense of beauty and health, arrogance of the human species, and the wanton disregard of nature are all shown to be both evil and destructive. We are warned, also, of the dangers of a philosophy that denies the importance of body and earth; Lewis's book provides an imaginative glimpse of the consequences that flow from such a philosophy. And we are warned about the sort of propaganda used to bring about the destruction of healthy agricultural ways. At the very least, we have in the picture of the N.I.C.E. a vision of what to avoid.

But Lewis's imaginative novel doesn't stop there. Readers are also given a glimpse, through the experiences of the other protagonist, Jane Studdock, of a healthy community at St. Anne's-on-the-Hill, and of what that means to ecology. At St. Anne's, readers see a compelling model of how to live in healthy relationships with other people, with other creatures, and with the earth. Indeed, many scholars have noted the striking narrative balance between St. Anne's and Belbury, not only in the similar number of sections and length of narrative devoted to Jane and Mark, but even in the identical number of important characters in the two organizations. Evan Gibson observes that "of the eighty-five episodes in the book, Jane Studdock appears in thirty-three and Mark Studdock in thirty-four." He goes on to note the same balance between the community at St. Anne's and what we might call the anticommunity at the N.I.C.E. "The number of characters in each which come into focus is exactly the same: nine, if we do not count Mark and Jane. On each side there is a supernatural possession—Alcasan [at the N.I.C.E.] and Merlin [at St. Anne's]—and a characteristic relationship to animals; in one, ideal, in the other, devilish."[35] We will return to the relationship with animals, as it is an important aspect of the ecologies of these two groups. For now, we just comment more broadly on the importance of contrasts. Donald Glover notes, "What strikes us at once is the elaborate system of parallels mentioned earlier. Their effect is to place the opposing camps of St. Anne's and Belbury in positions of matched opposition. . . . By moving between his two characters and keeping their penetration into the circles of Belbury and St. Anne's approximately parallel, Lewis . . . gives ample opportunity for the ironic comparisons afforded by the structural and thematic parallels."[36]

One of the first contrasts, made more obvious by the parallel structure of the story, comes in the initial descriptions of the two headquarters. Mark's initial journey to Belbury is in an ostentatious car (driven by Lord Feverstone) speeding along back roads with reckless disregard for animals and pedestrians alike—they kill at least one chicken—and no time to enjoy the countryside, which is described as being "devoured" behind them. By contrast, Jane first travels to St. Anne's by train, in which "autumn sunlight grew warm on the window pane and smells of wood and field from beyond the tiny station floated in and seemed to claim the railway as part of the land." Whereas Mark's first view of the N.I.C.E. headquarters at Belbury is of "a widespread outgrowth of newer cement buildings, which housed the blood transfusion office," Jane's walk up to St. Anne's brings her past "a row of beech trees and unfenced ploughland falling steeply away, and behind that the timbered midland plain spreading as far as she could see and blue in the distance" (*THS*, 2.4). The initial description is not deceiving; St. Anne's exists in harmony with the world around it, including both agricultural landscapes nearby and more distant forests and wilderness. It also exists in harmony with the creatures who dwell in that world, including wild creatures such as bears and potential pests such as mice. For Lewis, there is an intimate connection between harmonious beauty and goodness. The health of land is not just measured; it is also *felt*. Of course, Lewis urges us to see beyond superficial beauty and to see the land with the eyes of love. As in romance, prettiness is only the first part of beauty. True beauty lies much deeper and cannot be pried out by machinery or money; it must be courted.

While members of the N.I.C.E. are intent on defoliating the landscape and separating themselves from nature, those in the community of St. Anne's seem to love the land around them. They even love the weather, as Jane learns when she goes on a picnic with Frank and Camilla Denniston. When Camilla invites her for lunch, Jane suggests that they eat inside her flat. Camilla's idea, however, is to go "up to the woods beyond Sandown." Jane responds, "It's hardly a day for picnicking." Camilla concedes that it might get cold and foggy, but Frank asks, "Don't you like a rather foggy day in a wood in the autumn?" Jane is taken aback, but Frank makes his point more strongly, and it is a point in defense of enjoying nature rather than trying to subdue it. "Everyone begins as a child by liking Weather. You learn the art of disliking it as you grow up. Haven't you ever noticed it on a snowy day? The grown-ups are all going about with long faces, but look at the children—and the dogs? *They* know what snow's made for." And Camilla adds, "Any child loves rain if it's allowed to go out and paddle about in it." Thus while Mark is eating in a stuffy and smoky cafeteria at Belbury, and hating almost every minute of it, the Dennistons are taking Jane off the road, where they go "bumping across grass and among trees and finally [to] a sort of little grassy bay with a fir thicket on one side and a group of beeches on the other. There were wet cobwebs and a rich autumnal smell all around them" (*THS*, 5.3).

This is not a trivial observation. Several Lewis scholars have commented on the importance of this scene and the view of weather. Thomas Howard observes that the Dennistons at St. Anne have "a disarming sort of simplicity in them." He goes on to explain that "far from being bothered by fog on a day when they had planned to take Jane on a picnic, they both like Weather. . . . They must eat the picnic in the car, but it is in a scene that spells goodness in any Lewis narrative."[37] Wayne Martindale also links this to a broader appreciation among those in the St. Anne's community of the goodness of the physical, created earth and its pleasures when rightly enjoyed. Repeating an idea we have already attributed to Lewis, he writes "God invented all the pleasures . . . and anytime we take them as intended by God, we are in his territory. We move out of ourselves, a first step toward God himself. The Dennistons have all of Lewis's own sense of gusto in weather of all kinds and in the manifold riches of nature."[38] As even Mark himself eventually realizes, those at St. Anne's, "like Denniston, like the Dimbles," were the ones "who could enjoy things for their own sake" (*THS*, 11.3).

Perhaps the biggest contrast between the two organizations has to do with community. Belbury is a mockery of community. Nobody trusts anybody. Everybody seems intent on getting ahead of everybody else. Wither and Frost, the two leaders, rule by fear and intimidation. At St. Anne's, however, everybody is understood to have equal worth and value, even while they celebrate their differences and the different roles they have in the community. Again, Jane is at first taken aback by this, and in particular by the fact that her former house cleaner, Ivy Maggs, is a part of the community at St. Anne's—and not just a part of the community as a maid or a servant but as one who is taken seriously when community members meet to discuss their plans. "Mrs. Maggs seems to make herself very much at home here," she complains to Mrs. Dimble, affectionately known as Mother Dimble around St. Anne's. "My dear," Mother Dimble replies, "she *is* at home here." "As a maid, you mean?" Jane asks. Mother Dimble's reply is clear. "Well, no more than anyone else. She's here chiefly because her house has been taken from her." Jane, apparently desperate to interpret this in some way that will allow her to feel superior to Ivy, suggests that this is an act of charity on the part of Ransom, the Director. She then adds, "I hope I'm not being snobbish." Which, of course, she is. Mother Dimble replies by pointing out that she and her husband, Cecil, are also the Director's charities. In every attempt of Jane to suggest some social or even spiritual hierarchy of superiority—as there certainly is at Belbury—Mother Dimble is quick to suggest just the opposite, eventually just cutting to the chase and telling Jane outright, "you were never goose enough to think yourself *spiritually* superior to Ivy" (*THS*, 8.2).

We could go on for several chapters exploring the community at St. Anne's and contrasting it with Belbury—pointing out, for example, how the community at St. Anne's has no servants, but all the members work together at such common but important tasks as gardening and preparing meals, which many modern environmental writers have commented are very important practices. But many other Lewis scholars have already written extensively on the differences between the two communities, and have done so well. Again, Thomas Howard and Ed Chapman provide perhaps the best short summaries of the contrasts between St. Anne's and the N.I.C.E., particularly as they relate to ecology. Howard writes, "On the one hand, good health and normality and humility and loyalty and merriment and candor and courtesy; and on the other disease and cruelty and treachery and mockery and apostasy and the unnatural, all carried on under the self-congratulatory assumption that we are the 'thoughtful people' and that this is progress and enlightenment."[39] Chapman, who set out explicitly to explore ecological issues, is even more specific: "Ecological sanity is embodied at St. Anne's, in contrast to the sterility images and the worship of technology represented by Belbury. The people at St. Anne's spend much of their time gardening, a metaphor for the proper treatment of nature. All life, including mice, is treated with respect at St. Anne's, and the management of the household is exemplary of a loving ecological relationship between man and nature. But St. Anne's symbolizes more than mere ecological sanity; it represents a movement back to a sacramental relationship with nature."[40]

Though we won't continue with all the contrasts, there are two specific aspects of the contrasting communities that need to be commented on as they relate directly to issues of ecology, or to underlying worldviews about human relationships with the rest of nature. The first contrast has to do with the different views toward animals, as this is very revealing of the different broader perspectives on nature. The community at St. Anne's is one that is welcoming not only of all humans, regardless of their stations in life, but of animals as well. Jane comes across not only common household animals such as cats, but also jackdaws, mice, and even a bear, all of whom make St. Anne's their home. It is at St. Anne's that Jane "saw mice for the first time as they really are—not as creeping things but as dainty quadrupeds, almost, when they sat up, like tiny kangaroos, with sensitive kid-gloved forepaws and transparent ears" (*THS*, 7.2). Of course, these are things one sees only when one appreciates the mouse enough to really look at it. These are the eyes of love that are seeing.[41] Ransom, the Director, respects the role that even mice play in the world and helps Jane to understand this. As for Mr. Bultitude, the big brown bear, Jane never quite gets used to him, but it is clear that he has a place at St. Anne's also, even as his wildness is also respected. By contrast, at Belbury animals are viewed only as objects to be experimented on. Some of the scenes describing this are horrific. The community at St. Anne's is as respectful of all of life and nature as Belbury is disrespectful. One of the key moments in the narrative is when Mr. Bultitude takes part in the destruction of Belbury, including freeing all the tortured animals—without which the victory over the N.I.C.E. would be incomplete, since part of the evil to be fought is the mistreatment of animals. Lewis adds, significantly, that when these animals are freed, they migrate toward St. Anne's.

Merlin, Nature, and a Conclusion

The final contrast between St. Anne's and Belbury, as it relates to ecology, is less direct but no less important. *That Hideous Strength*, though set in what for Lewis was present-day England, is nonetheless a fantasy novel. The conclusion of the story—and, indeed, the entire plot and the purposes of both the N.I.C.E. and St. Anne's—hinges on the wizard Merlin awakening from enchanted sleep and returning to England. This, it turns out, is the real reason that the leaders of the N.I.C.E. wanted to acquire the Bragdon Wood in the first place, because it is believed to be the location of Merlin's tomb. The question readers have early on is which side of the battle Merlin will take if and when he does awaken. Both sides assume that his druidic power will be very influential in the outcome. Wither and Frost want to exploit that power, to merge the significant technological power at their disposal with the magical power of Merlin, and they assume they will be able to. Ransom, the Director at St. Anne's, fears this. Both sides are in a race to be the first to find Merlin.

When Merlin does awake, his power turns out to be even greater than either side might have guessed. And for that reason, the searches of both sides to find him prove to be irrelevant. Merlin is far too powerful to simply be caught and brought as a prisoner to either Belbury or St. Anne's. He makes his own decision. His decision is to go to St. Anne's. It is there that he senses a real leader resides who has the true authority to lead England along a proper path. This is the person of Ransom; Ransom is the Pendragon, the modern Arthur. Merlin recognizes that authority, but he also recognizes something more. Everything important about the community at St. Anne's, including what we would call its ecology and the moral and philosophical roots of that ecology, are in line with what the Christian druid Merlin believes. By contrast, everything about Belbury, and especially its view of the earth, stands in violent opposition to what Merlin cherishes and holds to be true.

At the heart of this all is Merlin's view of nature. Ransom explains this to the community at St. Anne's, which is feeling suspicious of having a powerful druid in its midst: "For [Merlin] every operation on Nature is a kind of personal contact, like coaxing a child or stroking one's horse. After him came the modern man to whom Nature is something dead—a machine to be worked, and taken to bits if it won't work the way he pleases. Finally, come the Belbury people, who take over that view from the modern man unaltered and simply want to increase their power by tacking on to it the aid of spirits—extra-natural, anti-natural spirits" (*THS*, 13.4). Note the striking contrast. For the modern man, represented by Belbury, nature has no intrinsic worth but is merely something to be exploited for profit or power. Its parts are like the parts of a machine, extractable and replaceable. The whole of nature, as understood by the leaders of the N.I.C.E., is only the sum of its parts. For Merlin, nature is alive and meaningful. It is not to be exploited. Rather, we are to exist in relationship with it, like a parent and child—a relationship that ought to be lived out with love and nurture. This is also the view held by Ransom and modeled in his community. It is evident in the descriptions of St. Anne's-on-the-Hill, from the natural surrounding landscapes to its treatment of mice, bears, and jackdaws. This is what a healthy ecology should look like. It is why Merlin was drawn there and why Ransom was able to incorporate him into their plans; they were already natural allies, and allies with respect to nature.

Ransom makes this even clearer a moment later, when he describes the nature of Merlin's magical power, *magia,* in contrast with the sort of technological power employed by the N.I.C.E., which he associates with another type of magic, *goeteia. Magia* makes use of the inherent power of the earth itself: the power of enchanted nature, or what J. R. R. Tolkien calls Faërie. *Goeteia* is a sort of magic that works through conjuring powerful spirits and then controlling those spirits. The genie in the lamp is an example of the latter: whoever possesses the lamp controls the genie; the genie, or conjured spirit, is a slave and must do as he is told. As such, *goeteia* works through exploitation, oppression, and domination. And, in the understanding of Ransom (and Lewis), *goeteia* is associated with modern industrial technology when used only as a means toward power. Ransom explains why this is important, when he explains the misconceptions of the rulers of the N.I.C.E. "They thought the old *magia* of Merlin, which worked in with the spiritual qualities of Nature, loving and reverencing them and knowing them from within, could be combined with the new *goeteia*—the brutal surgery from without" (*THS*, 13.4). The point here is that Belbury was wrong. These two powers cannot be combined. The good, the healthy, the right, involves recognition of the spiritual qualities of nature, and a corresponding love and reverence for creation. It should lead to a desire to know (which is the heart of science)[42] rather than to exploitation and simply making use of (applied science and technology). The former is love; the latter is contempt.

Perhaps the most telling comment, and the appropriate end to this chapter, is what Ransom says next, in pointing out that Belbury had the wrong assumptions all along. "No. In a sense Merlin represents what we've got to get back to in some different way. Do you know that he is forbidden by the rules of his order to use any edged tool on any growing thing?" (*THS*, 13.4). Ransom, the great hero of the Space Trilogy, sees in Merlin an important aspect of what Lewis saw as a healthy understanding of nature and as a Christian ecology and indeed a Christian moral principle. This is something, according to Ransom and Lewis, that we've "got to get back to" (though without all of the aspects of paganism, which the Christian druid Merlin also had rejected). We must again view nature as something spiritual and come back into love for, reverence for, and an understanding of her. Merlin's refusal to use edged tools and Lewis's to use mousetraps are perhaps unwarranted extremes. But it would be better to go to the extremes of not using mousetraps and not using an edged tool on any growing thing than to accept the other extreme that seems to have characterized modern technological society.

Chapter 8

The Re-enchantment of Creation

But we need not surrender the love of nature . . . to the debunkers. Nature cannot satisfy the desires she arouses nor answer theological questions nor sanctify us. . . . But the love of her has been a valuable and, for some people, an indispensable initiation.
—C. S. Lewis, *Four Loves*

Enchantment's end is the surrender, or submission, of the soul to the beauty of nature and art. Technology's end is the conquest of nature by power.
—Peter Kreeft, *The Philosophy of Tolkien*

In the title of this chapter, we use the word *enchantment*. We have used the word often throughout this book, but so far haven't stopped to say exactly what we mean by it. Part of the reason is that it has multiple meanings, and we have made use of more than one.

Enchantment may be a subjective feeling. Something—in the context of this book, that "something" is nature, or creation—may make us *feel* enchanted. In an essay with the curious title "Talking about Bicycles," Lewis describes this sort of enchantment by means of explaining the way one might feel about (for example) bicycling. The essay takes the form of a (possibly fictional) dialogue with an unnamed friend, in which Lewis plays something of a cynical oaf. The friend describes four possible stages (or ages) in one's lifetime relationship with bicycles: the Unenchanted Age, the Enchanted Age, the Disenchanted Age, and the Re-enchanted Age. In the first, one has simply never experienced bicycles—that is, really *experienced* them by riding one. In the second, one is entirely enamored by them, with a sort of romantic splendor, "when to have a bicycle, and to have learned to ride it, and to be at last spinning along on one's own, early in the morning, under trees, in and out of the shadows, was like entering Paradise." In the third stage, the Disenchanted Age, the romantic feelings are gone; if one has only a bicycle, and must rely upon it for one's livelihood or for a daily commute, it can become sheer drudgery "pedaling to and fro from school . . . in all weathers" (TaB, 67). The promises that it was a gateway to paradise have proven false, and one knows it.

The fourth stage, the Re-enchanted Age, is the interesting one. It does not deny the reality of the drudgery, nor does it deny that the romantic feelings are often misleading illusions. It acknowledges both. But it also realizes that there was something true in that romance as well. As the friend describes in the dialogue,

> I recover [in the fourth age] the feelings of the second age. What's more, I see how true they were—how philosophical, even. For it really is a remarkably pleasant motion. To be sure, it is not a recipe for happiness as I then thought. In that sense the second age was a mirage. But a mirage of something. . . .
>
> Whether there is, or whether there is not, in this world or in any other, the kind of happiness which one's first experience of cycling seems to promise, still, on any view, it is something to have had the idea of it. The value of the thing promised remains even if that particular promise was false—even if all possible promises of it are false. (TaB, 67–68)

Bicycles, of course, are merely the image used to make a point. These four stages find relevance with many things. As the friend suggests, relationships in general and marriages in particular are areas of life to which this analysis may apply. A honeymoon is perhaps the supreme example of the Enchanted Age, when the married couple is quite sure that marriage will not only be a recipe for happiness, but will be nothing other than happiness and paradise. Most couples then enter a Disenchanted Age when the flaws of the new partner are exposed. That is when we say "the honeymoon is over"—an expression that has become an idiom for what Lewis would call the Disenchanted Age. Some marriages emerge into the Fourth Age. Some do not. In the Fourth Age, one can look at one's partner, see the faults, and know that the marriage takes hard work, but still enjoy the feelings brought on by the romance and even by the memory of the honeymoon, knowing that while the promises weren't all true, they were all good.

Our view of nature, or relationship with nature, is a third area to which this analysis may apply, and the area of particular interest for this book. Though the essay doesn't explicitly list "nature" or "creation" as a category of application, the friend at least suggests it with a reference to the way we feel about the mountains. It is "a fact about mountains—as good a fact as any other—that they look purple at a certain distance" (TaB, 71). His point is that for those in a Disenchanted Age with respect to nature, the *purple* may be written off or explained away in terms of optics and physics and the properties of light. For the re-enchanted, the physics of light is not dismissed or ignored, but neither are the feelings brought about by the shade of purple and all its connotations simply because they can be explained—or because the promise once made by the beauty of nature has given way to the reality of the ugliness of much of our world and its history.

We will return to this type of re-enchantment and the underlying meaning of enchantment, but we note also that there is a more objective meaning of the word. One may have enchanted feelings about something because it really is, in some way, enchanted. An enchantment, in the narrowest sense, is a spell cast over something, but more broadly it may be a sort of *in-habitation*. If pixies really dwelt in flowers, or dryads in the trees, or naiads in the rivers, then one might feel the flowers and trees and rivers to be enchanted because they *really are*. Or the sense of enchantment one has in trees may come from something else that is *real*—though not literally the same thing as a dryad. This seems to be part of what Lewis was getting at in a letter we quote previously in greater length: "The feeling about home must have been quite different in the days when a family had fed on the produce of the same few miles of country for six generations, and that perhaps this was why they saw nymphs in the fountains and dryads in the wood—they were not mistaken for there was in a sense a *real* (not metaphorical) connection between them and the countryside."

Yet a third way the word *enchantment* is used is as a rough synonym for *magic*. In literature, this may relate to the second meaning:

an object (personal or impersonal) is *enchanted* if some sort of spell has been cast upon it. Now in literature, magic and the supernatural are not the same thing; something may be magical—again, we are speaking of literature—and still be a part of nature. Despite the presence of magic in most of the Narnia stories as well as in *That Hideous Strength,* this is the sense of the word *enchantment* ("enchantment" = "magic") that we are least interested in. But if there really is a *super*natural reality, and if that supernatural reality does inhabit nature, then nature really can be said to be—and ought to be understood as—*enchanted* in a much deeper sense and with that second meaning. And our feelings about it ought to involve some sense of enchantment. Or, as we shall suggest, "re-enchantment." This, at least, is an important part of what Lewis was trying to do for his readers, and it has important ramifications for our ecological practices.

Disenchantment and Christian Re-enchantment

We hope that we have demonstrated sufficiently that in Lewis's fiction there is a consistent and strong ecological vision. This is a vision that emerges out of a number of sources, including Lewis's religion, his love for good stories and great literature, and his affinity for the late medieval Platonists. His vision also has its sources in his practices, including Lewis's love for walking and his care for animals with whom he shared his life. His fiction and his nonfiction alike—and perhaps most intensely his personal letters—show him to have been a man who attended to natural phenomena: weather, stars, phases of the moon, migrations, flora.

Lewis's ecology is characterized by integrity, plenitude, humility, reverence, and a grateful embracing of life. His desire to integrate all he believed meant that what he appreciated in nature could not help but be important to every other area of his life. From the Platonists Lewis adopted the idea of plenitude, that no portion of creation was void of purpose and meaning. He found nature to be rich with potential to help him understand himself and his world, and all of it is an "index, a symbol, a manifestation" of the divine, and therefore none of it is unimportant. Being or existence itself was found to be more richly textured than imagination could suppose, and since we cannot always see what is there, Lewis's ecology is marked by an insistence on the importance of deep humility and reverence. Ransom's passage through the caves of Perelandra purges Ransom of the arrogance of humankind: he sees that the creatures below the earth are not monsters but only his fellow beings; the monstrosity is in his own perception of them. The great charioteers he sees far beneath the earth may even be like "gods" in comparison to himself. Only great folly or great arrogance could lead a human to suppose that we are the rightful dominators and exploiters of all creation. What remains to be done, then, is to humbly and gratefully receive what is given to us in nature, including our own eventual death. If we only live to forestall our own death, we unwittingly advance it by making all our actions conform to it. Thoreau wrote in his essay "Walking" that "in Wildness is the preservation of the World."[1] Lewis would modify this: in cherishing and gratitude is the preservation of the world.

Perhaps the most surprising feature of Lewis's ecological vision, at least for some readers, is that it is not in conflict with his Christian faith. As we have seen not only in his religiously themed fiction but also in his theological and philosophical works, Lewis's ecology appears to be nurtured from the same sources that nurture his religious worldview. This is surprising because we are accustomed, in the present day, to thinking of religion as a primitive way of thinking that puts us in opposition to this world. We may ask, How can religion and ecology live together? Lewis's answer is that this is the wrong question. The real question is, How can a disenchanting story about the world help us to care for nature?

Lewis differs from philosophical naturalists such as Daniel Dennett who argue that religion arises out of a response to hostile nature. Dennett, in his book *Breaking the Spell: Religion as a Natural Phenomenon*, argues that religion is an enchantment, one whose origins once gave us an evolutionary advantage, and one that we ought to outgrow. A disenchanted world is a better one, because then we no longer populate the world with false beings and false intentions.

The problem with naturalistic philosophies like Dennett's is that they reduce the objects of religious worship to a simple ontology that cannot account for the richness of our experience (including our moral experience); and they also wind up making enemies out of humans and nature: if our religion arises out of nature, then it arises as an insistence that nature must be viewed as hostile. Nature thus demands the mediation of religion to keep the hostile gods at arm's length; prayers and priests are only there to keep us out of the way of nature until we can learn to monitor and control nature scientifically. The effect of such natural religion as Dennett proposes is the disenchantment of the world. Religion and religious stories are no longer needed once we have advanced to scientific maturity, because now we have a scientific story to tell, one that chases away the ghosts of our primitive experience. In stories like Dennett's, the chief interest of humankind is the avoidance of death; nature's meaning to us is death, and there can be no rapprochement between humans and nature until one party is tamed and dominated by the other.

Lewis insisted that his faith did not arise out of nature, and even that nature could be a distraction for those wishing to pray. Nonetheless, he also insisted that nature provides the language for articulating faith. Very often it also provides the spark to ignite faith, and it is not to be understood as wholly alien to that which one worships. The God whom he worshiped was not a God who stood between him and nature or protected him from nature's ravages. Lewis's God was the author of nature, who gave humans and the world to each other and who, in this giving, gave not just nature but also the possibility of knowing the divine.

We see this in the final chapter of *Perelandra*, where Maleldil's (God's) representatives, the eldila (angels), give the world Venus to those who dwell on it. We see it again in *The Magician's Nephew* when Aslan gives the animals first themselves and then the world: "'Creatures, I give you yourselves,' said the strong, happy voice of Aslan. 'I give you forever this land of Narnia. I give you the woods, the fruits, the rivers. I give you the stars and I give you myself. The Dumb Beasts whom I have not chosen are yours also. Treat them gently and cherish them'" (*MN*, x). In this giving, the gift of Narnia and the gift of Aslan are offered at the same time; that is, the gift of the world is not distinct from the gift of the possibility of communion with the One who sang the world into being. There is no primal hostility here, no fear of death, no antagonism between creatures and the world. All of nature, all of life, is conceived as a fitting and hospitable gift.

As far as Lewis was concerned, not only are myth, story, and Christian faith compatible with good ecology, but it is even difficult to see how our view of nature can avoid the kind of antagonism often portrayed in naturalistic philosophies without being "enchanted" by something like the Christian myth. "As long as one is a Naturalist," he writes, "'Nature' is only a word for 'everything.'—And Everything is not a subject about which anything very interesting can be said or (save by illusion) felt. . . . But everything becomes different when we recognize that Nature is a *creature,* a created thing, with its own particular tang or flavour." He goes on to add that "only Supernaturalists really see Nature" (*Mir,* 64–66). We may disagree with him on this last point, but it is certainly the case that Lewis himself felt that his own appreciation for creation, and his motivation to care for it, came because of his Christian worldview and not despite it.

Supernaturalism as Enchantment

This point ought to be explored. Consider again for a moment an entirely pragmatic ecology—one that evaluates all actions and courses of action, potential and actual, only on their effects, without any appeal to an objective system of values or morals. Such a system would call us to avoid behaviors that have short- or long-term effects deemed to be (environmentally) undesirable. To use an obvious example, we know that dumping toxins into our soil or water or air will seriously harm both us and the earth on which we live. So we argue that any financial benefits of such activities to the few are far outweighed by the harmful impact on the many, and we seek to eliminate this behavior. Lewis's works of fiction that we have explored in this book certainly provide numerous good illustrations both of principles and practices that should help bolster a healthy pragmatic ecology. Thus Thomas Howard's observation about *That Hideous Strength* cited in the previous chapter: "If you will reject and violate Nature—Nature in all of its manifestations . . . then Nature will spring back upon you and destroy you, which is what happens with the unleashing of animals at Belbury." One need not have any transcendent morality in order to live the sort of healthy ecological practices that Lewis modeled and that are so desperately needed in the world today: reducing consumption, eschewing exploitation of the earth and our fellow creatures, living sustainably, eating locally, and simply treating the earth with care and respect. Lewis shows that if we fail to do these things, our actions will come back to haunt us.

Though Lewis certainly had a morality—in particular, a Christian morality—behind the healthy ecology modeled in his books, this particular morality is not a prerequisite for living consistently with those principles. One needs only to realize the fundamental law of consequences to have some motivation to care for the earth even at a selfish level, and of course any care or love for fellow creatures should also provide motivation. Observing in Lewis's writing what Howard observed should also put Lewis's ecology on friendly terms with nearly all elements of modern environmentalism, including those whose metaphysical beliefs are most distant from those of Lewis.

But, as we have suggested, there are shortcomings in a merely pragmatic ecology. One problem is that it is often very difficult to foresee the ecological consequences of many of our actions. This is true even with the supposedly twenty-twenty vision of hindsight. The debate over the extent to which global climate change has been caused by us is sufficient evidence to illustrate this point. Another problem is that, even if we agree on the outcomes of our actions, we don't necessary agree on the desirability of competing outcomes. It may well be that even if individuals are fully aware of possible harmful effects of their choices, they may make the same choices anyway for entirely selfish reasons. This becomes much easier if one doesn't see any transcendent value in nature, but only the pragmatic impact of its health upon one's own health. It is vital, it seems, to have some understanding of the inherent goodness and value of the physical earth.

In the first chapter of this book, we discuss Lewis's rejection of any philosophy—including interpretations of Platonism to which he had earlier held—that denies the inherent value of the physical world and of human bodies. This change in his thinking corresponded with his conversion to Christianity; it followed *from* his Christian faith. His belief in the world and our bodies as the creation of a good creator, and in the incarnation of God into the flesh in the person of Jesus, and in the goodness even of physical pleasure (when rightly enjoyed) as a gift from God, all informed and shaped his worldview that nature is good and important and valuable. Now this view of the goodness of the physical world and of the bodies of humans—the vehicles through which we interact with the world—is vitally important to shaping Lewis's ecology. One's care for nature, like one's refusal to exploit nature, comes in part from a recognition of its worth and importance. This idea surfaces in every chapter of this book, in our exploration of every one of his works of fiction. From the creation account in *The Magician's Nephew* to the portrayal of the evil of the N.I.C.E in *That Hideous Strength* and its attempt to disembody man, the goodness of nature and of the body is continually affirmed in Lewis's writing, as is the importance of our care for and nurture of that creation.

This is also a view most modern environmentalists would appreciate, even those who fundamentally *disagree* with the underlying Christian worldview that for Lewis shapes that belief (but which is by no means the only metaphysical system in which people see the importance of a physical world). Other than the pragmatic ecology described above, it is difficult to conceive of an ecological vision that is committed to caring for the earth that does not stem from recognition of the goodness and importance of that earth, and the material universe, and of our own physical existence. In short, those who do not share Lewis's Christianity can still appreciate his imaginative portrayals of a healthy ecology and agree with his valuing of creation (though these readers would prefer to call it "nature"). On this count, also, Lewis is on the same page as the majority of the most respected environmentalists of our day. It is an area where bridges can, and indeed must, be built.

However just as Lewis saw it as both wrong and unhealthy to affirm *only* the world of ideas, or of some spiritual reality, and to deny the physical world, he also saw it as equally unhealthy to affirm *only* a material universe and to deny the reality of the spiritual. For Lewis, the material world—including humans as bodily creatures—is not all there is: there is also a spiritual reality; and humans are also spiritual as well as bodily creatures.

Disenchantment

In the introduction to his book *The Narnian,* Alan Jacobs expresses this belief about C. S. Lewis and calls it the "keynote" of his book: "Lewis's mind was above all characterized by a *willingness to be enchanted* and it was that openness to enchantment that held together the various strands of his life," including "his delight in laughter, his willingness to accept a world made by a good and loving God."[2] Lewis meant that the world ought to feel enchanted to us—all of it, from the smallest flower to the distant stars in the cosmos. It ought to *feel* enchanted because it *is* enchanted. Which is to say, it has not just a magical quality, but a *spiritual* quality—a luminosity. It is alive. But modernity has made it feel disenchanted. In the view of modern physicalism, or metaphysical materialism, or what Lewis might call *scientism,* a tree is nothing more than a tree, and a flower no more than a flower. A star is just a flaming ball of gas. What this means is that all of these things, as well as human life itself, can be reduced to their physical components. We have lost touch with the spiritual, enchanted side of the earth. In an interesting twist, Lewis saw these precepts of modernity as functioning like an evil enchanter that had cast a disenchanting spell on the world. "Spells are used for breaking enchantments as well as for inducing them," he writes in *The Weight of Glory.* He goes on to say, "and you and I have need of the strongest spell that can be found to wake us from the evil enchantment of worldliness which has been laid upon us for nearly a hundred years."[3] For just as it is destructive to ignore or despise the physical reality in favor of a world of Platonic ideals, so, argues Lewis, is it also dangerous to ignore the spiritual and see only the physical. As Jacobs notes, Lewis was thus making "an attempt to reverse . . . the disenchantment of the world."[4]

One of the most tragic moments in all of the Narnia stories comes toward the end of *The Last Battle* when the dwarfs start shooting their fellow Narnians, beginning with the talking horses. It is Jill who first sees this. "It was the Dwarfs who were shooting and—for a moment Jill could hardly believe her eyes—they were shooting the Horses." It is the worst betrayal in any of the seven books—worse even than Eustace's betrayal of his siblings. Eustace may have deceived himself, but he really didn't want his siblings killed, and he later repents of his actions. The dwarfs never repent. They are gleeful in their evil. "We don't want any Talking Horses," they shout. "We don't want you to win any more than the other gang. You can't take *us* in. The Dwarfs are for the Dwarfs" (*LB,* ix). In that second to last sentence lies the heart of the issue; the dwarfs have been fooled by a counterfeit Aslan or, more generally, a counterfeit spirituality and morality, and so they reject altogether *any* notion of spirituality. All that exists for them is what they can feel and touch with their hands. Pragmatically, the dwarfs believed (correctly or incorrectly) that they would be better off if they could kill not only all the Calormenes, but also the talking beasts who are their fellow Narnians. And since there is no room in their beliefs for any transcendent meaning, there is also no reason for them to care about Narnia and their fellow creatures, except as it serves them. (We will return to this in the next section.)

In short, the dwarf's world has been disenchanted. And so powerful is that disenchantment that when Aslan later appears and provides for them a glorious enchanted feast, even better than the ones provided by Father Christmas in *The Lion, the Witch and the Wardrobe* or at the Island of Ramandu in *The Voyage of the Dawn Treader*, they cannot enjoy it.

> Instantly a glorious feast appeared on the Dwarfs' knees: pies and tongues and pigeons and trifles with ices, and each Dwarf had a goblet of good wine in his right hand. But it wasn't much use. They began eating and drinking greedily enough, but it was clear that they couldn't taste it properly. They thought they were eating and drinking only the sort of things you might find in a Stable. One said he was trying to eat hay and another said he had got a bit of an old turnip and a third said he'd found a raw cabbage leaf. And they raised golden goblets of rich red wine to their lips and said "Ugh! Fancy drinking dirty water out of a trough that a donkey's been at! Never thought we'd come to this." But very soon every Dwarf began suspecting that every other Dwarf had found something nicer than he had, and they started grabbing and snatching, and went to quarrelling, till in a few minutes there was a free fight and all the good food was smeared on their faces and clothes or trodden under foot. (*LB*, xiii)

To put this all another way, we could say that the dwarfs have denied the existence of all that has previously enchanted Narnia, and as a result they are not able to appreciate the goodness that nature has to offer them. The particularly ironic aspect of this is that the dwarfs are actually proud of this. "Well, at any rate there's no Humbug here. We haven't let anyone take us in. The Dwarfs are for the Dwarfs." There is little doubt that Lewis was drawing on modern beliefs that have also denied anything that might enchant our own world. And so Aslan's assessment of the dwarfs is one Lewis might also apply to the world today. "They have chosen cunning instead of belief. Their prison is only in their own minds, yet they are in that prison; and so afraid of being taken in that they can not be taken out" (*LB*, xiii).

Transcendence and the Framework of Objective Morality

There is yet another effect, Lewis thought, of living in a disenchanted world, or of denying the reality of anything spiritual or nonmaterial. If nothing exists that transcends nature, then there exists no objective moral system that could also transcend nature. If nature is all there is, then—well—nature is all there is. We may at first disagree with Lewis's assessment that "everything is not a subject about which anything very interesting can be said or . . . felt," and the implied conclusion: if "'Nature' is only a word for 'everything,'" then there isn't much that can be said or felt about Nature. But consider a point made by Pulitzer Prize–winning nature writer Gary Snyder. Snyder argues that the word *nature* should have a "broader definition" than it is usually given; it should include "'the material world or its collective objects and phenomena,' including the products of human action and intention." Snyder is astutely point-ing out that if humans are entirely physical creatures, or *merely* physical creatures, with no spiritual or supernatural life—nothing correspond-ing to an eternal *soul*—then by definition we also are a part of nature, and everything we do is natural. This is the viewpoint he would have us take. "Science and some sorts of mysticism," he goes on to say, "rightly propose that *everything* is natural. By these lights there is nothing unnatural about New York City, or toxic wastes, or atomic energy, and nothing—by definition—that we do or experience in life is 'unnatural.'"[5] In a *dis*-enchanted world, it is as natural for a human to dump toxins in the water as for a bear to defecate in the woods.

There are moral implications as well. If there is no transcendent value, then individuals may create their own moral systems, but there is nothing to say that any one is any better than any other. Objective or transcendent morality is gone. What remains? At best a subjective system. And while on the surface the subjective system may be based on potential outcomes of our actions, at an ultimate level these actions are based only on personal preference because we have no objective way of saying that one outcome is better than another. Again, as we pointed out at the start of this chapter, a known and established objective moral system is not necessary for healthy ecological practices. (As has been noted in this book as elsewhere, plenty of folks who claim to accept the same religion as Lewis fail dramatically to live out its principles in their ecology, and many who disagree fundamentally with Lewis's religious tenets live out many of the same practices—sometimes for very similar reasons, and sometimes for different ones.) A realization of the consequences of all our actions, or a love for our fellow beings, should lead to sound ecology, and Lewis illustrates and motivates us in these things powerfully.

Nonetheless, for C. S. Lewis a recognition of transcendent meaning and morality in the universe pulls everything together and provides a backbone to his ecological understanding. To put this on a more concrete level, we might point out that the world's ecological systems are constantly threatened by exploitation. A host of environmental troubles face our planet today. But why should anybody care, other than for personal reasons (*It might hurt me*)? In fact, there are obviously many individuals who prefer the immediate pleasures and luxuries afforded by wanton consumption (of energy as well as resources) more than they prefer the long-term "benefits" of living more ecologically healthy lives. Health itself is a personal preference. Any ecological argument is lost. If a person has no reason to care what the world is like in thirty years, and no moral basis for living responsibly, what argument can be given?

Here is another side of this. According to naturalism, whatever happens is justified simply because it happened. Indeed, in a materialist universe, where everything is predetermined from the big bang until the final erg of usuable energy has given way to entropy, whatever happens is not only justifiable but it is unavoidable. Whatever has happened *must* have happened—including pollution and extinctions. Consider the implications of Snyder's conclusion that humans are part of nature, and that nature is entirely deterministic. Fred Van Dyke, David C. Mahan, Joseph K. Sheldon, and Raymond H. Brand discuss this in their book *Redeeming Creation*.[6] They explore the commonly held view of evolution not merely as a biological process, but as an irresistible force of destiny "imbued with value regardless of the outcome it produces." This results in arguments such as those of Norman Levine that "extinction is an inevitable fact of evolution, and it is needed for progress. New species continually arise, and they are better adapted to their environment than those that have died out." Interestingly, Van Dyke and his colleagues note that Levine's view is represented by the villain Weston in *Out of the Silent Planet* and *Perelandra*. C. S. Lewis, obviously, had a very different view, in which nature is enchanted by something that transcends nature and provides a transcendent morality, in which exploiting the earth, the water, or our fellow creatures is not merely inconvenient but morally wrong.

Just a Hopeless Romantic?

Still, we may justifiably look askance at the kinds of worlds that Lewis offers us. While their consistency and mythic power may be attractive, does Lewis really offer us anything we can take home from Narnia, Malacandra, or Perelandra? Nowhere in any of these worlds do we see cities, homes, or farms like our own. In Weston's speech to Oyarsa in *Out of the Silent Planet,* he rightly points out that every society he has seen on Malacandra is primitive in comparison to our own. Perhaps this is only snobbery, but it raises an important question about the practicality of Lewis's views. We have argued all along that Lewis's narratives may be helpful for thinking about terrestrial ecology, yet the landscapes in Lewis's worlds simply do not correspond to our own. Narnia is founded as an agrarian state; Perelandra and Malacandra have intentionally small populations. It is quite difficult to imagine trying to persuade our world to adopt widespread agrarianism, and even more difficult to imagine trying to implement economies like those in Lewis's worlds.

One important critique of Lewis's agrarianism comes, indirectly, from Victor Davis Hanson.[7] In his book *Fields without Dreams: Defending the Agrarian Idea,* Hanson reminds us that many agrarian books are simply laments written by romantics with no practical agrarian experience and little knowledge of the history of agrarianism. What we need is not more romance but a practical understanding of what agrarianism means and what we stand to lose if it vanishes. Hanson, an agrarian farmer writing about the demise of agrarianism in America, says

> We are at the end of a historical cycle in America, which has occurred many times in the history of civilization. Agrarianism emerges on the detritus of a failed complexity; it creates a stability that leads to affluence and greater freedom; that bounty invariably leads to a rejection of a now boring and unimaginative community of small and blinkered farmers. Any book about farming must now not be romantic nor naive, but brutally honest: the American yeoman is doomed; his end is part of an evolution of long duration; and so for historical purposes his

last generation provides a unique view of a world—a superior world I will argue—that is to be no more.[8]

So we have two important questions to put to Lewis: first, does Lewis seriously mean for us to adopt systems and states such as those we see in his fiction? And second, is Lewis just a hopeless romantic? Is he, like so many other academic writers about agrarianism, just another urbanite who has read and admired his Emerson or his Wordsworth and now, as a shopping mall rises in his favorite meadow, is coming to lament a time or an ideal that never really was?

The answer to both questions is a modified yes. Lewis does seem to intend for his stories to affect us, though not in the way it might seem at first glance. And Lewis is in one way a romantic, though he is far from hopeless. His hope lies in the power of story to re-enchant the world, and in his insistence that individual lives and decisions matter. Consider, for example, that Lewis himself was well aware of the dangers of romanticism, especially with respect to our view of nature. In his book *The Four Loves*, he writes,

Nature-lovers want to receive as fully as possible whatever nature, at each particular time and place, is, so to speak, saying. The obvious richness, grace, and harmony of some scenes are no more precious to them than the grimness, bleakness, terror, monotony, or "visionary dreariness" of others. The featureless itself gets from them a willing response. It is one more word uttered by nature. They lay themselves bare to the sheer quality of every countryside, every hour of the day. They want to absorb it into themselves, to be coloured through and through by it. This experience . . . has been debunked by the moderns. And one must certainly concede to the debunkers that Wordsworth, not when he was communicating it as a poet, but when he was merely talking about it as a philosopher . . . said some very silly things. (*FL*, 34–5)

"Nature-lover" is not a derogatory term here. Lewis praises nature lovers' ability to learn from nature at all times and their appreciation of the "grimness, bleakness, terror, monotony, or 'visionary dreariness'" of nature as well as the more obvious scenes of beauty. We would all be better, Lewis seems to be suggesting, if we had more willingness to hear the words uttered by nature and to be colored by what we hear. The problem is that, for many "moderns," nature has been disenchanted. In the same breath, however, Lewis also seems to warn against overly romanticizing nature as he feels Wordsworth does when he tries to move from poetry to philosophy. Although from this passage alone we might not conclude too much, the bigger picture brings us back to the bicycle: Lewis seems to be calling not merely for enchantment as romanticism, but for a re-enchantment that moves beyond disenchantment.

Consider the observation made by Gregory Wolfe in his article on Lewis's debt to George MacDonald: "When, as a mere Romantic, Lewis experienced a moment of Joy, he naturally associated it with another world—the North, fairy land, a story. Even when the joy was linked to clouds or mountains, Lewis said, they did not lead him to think differently about the particular clouds and mountains he knew. Instead, after the moments of joy, he experienced a dissatisfaction with the world. But in *Phantastes* Lewis was confronted by a reversal of the Romantic experience in that now moments of joy did not cause dissatisfaction; they enhanced the real world."[9] The "mere Romantic" stage Wolfe describes is the stage before Lewis's conversion to Christianity, when he was drawn to a rationalist philosophy. Lewis still had the romantic, or enchanted, response to nature, but this rationalist philosophy was disenchanting him. The romantic could take moments of joy from nature but end up more dissatisfied than before. The re-enchanted Lewis—the Lewis affected by Christianity experienced indirectly in the writings of George MacDonald, and later more directly—could appreciate the old romantic feelings without the dissatisfaction, because he could see beyond it not to its debunking, but to a deeper truth. Thus for Lewis, the very sort of romantic enchantment of the fairy-tale presentation of nature—the nature of Narnia or Malacandra or Perelandra—led to a re-enchantment of his own world and an enhancement of it.

The Power of Story and a Practical Upshot

And we are back again to the power of story. Literature is dangerous in many ways, and one great danger presents itself to anyone who claims to find practical significance in a work of fiction. That danger is that we will eviscerate the living story in order to salvage our favorite portion of it. If we approach Lewis's stories only as sources of certain positive doctrines, we will miss the most important part of the stories: the stories themselves. As Lewis writes at the end of *Out of the Silent Planet*, his hope was to use the mode of mythic fiction as a way of beginning to make a change in the way we think. This is not to say that he was simply trying to smuggle theology or ideology in through the door of fiction. Rather, he knew that stories are a powerful tool both for helping us to become familiar with new ideas and for testing them out. Meeting an idea in a textbook can be like meeting a specimen in a jar: the organism is intact, but it is excised from its natural environment, and it is dead. On the other hand, when we meet an idea in a story, we are able to observe it in its natural environment. We meet it alive and fully functioning. Just as a limp or a strong gait can better be seen when the runner is in motion than when she is still, so the strengths and weaknesses of ideas reveal themselves when those ideas are encountered in the context of stories. Lewis often referred to his stories as "romances," that is, novels. Lewis was, in this sense, unashamed to be a "romantic."

It is important to note that he did not consider his stories to be "pamphlets" or "tracts" or "polemics." Polemics hope to advance a doctrine, adducing strong arguments to persuade the reader to adopt the doctrine. Lewis apparently hoped to offer not a doctrine but a picture, and to advance it not so much through argument as through the beauty of the picture itself. The figure of Mark, employed by the N.I.C.E., makes plain that Lewis was aware of the power and dangers of merely polemical writing that, ignoring the voice of the writer's conscience and the consequences for individuals, calls for political and cultural change. Mark's writings contributed to considerable violence against people, animals, plants, rivers, air, and the land, because he wrote what was in line with the dictates of his party. Lewis's fiction doubtless contains strong depictions of Lewis's own views, but he offers them to us mediated by their context. His stated intention is that the stories would be a catalyst by means of which we would discover on our own how we ought to live our lives. The intention is not to convert people but to show them something lovely in order that they might recognize its loveliness on their own and so genuinely respond to it, without coercion.

So does Lewis intend for us to become agrarians? If we are asking whether Lewis intends for agrarians to take over the state, the answer is plainly no. Lewis's novels also offer a picture of what Lewis considered healthy politics, and strong-armed revolutions that show no regard for individuals do not fit that description. Shift the ape and the leadership of the N.I.C.E. move forward under cover of obfuscatory jargon, deception, and secrecy, all of which point to an essentially exploitive set of methods. At St. Anne's none are coerced to do what their consciences oppose, and those who are expected to act are told what they need to know in order to make good decisions. Clearly Lewis took individual, well-informed decisions to matter. For that reason, agrarian reforms cannot be simply imposed from the top down. (Besides, if they were institutional reforms, would they really be *agrarian* reforms?) But if the question is whether Lewis hopes that we will see the beauty of agrarian ideals and so desire to live well, the answer is yes. In other words, Lewis's stories are not about bringing about revolutionary social change; they are about laying the groundwork, through the sense of beauty, for individuals to choose to live well and to do what is best—and all for the right reasons.

So Lewis's integrated worldview in fact matters: his Christian story is one that calls the world good and hospitable and that calls for a reverential and humble response on the part of humans. His is a voice that gives the lie to the "Abrahamic" narrative of domination. Practically speaking, what does that mean? We may deduce a few principles from Lewis's writings.

First, as we have said above, both the community and the individual matter.

Second, we should not do harm without cause. While this may seem like common sense, it also plays a constant role in Lewis's ecology. The two human figures who have the closest communion with nature in Lewis's stories are Merlin and young Digory, both of whom are effectively prohibited from using edge tools on living things. In Narnian battles, the rule all Narnians obey is one of mercy.

Third, there is a constant emphasis on the human obligation to improve other creatures and to help them to "perfect their natures." What precisely this means is, on the one hand, very difficult to tell. What is the nature of a mouse, and how do we improve it? Uncle Andrew argues that the purpose of rodents is to be bought and experimented on, and this is evident because they are lower creatures whose deaths and sufferings are not ultimately important to him. On the other hand, it seems obvious that we should not be cruel. But may we exterminate mice if they come into our homes? Lewis liked them, but we also know them to be bearers of hantavirus, and allowing them in our homes may not be the best way to love our families. Here we see one of the limitations of turning to stories for ecological doctrines only. If we hope to extract a mouse policy from Lewis's texts, we might do so in vain. But if we look at his treatment of mice, we see that his kindness toward them evinces good and imitable character *in general,* while the unkindness shown toward Reepicheep by various Telmarines and initially by Eustace, or Andrew's cruelty toward guinea pigs, or Weston's mutilation of frogs on Perelandra evinces what can only be decadence, vice, and improper domination.

Fourth, Lewis's texts consistently advocate humility toward what we do not know. This is also plain from the same examples of Eustace (when he first appears), Miraz, Andrew, and Weston. Each of them arrogates to himself the right to use animals as he will. But this arrogation is far reaching, since it requires as well that each of them act as though he knows that there is nothing above him that prohibits this action, no higher being to whom these creatures belong, no higher law than his own will. In Lewis's writings about medieval and Renaissance literature, the principle of plenitude is, of course, a metaphysical point about the fullness of being, the importance of all things and all places, and about the significance of creation. We think Lewis intends all that to be taken seriously today, but ultimately this is not a metaphysical point but rather an ethical one. That is, it does not matter so much that we think we can prove there are beings everywhere. However, the metaphysical doctrine comes with a story about the meaning of the world and about our responsibilities in it. The plenitude or fullness of being means we always have neighbors. Nothing we do happens in a vacuum (which, apparently, nature abhors), but it occurs in a neighborhood, and our actions have consequences both for other creatures and for the future. This can be an important corrective to human hubris and the corrosive actions that are sometimes dictated by efficiency or expediency.

This brings us to our fifth and final point: stories may be an important but largely missing element in ecological—and perhaps in all scientific—education. Of course, already in Francis Bacon's time we discovered that science moves excruciatingly slowly if we have to consult the priests about the metaphysical status of mice and whether or not there are angels that prohibit our testing medicines on them. We are not proposing attempting to bring angelology back into the laboratory. Bacon famously, in his *Novum Organon,* dismisses attempts to determine ideal, formal, and ethical causes of natural things, preferring to let empirical science advance chiefly by investigating matter and energy. This uncoupling of metaphysical and physical branches of inquiry gave a helpful boost to the empirical sciences. Still, perhaps we have gone too far in "disenchanting" science. If religious dogma and the pronouncements of metaphysicians fetter science, stories like Lewis's can help to provide scientists with a basis for moral reasoning that is instructive but not dogmatic. They do so by grounding the ethical issues in lived situations and by giving all who read them a common "language" of ethical anecdotes.

C. S. Lewis's stories offer us a vision of the world brimming with life and goodness, full of purpose, rich with value, every part enmeshed in deep and ethical relations with every other part. His is a world of spirit—spirit dwelling in the trees, rivers, and stones, hovering over the deep and upon the mountains. This is a less popular notion in some modern circles, and yet it is a vital part of Lewis's ecology: for millions of readers, Lewis succeeded in enchanting, or rather *re-enchanting* nature. He brought the woods and fields and rivers and seas, and the animals that live in them, alive with mythical and spiritual significance, helping us not only to see them in new ways, but also to care for them more deeply. And even for those who disagree with any of its theistic aspects, this vision of the fullness and goodness of the universe might be Lewis's greatest contribution to modern ecology—and the greatest positive influence he has had.

Notes

Introduction

1. The word *ecology* has both a narrow meaning and a broad one. In the narrower sense, the word refers to the study of the relationships of living things; in this sense it is like the terms *biology* or *geology,* and simply refers to a science. Taken more broadly, however, it refers not only to the study of the relationships of living things, but to those relationships themselves and our ideas about them. In this broader sense, for example, *Yellowstone ecology* would refer not merely to a study of the interactions of living things in Yellowstone National Park, but also to actual relationships of those living things and to our intentional consideration of those relationships and principles that govern them. In this broader sense, the word *ecology* includes an ethic—that is, an idea not just of what the relationships are, but what proper relationships *should* be. Thus an ecology can also be a construct—an idea, or set of ideals—that one holds as a proper or healthy way to interrelate. Ecological ideas, of course, may emerge from our *study,* that is, from the science of ecology as understood in the narrower sense, but they also impact our *practice.* Throughout the book, we use the term *ecology* in this broader sense to include our study and ideas about relationships among living things, as well as the ideals and practices that emerge from those ideas.

2. Kathryn Lindskoog, *The Lion of Judah in Never-Never Land* (Grand Rapids, Mich.: W. B. Eerdmans, 1973).

3. Ed Chapman, "Toward a Sacramental Ecology: Technology, Nature, and Transcendence in C. S. Lewis's Ransom Trilogy," *Mythlore* 3 (June 1976): 10–17.

4. Ibid., 11.

5. The question "Why story?" is a question that Lewis foresaw, thought about considerably, and addressed in many places. The authors of this book have written a previous book, *From Homer to Harry Potter: A Handbook of Myth and Fantasy* (Grand Rapids, Mich.: Brazos Press, 2006), exploring fantasy literature more broadly, looking at its worth and how to understand its truth. This previous book draws upon a much broader array of Lewis's writing on the subject of story.

6. Alan Jacobs, *The Narnian: The Life and Imagination of C. S. Lewis* (San Francisco: HarperSanFrancisco, 2005), x–xi, xviii.

7. See chapters 1 and 2 of *From Homer to Harry Potter,* as well as Lewis's essays "On Science Fiction."

8. Lewis writes in "On Science Fiction" (OSF, 64), "When I put canals on Mars I believe I already knew that better telescopes had dissipated that old optical delusion. The point was that they were part of the Martian myth as it already existed in the common mind."

9. See 2 Samuel 11–12. When the prophet Nathan came to King David with a story about a wicked rich man who stole his poor neighbor's only sheep in order to feed a visitor, David reacted with appropriate rage against the injustice. It turns out that the story was about David himself stealing Bathsheba, the wife of one of his army officers named Uriah. Had Nathan told the tale about David, the king probably wouldn't have listened. David had to hear the truth in the form of *fiction* or *story* before he could hear the *fact.*

10. Thomas Howard, *Narnia and Beyond: A Guide to the Fiction of C. S. Lewis* (San Francisco: Ignatius Press, 2006), 60.

11. Ibid., 79.

12. J. Robert Barth, *Romanticism and Transcendence: Wordsworth, Coleridge, and the Religious Imagination* (Columbia: University of Missouri Press, 2003), 4.

13. Cal Dewitt, personal interview with Matthew Dickerson, February 15, 2006.

14. Peter Kreeft, *The Philosophy of Tolkien: The Worldview behind the Lord of the Rings* (San Francisco: Ignatius Press, 2005), 23.

15. Philip N. Joranson and Ken Butigan, eds., *Cry of the Environment: Rebuilding the Christian Creation Tradition* (Santa Fe: Bear and Company, 1984), 277.

16. Norman Wirzba, "Introduction: The Challenge of Berry's Agrarian Vision," in *The Art of the Commonplace: The Agrarian Essays of Wendell Berry,* edited by Norman Wirzba, vii–xx (Washington, D.C.: Shoemaker and Hoard, 2002).

17. Cf. Aldo Leopold, *Sand County Almanac* (New York: Oxford University Press, 1968), viii. Leopold speaks pejoratively about the "Abrahamic" vision of land in his preface, suggesting hostility toward Judeo-Christian land ethics. But this is not the whole story. In the third section of his book, "The Land Ethic," Leopold writes that "individual thinkers since the days of Ezekiel and Isaiah have asserted that the despoliation of land is not only inexpedient but wrong. Society, however, has not yet affirmed their belief. I regard the present conservation movement as the embryo of such an affirmation" (203). In effect Leopold is identifying two distinct strains within the Jewish and

Christian narratives. One narrative is the one that makes land into mere property and so makes usefulness its highest imaginable quality. This narrative, the "Abrahamic," excludes the land from being an ethical agent. The other narrative is the narrative of an ethic that is slowly growing and expanding to include the land within an ethic and as an agent or participant in that ethical system. This strain is currently more muted but it is the greater, and it must become greater still, Leopold implies, if we are to take our ethical obligations seriously. So Leopold sees the Jewish and Christian traditions as a mixed bag, offering both a positive and a negative ecology. In other words, Leopold's reply to Lynn White and others who say that Christianity is to blame for ecological crises is that they have seen only the first chapter of the story. What follows later in the story is the development of a greater ecological ethic precisely out of the same source in the law and the prophets.

18. Jim Nollman, *Why We Garden,* cited by Vigen Guroian in *Inheriting Paradise: Meditations on Gardening* (Grand Rapids, Mich.: Eerdmans, 1999), 6. In response, Guroian suggests that Nollman's "real knowledge of biblical faith is limited" and points to Psalm 148 as a counterexample to Nollman's claim. This book will also present numerous counterexamples in the form of the teaching provided by the Christian writer C. S. Lewis, who also comments on Psalm 148.

19. Sallie McFague, "Intimate Creation—God's Body, Our Home," *Christian Century,* March 13, 2002.

20. Regarding God as King, see Matthew 27:11 and Luke 23:3. See also Psalm 24:7; Psalm 44:4,7; Matthew 2:2; I Timothy 1:17; and so on. It is important to note, however, that the Bible speaks of God as Creator, while also using the metaphors of God as father and shepherd, and elsewhere using the imagery of God as nurturing and protective mother.

21. Sallie McFague, "A Square in the Quilt: One Theologian's Contribution to the Planetary Agenda," in *Spirit and Nature: Why the Environment Is a Religious Issue: An Interfaith Dialogue,* edited by Steven C. Rockefeller and John C. Elder, 39–58 (Boston: Beacon Press, 1992). Lecture presented at the "Spirit and Nature" symposium at Middlebury College in 1990.

22. Ibid., 48.

23. Ibid., 44.

24. Rockefeller and Elder, *Spirit and Nature,* 4.

25. Lynn White Jr., "The Historical Roots of our Ecologic Crisis," *Science* 155, no. 3767 (March 10, 1967): 1203–7.

26. Ibid., 1206.

27. See, for example, Steven Bouma-Prediger, *For the Beauty of the Earth* (Grand Rapids, Mich.: Baker Academic, 2006), especially chapter 3. This is not to imply a lack of culpability on the part of many Christians. Bouma-Prediger

agrees that the Christian church must accept a measure of guilt for poor ecological practices, or for bad teaching leading to such unhealthy practices. Lewis would add that this is true of any aspect of Christian doctrine, such as commands to love your neighbor, honor God, and not covet. The problem in these areas, argued by Bouma-Prediger and others, is not the biblical teaching on ecological (and other) issues, but rather the failure on the part of the church to follow those teachings and to teach those teachings. Lewis was very fond of the writings of G. K. Chesterston, who noted in his book *What's Wrong with the World* that "the Christian ideal has not been tried and found wanting; it has been found difficult and left untried." Ecologically speaking, this is also one of the premises of this book, which we hope to show through an exploration of the writings of C. S. Lewis.

28. White, "Historical Roots," 1205.

29. Ibid., 1205–6.

30. Lindskoog, *Lion of Judah,* 29.

31. Ibid., 47.

32. White, "Historical Roots," 1207.

33. Ibid., 1207.

34. See, for example, Philippians 2:3–8, as well as Matthew 18:4, Luke 18:14, and James 4:10.

35. White, "Historical Roots," 1205.

36. Rockefeller and Elder, *Spirit and Nature,* 3.

1. What He Thought about Everything

1. Owen Barfield, "Preface," in *The Taste of Pineapple,* edited by Bruce L. Edwards (Bowling Green, Ohio: Bowling Green State University Popular Press, 1988), 2.

2. Alan Jacobs, *The Narnian: The Life and Imagination of C. S. Lewis* (San Francisco: HarperSanFrancisco, 2005), xx–xxi.

3. Dr. Bruce Edwards, quoted from http://cslewis.drzeus.net/papers/tribute.html (accessed June 5, 2008); available at personal.bgsu.edu/edwards/blade.htm (accessed June 17, 2008).

4. Lewis took three "Firsts" or degrees of the first class, at Oxford. His first degree, in Greek and Latin, went by the name *Honours Moderations,* or *Honours Mods* for short. His second degree was in "Greats," that is, philosophy and ancient history. His third "First" was in English. Cf. Jacobs, *The Narnian,* 99ff.

5. Jacobs, *The Narnian,* 106.

6. We are referring primarily to C. S. Lewis after his conversion to Christianity in 1929. Prior to his rejection of a materialist worldview, various

biographers and chroniclers of his thinking describe inconsistencies especially in Lewis's simultaneous interest in, on the one hand, myth and imaginative poetry, and on the other, a commitment to Enlightenment rationalism, which rejected the validity of the former as a path toward knowledge or wisdom. Alan Jacobs chronicles this time, referring to "two sides of Lewis at odds with each other": the one side that was an "imaginative lover of poetry," and the other the "dialectician" (*The Narnian*, 90). For a time, the imaginative side of Lewis was, as Jacobs puts it, being starved. After his conversion to Christianity—and as an important step leading to that conversion—philosophy and literature, more specifically reason and imagination, ceased to be at odds for Lewis.

7. Ed Chapman, "Toward a Sacramental Ecology: Technology, Nature, and Transcendence in C. S. Lewis's Ransom Trilogy," *Mythlore* 3 (June 1976): 11–12.

8. Certainly the issue of deforestation had been addressed prior to Lewis's time, including by visible figures such as President Theodore Roosevelt in the United States. But many decades passed before the concern for the effects of deforestation received the wide-scale attention that it receives today.

9. Armand Nicholi Jr., *The Question of God: C. S. Lewis and Sigmund Freud Debate God, Love, Sex, and the Meaning of Life* (New York: Free Press, 2002), 27.

10. Jacobs, *The Narnian*, 4.

11. Nicholi, *The Question of God*, 49–50.

12. As Lewis himself would learn, philosophy is by no means opposed to creativity, poetry, myth, or imagination. But a certain strict rationalist philosophy perhaps offered an escape from the spiritual worldview implied by myth, while at the same time denying that the imagination, or indeed anything other than rationalism, such as poetry, story, or myth, could be a vehicle for discovering truth.

13. Jacobs, *The Narnian*, 100.

14. Ibid., 102.

15. Ibid., 108.

16. Ibid., 124.

17. See chapter 6 of our previous book, *From Homer to Harry Potter: A Handbook of Myth and Fantasy* (Grand Rapids, Mich.: Brazos Press, 2006), which traces this influence, giving several specific examples of devices, ideas, and characters from MacDonald's fantasies and fairy tales that can be seen in Lewis's own fantastic fiction.

18. C. S. Lewis, "Preface" in *George MacDonald: An Anthology*, edited by C. S. Lewis (New York: Macmillan, 1947), xxxii.

19. Ibid., xxxiii.

20. Cited in Jacobs, *The Narnian*, 63.

21. Rolland Hein, *The Harmony Within: The Spiritual Vision of George MacDonald*, rev. ed. (Chicago: Cornerstone Press, 1999), 93.

22. Excerpt from the poem "My Room," by George MacDonald, in *Works of Fancy and Imagination*, vol. 4 (London: Strahan and Company), 32.

23. Excerpt from the poem "The Tree's Prayer," by George MacDonald, in *Works of Fancy*, 18.

24. Timothy Johnson Bleeker, "The Christian Romanticism of George MacDonald: A Study of His Thought and Fiction" (Ph.D. dissertation, Tufts University, 1990), 24.

25. Jacobs, *The Narnian*, 64.

26. Bleeker, "Christian Romanticism," 23.

27. Gregory Wolfe, "C. S. Lewis's Debt to George MacDonald," *The Bulletin of the New York C. S. Lewis Society* 15, no. 2 (December 1983): 2.

28. Hein, *The Harmony Within*, 76.

29. Peter Kreeft, *The Philosophy of Tolkien: The Worldview behind the Lord of the Rings* (San Francisco: Ignatius Press, 2005), 11.

30. Peter Kreeft provides numerous direct quotations and specific examples for almost all of the fifty philosophical questions he addresses in the writings of J. R. R. Tolkien. Interestingly, however, on the question "Are Platonic Ideas real?" he does not cite any passage from Tolkien's work. Instead, he makes his point with a more general example. "In *The Lord of the Rings* everything seems to be more itself, more Platonic. The earth is more earth, nature is more natural, the history is more historical, the genealogies more genealogical, the tragedy more tragic, the joy more joyful, the caverns more cavernous, the forests more foresty, and the heroes more heroic" (*Philosophy of Tolkien*, 45). The nature of Kreeft argument suggests, then, that if Tolkien's fantasy does reflect medieval Platonism it does so less consciously than Lewis's. Kreeft's final comment regarding Platonism in Lewis and Tolkien speaks to the power of myth in the writings of both. "A great mythmaker awakes the longing for these Platonic archetypes, which are buried deep in human knowledge, through using a magic language: the language of myth" (ibid., 48).

31. Evan K. Gibson, *C. S. Lewis, Spinner of Tales: A Guide to His Fiction* (Grand Rapids, Mich.: Eerdmans, 1980), 114.

32. Norman Wirzba, "Placing the Soul: An Agrarian Philosophical Principle," in *The Essential Agrarian Reader: The Future of Culture, Community, and the Land*, edited by Norman Wirzba, 80–100 (Lexington: University Press of Kentucky, 2003), 82.

33. Ibid.

34. In an early sketch of his *Birth of Tragedy*, Nietzsche famously referred to his philosophy as "inverted Platonism," because, in his estimation, Platonism transposed all of this world's value to an ideal world, sapping this world of its

vitality. Nietzsche affirmed the present concrete reality of the world over the ideal but unreachable world of Platonic ideas. In the preface to his *Beyond Good and Evil,* Nietzsche calls Christianity "Platonism for the masses."

35. T. M. Moore, *Consider the Lilies* (Phillipsburg, N.J.: P&R Publishing, 2005), 100. Moore is summarizing Alister E. McGrath, *A Scientific Theology I: Nature* (Grand Rapids, Mich.: Eerdmans, 2001), 81ff.

36. Hein, *The Harmony Within,* xvi.

37. Wolfe, "C. C. Lewis's Debt," 3.

38. Philip Sherrard, *The Rape of Man and Nature* (Ipswich, U.K.: Golgonooza, 1987), 90.

39. Jacobs, *The Narnian,* x.

40. Matthew Dickerson and Jonathan Evans, *Ents, Elves, and Eriador: The Environmental Vision of J. R. R. Tolkien* (Lexington: University Press of Kentucky, 2006), xv.

41. N. T. Wright, "Heaven Is Not Our Home," *Christianity Today* 52, no. 4. (April 2008): 36–39.

2. Nature and Meaning in the History of Narnia

1. Wendell Berry, *Jayber Crow* (Washington, D.C.: Counterpoint, 2000).

2. *Letters,* 50, quoted from Alan Jacobs, *The Narnian: The Life and Imagination of C. S. Lewis* (San Francisco: HarperSanFrancisco, 2005), xxiv.

3. Kate Turner interview, 2000. In an interview with Kate Turner on April 2, 2000, Wendell Berry noted, "I am an admirer of C. S. Lewis and I love a lot of the things the he wrote. Especially I love his literary scholarship. . . . He did and said some things that are incalculably beyond my reach because of the way his life was and the way his persuasion led him. . . . And he was a superb steward of the things that he was given to take care of. . . . He was a great servant, C. S. Lewis was." Later in the interview, speaking of his own attempt to communicate reasons for good ecological practices to those who don't share his spiritual worldview, Berry again points to C. S. Lewis and his portrayal of a virtuous nonreligious "rationalist" or "rational materialist" in *That Hideous Strength.* Interestingly, Berry says the difference between himself and Lewis is not in their ideas, but in their different emphases, which stem from their different professions. "The fundamental difference between [C. S. Lewis] and me," Berry said, "is probably not one of belief but one of life. He was a scholar, a man whose life was devoted almost exclusively to books. And I'm an agrarian and a farmer." He goes on then to mention how Lewis had the same concerns with loss of community and the same observations about how things had gone wrong, but "Lewis in his time didn't *have* to think of the things we're having to think of now. The agrarian class, the agrarian tradition in England was more

intact in Lewis's time than it is now." Wendell Berry constrasts this with the characters in his own fiction. "My characters I think increasingly appear as the last of their kind, as a vanishing kind of humanity. And because of them, I began writing. . . . It was increasingly clear that the people who died were not being replaced." Berry certainly has objective data to show that things had changed very rapidly between the publications of *The Lion, the Witch, and the Wardrobe* and *Jayber Crow*. What is interesting, then, is that Lewis actually did seem to realize that the real agrarian was a vanishing kind due to the pressures already apparent in the mid-twentieth century; this is suggested by the character of Frank, the country boy forced to become a London cabby in *The Magician's Nephew*.

4. *The Magician's Nephew*, though it describes a much earlier time in the history of Narnia, was the sixth of seven books to be written.

5. Prologue to the second edition of *The Lord of the Rings* by J. R. R. Tolkien (Boston: Houghton Mifflin, 1954).

6. Dale Larsen and Sandy Larsen, *While Creation Waits: A Christian Response to the Environmental Challenge* (Wheaton, Ill.: Harold Shaw, 1992), 17.

7. We grant that in *The Horse and His Boy* Shasta and Aravis actually spend more time riding than walking, but then (as the title suggests) the horses Bree and Hwin are also important characters, and even when Shasta and Aravis are riding, the two horses are still walking (or trotting or galloping).

8. Gary Snyder, "The Etiquette of Freedom," in *The Practice of the Wild* (San Francisco: North Point Press, 1990), 18.

9. John Elder, *Reading the Mountains of Home* (Cambridge, Mass.: Harvard University Press, 1998), 53.

10. See Alan Jacobs, *The Narnian: The Life and Imagination of C. S. Lewis* (San Francisco: HarperSanFrancisco, 2005), 53–54, who also points out that Lewis's walks were both "times of meditation and reflection" as well as times to find Joy or the longing for Joy in "particular landscapes, or certain views of those landscapes." Regarding walking, Jacobs also notes that Lewis "early on became very aware of the ways in which the Irish landscape . . . differed from any of the English ones he had come to know." He suggests how much Lewis as a walker could be affected by these landscapes, and how observant he was of them—in particular how much "more overtly Irish" he became "when writing about the contours of County Down" (which was his favorite walk).

11. Philip Sherrard, *The Rape of Man and Nature* (Ipswich, U.K.: Golgonooza, 1987), 90.

12. Wendell Berry, "The Body and the Earth," in *The Art of the Commonplace: The Agrarian Essays of Wendell Berry*, edited by Norman Wirzba, 118–19 (Washington, D.C.: Shoemaker and Hoard, 2002).

13. Andrew Haile, senior thesis, Middlebury College, spring 2007.

14. If there is a more apt criticism of this pair of scenes, it might be that Lewis is anti-male; in both cases it is the females (whether students or teachers) who are shown to be wise and virtuous and who care about education, while the males are the villains.

15. See Jim Ball, "The Use of Ecology in the Evangelical Protestant Response to the Ecological Crisis," *Journal of the American Scientific Affiliation* 50, no. 1 (1998): 32–38.

16. There is no space even to *summarize* this extensive work here except to the extent that the ideas are directly evident in Lewis's writing. Among the most important points are: (1) The command to "rule" goes hand in hand with the doctrine that we are created in God's image, which means that humanity's rule over earth is carried out properly in the model of God's own rule, which is a loving rule most clearly modeled in the self-sacrificial model of Jesus, the servant king; (2) The command to populate the earth *follows* a statement that the creatures of the sea and sky also are supposed to "Be fruitful and increase in number" (Genesis 1:22, NIV); (3) That the earth and its creatures have just been proclaimed "good" five times, and that this goodness precedes and is independent of its usefulness to humanity or even of humanity's presence at all. Any exercise of dominion must take place with the understanding of the inherent goodness and value of the rest of creation; and (4) That this command to rule, subdue, and fill the earth is followed in Genesis 2:15 with a specific command for humans to nurture the earth. For further exploration, we recommend Steven Bouma-Prediger's *For the Beauty of the Earth* (Grand Rapids, Mich.: Baker, 2001).

17. Wherever possible, we have tried to use gender-inclusive language such as "humanity" instead of "man." As is evident from what we have cited so far, Lewis followed the older convention of using "man" as inclusive of both genders. Occasionally, as here, we follow Lewis's usage to avoid awkward constructions as we attempt to write in a way that is consistent with his narratives. Usually, as in this instance, our use of the singular but inclusive "Man" is intended to distinguish humans in Narnia from other sentient beings

18. *The Horse and His Boy* is somewhat different in that the human protagonists, Shasta and Aravis, never travel to our world. However Peter, Susan, Edmund, and Lucy do enter the tale, and they will eventually return to our world.

19. Bouma-Prediger, *For the Beauty of the Earth*, 74.

20. In *Reflections on the Psalms,* Lewis almost makes another point about similarities between ancient Judaism and paganism with respect to taking real unabashed delight in worship. Regarding King David dancing before the Ark of God (II Samuel 6)—dancing as Lewis describes it "with such abandon"—he comments: "This helps to remind us at the outset that Judaism, though it is the

worship of the one true and eternal God, is an ancient religion. That means that its externals, and many of its attitudes, were much more like those of Paganism than they were like all that stuffiness—all that regimen of tiptoe tread and lowered voice—which the word 'religion' suggests to so many people now. In one way, of course this puts a barrier between it and us. We should not have enjoyed the ancient rituals. Every temple in the world, the elegant Parthenon at Athens and the holy Temple at Jerusalem, was a sacred slaughterhouse. . . But even that has two sides. If temples smelled of blood, they also smelled of roast meat; they struck a festive and homely note, as well as a sacred" (*ROP,* 44–45).

21. Dick Keyes, *Beyond Identity* (Ann Arbor, Mich.: Servant Books, 1984), 21.

22. Steven Bouma-Prediger, "Creation Care and Character: The Nature and Necessity of the Ecological Virtues," *Perspectives on Science and Faith: Journal of the American Scientific Affiliation* 50, no. 1 (March 1998): 6–21.

23. Barbara Kingsolver, foreword to *The Essential Agrarian Reader: The Future of Culture, Community, and the Land,* edited by Norman Wirzba (Lexington: University Press of Kentucky, 2003), xiii.

24. Bouma-Prediger, "Creation Care," 6–21.

25. Norman Wirzba, "Introduction: Why Agrarianism Matters—Even to Urbanites," in *The Essential Agrarian Reader,* ed. Wirzba, 8.

26. Lisa Zinn, interview with Matthew Dickerson, July 8, 2006, at the Au Sable Institute in Mancelona, Michigan.

27. Larsen and Larsen, *While Creation Waits,* 7.

28. One might point to the Witch's castle and say that it is, in fact, a "community" including at least one dwarf and several wolves. The same could be said of Miraz's court. But if these are "communities," they are not communities that model any of the *virtues* of community. Rather, they are a mockery of real community. They are characterized by fear, injustice, and betrayal rather than loyalty, trust, or companionship. Two of Miraz's own nobles plot his assassination, even as Miraz plots the murder of his nephew. A more explicit contrast between healthy community and its antithesis is explored in chapter 7 of *That Hideous Strength.*

29. See, for example, the essays in *Rooted in the Land: Essays on Community and Place,* edited by William Vitek and Wes Jackson (New Haven, Conn.: Yale University Press, 1996).

30. See www.ausable.org/au.ausableidea.cfm (accessed June 5, 2008).

31. Bill McKibben, "A Deeper Shade of Green," *National Geographic,* August 2006, 33–41.

32. Jacobs, *The Narnian,* 189–90.

33. Ibid., 55.

34. Lewis was referring here to 1 John 4:20, which in the King James

Version reads, "If a man say, I love God, and hateth his brother, he is a liar: for he that loveth not his brother whom he hath seen, how can he love God whom he hath not seen?"

35. Larsen and Larsen, *While Creation Waits,* 9.

36. Richard Foster, *Celebration of Discipline* (San Francisco: Harper and Row, 1978), 70, 79–81.

37. Jacobs, *The Narnian,* 189.

38. This is a device that C. S. Lewis borrowed from Scandinavian myths and particularly the *Völsunga Saga,* though there are many variations of the story of the hero Sigurth, including the *Niebelungenlied.* In the tale, Fáfnir kills his father in order to gain his father's gold. As a result of the gold lust, Fáfnir is turned (or turns himself) into a dragon. He is later killed by Sigurth, the foster-son of his brother Regin, whom Fáfnir had earlier driven away and with whom he had refused to share the treasure. Lewis's solution, however, is unique: the un-dragonizing—that is, the restoration to humanity—of the dragon, rather than his slaying. Lewis is certainly suggesting that there is hope of learning contentment even for the chronically discontented such as Eustace.

39. As the narrator tells us about Lucy's situation, "it is a terrible thing to have to wake four people, all older than yourself, and all very tired, for the purpose of telling them something they probably won't believe and making them do something they certainly won't like" (*PC,* x).

40. Fred Van Dyke, David C. Mahan, Joseph K. Sheldon, and Raymond H. Brand, *Redeeming Creation* (Downers Grove, Ill.: Intervarsity Press, 1996), 53.

41. Wendell Berry, Kate Turner interview.

42. Don W. King, *C. S. Lewis, Poet: The Legacy of His Poetic Impulses* (Kent, Ohio: Kent State University Press, 2001), 187. "Under Sentence" first appeared on September 7, 1945, in *The Spectator,* 175.

3. *The Magician's Nephew*

1. Lewis shared a draft of what came to be known as "the Lefay Fragment" with Roger Lancelyn Green in June 1949. *The Magician's Nephew* apparently grew out of that fragment, which would put its initial conception shortly after *The Lion, the Witch and the Wardrobe,* though it wasn't developed until later (Walter Hooper, *C. S. Lewis: A Companion and Guide* [New York: HarperCollins, 1996], 403).

2. Examples include the decadent city of Tashbaan in Calormen (*The Horse and His Boy*), the city run by slavery and enchantment in the Emerald Witch's underground empire (*The Silver Chair*), and Narrowhaven in the Lone Isles, which must be cleansed of its slavery and corrupt governor (*The Voyage*

of the Dawn Treader). There are hints of developed towns in Narnia under the wicked rule of Miraz and the Telmarines (*Prince Caspian*), but it is not until the final book that there is a city in Narnia proper. In *The Last Battle,* Cair Paravel is first described as a city, presumably having developed into one over the years. Interestingly, the king feels a need to escape the city for the quiet of the countryside, and it is also in this book (after Cair Paravel has become a city) that Narnia falls.

3. Here we see Lewis's notion of *proper* kingship, which is not hostile domination but natural responsibility for ensuring the well-being and growth of those in one's care. This stewardship improves both the king and the subjects.

4. Peter Kreeft, *The Philosophy of Tolkien: The Worldview behind the Lord of the Rings* (San Francisco: Ignatius Press, 2005), 85.

5. David Orr, "The Uses of Prophecy," in *The Essential Agrarian Reader: The Future of Culture, Community, and the Land,* edited by Norman Wirzba (Lexington: University Press of Kentucky, 2003), 82.

6. Lewis makes another interesting point here: for the Norse, a dragon is both natural and a pestilence; the Norse sees himself in conflict with nature. For the Jew, the Leviathan is a thing of beauty—dangerous, and to be respected in its place (*RoP,* 84).

7. As we will see in the Space Trilogy books, Lewis spent a good deal of time arguing against philosophers like Henri Bergson, who attempted to make the maker and the made one and the same, as in his book *Creative Evolution* (1907; New York: Modern Library, 1944).

8. Philip Sherrard, *The Rape of Man and Nature* (Ipswich, U.K.: Golgonooza, 1987), 93.

9. Steven Bouma-Prediger, *For the Beauty of the Earth* (Grand Rapids, Mich.: Baker Academic, 2006), 142.

10. Peter Kreeft, *Heaven, the Heart's Deepest Longing,* expanded ed. (San Francisco: Ignatius, 1980), 228.

11. Bouma-Prediger, *For the Beauty of the Earth,* 94–96.

12. Alan Jacobs, *The Narnian: The Life and Imagination of C. S. Lewis* (San Francisco: Harper San Francisco, 2005), 170–71.

13. Lewis explicitly mentions that all the animals are killed, along with all the humans, to indicate that animals have moral worth also and that to kill them is a crime.

14. T. M. Moore, *Consider the Lilies* (Phillipsburg, N.J.: P&R Publishing, 2005), 7–8.

15. Hooper, *C. S. Lewis,* 431–42.

16. Jacobs, *The Narnian,* 188.

17. This is one of many places in which Lewis affirms or argues for a conception of nature akin to the medieval Christian notion of Plenitude, for

instance in Bernardus Silvestris or Alanus ab Insulis: everything has a natural place and wants to be in it.

18. Hooper, *C. S. Lewis*, 403.

19. Ibid., 404.

20. Ibid., 397.

21. Peter Kreeft, *The Philosophy of Tolkien*, 85–86.

22. Ibid., 86.

23. This idea has a long tradition in Christian ethical theology. St. Augustine, for instance, argues in his *Confessions* that all sin is an imitation of God; and St. Thomas Aquinas describes sin as the choosing of lesser but more readily accessible *proximate* goods over greater *final* goods. This tradition draws on the passage in Genesis in which God, creating the world, declares all things to be good. This means that no one can choose a bad thing; one can only choose from a multitude of good things—albeit in bad ways or for bad ends.

24. Hooper, *C. S. Lewis*, 560.

25. This is much more difficult to apply in the context of a merely consequentialist ethics, since it presupposes a hierarchy of goods, and that supposition is not necessarily supported by consequentialist ethics. Still, even consequentialists wind up with some notion of the ordering of goods; those goods are best that offer the best consequences. Here, we consider how it might cash out in a Christian framework such as that of C. S. Lewis.

4. *The Last Battle* and the End of Narnia

1. Lewis began writing *The Magician's Nephew* before he began *The Last Battle*, but he struggled to complete *The Magician's Nephew*. So *The Last Battle* was both begun and published after *The Magician's Nephew*, but was completed before it (Alan Jacobs, *The Narnian: The Life and Imagination of C. S. Lewis* [San Francisco: HarperSanFrancisco, 2005], 248). The story of the end of Narnia may have provided Lewis with the material or inspiration to complete the story of Narnia's beginning in *The Magician's Nephew*—which would further attest to the importance of *The Last Battle*.

2. *The Voyage of the Dawn Treader* does not have a castle such as Cair Paravel or the castles of Miraz or the White Witch, but the story does bring us to the governor's palace. Likewise, *The Magician's Nephew* brings us to Jadis's palace, though it is in ruins. Though Cair Paravel is mentioned in *The Last Battle*, the narrative never actually brings us there.

3. Mr. and Mrs. Beaver in *The Lion, the Witch and the Wardrobe*, with their sewing machine, frying pans, locking doors, etc., are entirely anachronistic and belong to the world of *The Wind in the Willows* (which Lewis loved) rather than to Narnia, especially the Narnia of the subsequent six books. With

the exception of Reepicheep, in the later books even the talking animals of Narnia fight with tooth and claw and hoof, like real animals, rather than with human weapons as do, for example, the animals of the Brian Jacques *Redwall* books.

4. This explains Puddleglum's horror in *The Silver Chair* only *after* he discovers that meat he was eating comes from a *talking* stag shot by the evil giants of Harfang (*SC*, ix). Likewise, Tirian is hunting at the start of *The Last Battle*, and other heroes hunt dumb beasts at times during the stories, but in *Prince Caspian*, when Susan shoots a bear she is very concerned that it might have been a talking beast. "I was so afraid it might be, you know—one of our kind of bears, a *talking* bear" (*PC*, ix).

5. Lynn White Jr., "The Historical Roots of our Ecologic Crisis," *Science*, 155, no. 3767 (March 10, 1967): 1203.

6. Clyde S. Kilby, *The Christian World of C. S. Lewis* (Grand Rapids: Eerdmans, 1964), 91.

7. This principle can be found in many of the world's religions. It appears in Christianity, especially in Luke 6:31, which reads in the New International Version, "Do to others as you would have them do to you."

8. We assume from his presence at a hunting lodge that Tirian was hunting. We note that it is a popular view today, especially in urban areas, to disdain hunting as somehow particularly inhumane. While it is not the goal of this book to defend hunting, we must remember that many cultures, such as those of indigenous North American peoples—whom modern Americans often view as being closely in touch with the earth—were hunting cultures. Few humans today still hunt for their own meat; we prefer to purchase our beef in restaurants or prepackaged in grocery stores, where we needn't be reminded that it was once walking around on legs. Yet anyone who is not a complete vegetarian is ultimately responsible for the killing of some animals, and even vegetarians are indirectly responsible for the deaths of animals—or directly, when they stop a mosquito. Lewis, though opposed to inhumane treatment of animals, was well aware that hunting is no more inhumane than other means of slaughtering animals for food, and it is much more humane than some. Barbara Kingsolver, in her foreword to *The Essential Agrarian Reader*, makes an even stronger point. "Recall that farmers and hunters, historically, are more active environmentalists than many progressive, city-dwelling vegetarians" (Lexington: University Press of Kentucky, 2003), xii.

9. Wendell Berry, "Conservation and Local Economy," in *The Art of the Commonplace: The Agrarian Essays of Wendell Berry*, edited by Norman Wirzba, 195–96 (Washington, D.C.: Shoemaker and Hoard, 2002).

10. Bill McKibben, "A Deeper Shade of Green," *National Geographic*, August 2006, 33–41.

11. Lewis was acquainted with Gerard Manley Hopkins's nephew Gerard Walter Sturgis Hopkins, who worked at Oxford University Press.

12. Published February 10, 1938, in *The Oxford Magazine*, 56.

13. Don W. King, *C. S. Lewis, Poet: The Legacy of His Poetic Impulses* (Kent, Ohio: Kent State University Press, 2001), 187.

14. Wendell Berry, "Conservation and Local Economy," printed in *Sex, Economy, Freedom, and Community: Eight Essays* (New York: Pantheon Books, 1992), 4.

15. In one personal letter, J. R. R. Tolkien wrote, "By [Magic] I intend all use of external plans and devices (apparatus) instead of development of the inherent powers or talents—or even the use of these talents with the corrupted motive of dominating: bulldozing the real world, or coercing other wills. The Machine is our more obvious modern form though more closely related to Magic than is usually recognized" (*The Letters of J. R. R. Tolkien*, edited by Humphrey Carpenter with Christopher Tolkien [Boston: Houghton Mifflin, 1981], 145–46). C. S. Lewis points out that even in our world, historically, the pursuit of magic and applied science have shared a common purpose. Writing about the scientific pursuits of Francis Bacon, he notes that "his endeavor is no doubt contrasted in our minds with that of the magicians: but contrasted only in the light of the event, only because we know that science succeeded and magic failed. That event was then still uncertain. Stripping off our knowledge of it, we see at once that Bacon and the magicians have the closest possible affinity. Both seek knowledge for the sake of power (in Bacon's words, as "a spouse for fruit" not a "courtesan for pleasure"), both move in a grandiose dream of days when "Man shall have been raised to the performance of 'all things possible.' . . . Nor would Bacon himself deny the affinity: he thought the aim of the magician was 'noble'" (ELISC, 13–14).

16. In this letter, Lewis uses the word *technique,* which shares with the word *technology* the same Greek root *tekhne,* which means art, craft, or skill. Lewis, with his knowledge of Greek, was certainly aware of that meaning, and so not only is the use of the word *technique* significant in the letter, but in *The Last Battle* in the ape's clever use of his skills we are seeing "technology" at work in a real sense of that word.

17. J. R. R. Tolkien, *The Hobbit* (New York: Houghton Mifflin, 2002), 108–9.

18. Louis D. Rubin Jr., "Introduction," in *I'll Take My Stand: The South and the Agrarian Tradition* (Baton Rouge: Louisiana State University Press, 1977), xv.

19. Ibid., xx–xxi.

20. For a more thorough exploration of the pitfalls of romanticism regarding agrarian life, and how Tolkien's writing transcends it, see Matthew

Dickerson and Jonathan Evans, *Ents, Elves and Eriador: The Enviromental Vision of J. R. R. Tolkien* (Lexington: University Press of Kentucky, 2006).

21. The narrator answers Puzzle's question. "A Hunter, a Man, had killed and skinned this lion somewhere up in the Western Wild several months before. But that doesn't come into the story" (*LB*, i). Though this explanation seems merely factual and free of judgment, it is an interesting side note. The man was probably not hunting a lion for food. But the fact that it happens in the wild, and not near some settlement, suggests that it wasn't in defense either. So presumably the lion was killed only for sport. If this "doesn't come into the story," then why does the narrator present this fact? Perhaps this person killing a noble beast for mere sport bears some culpability in the events that follow.

22. In Berry, *The Art of the Commonplace*, 201.

23. This lecture became a part of his book *Mere Christianity*.

24. When the narrator notes that Shift "did not want anyone to see what he was doing" (*LB*, i), it may be because the ape has a guilty conscience; though he tries to deny any moral obligation on his actions, he still has a deeper knowledge that what he is doing is wrong. This interpretation would be consistent with some of Lewis's arguments about human nature and our moral conscience. It seems more likely, however, that Shift is thinking entirely practically here; his plan of deception will work only if nobody knows what he is doing. He has worked to eliminate in himself all question of right and wrong, and to consider only technological questions of what will work.

25. Jim Ball, "The Use of Ecology in the Evangelical Protestant Response to the Ecological Crisis," *Journal of the American Scientific Affiliation* 50, no. 1 (1998): 32–38.

26. Alan Jacobs, *The Narnian: The Life and Imagination of C. S. Lewis* (San Francisco: HarperSanFrancisco, 2005), 307.

27. Wayne Martindale, *Beyond the Shadowlands: C. S. Lewis on Heaven and Hell* (Wheaton: Crossway Books, 2005), 16. Martindale gives biblical references to I Peter 2:11 and Philippians 3:20.

28. See, for example, Jesus' teaching in Matthew 21:33ff; 25:14ff.

29. This suggestion had already been raised by others, for instance, Camus in the opening lines of his *Myth of Sisyphus*.

30. Martindale, *Beyond the Shadowlands*, 42.

5. Out of the Silent Planet

1. Here is that walking theme again, so prevalent in the Narnia stories, and not insignificant if Gary Snyder is right.

2. See *L3*, p. 968, n. 134: "*Arbol,* the Spanish word for 'tree,' becomes in

Lewis's interplanetary stories the Old Solar word for the Sun. Thus, 'the field of Arbol.'" This is a note from a letter to R. L. Greene, in which Lewis talks about his own love for names and gives "Arbol" as an example, making it seem likely Lewis didn't just make it up at random. Lewis uses both "field" and "fields" in *Perelandra*.

3. Paul E. Lutz, "Interrelatedness: Ecological Pattern of the Creation," in *Cry of the Environment: Rebuilding the Christian Creation Tradition,* edited by Philip N. Joranson and Ken Butigan, 253–74 (Santa Fe: Bear and Company, 1984).

4. St. Augustine, *The Literal Meaning of Genesis,* vol. 2, translated by John Hammond Taylor, S.J. (New York: Newman Press, 1982), 227.

5. We should point out here that Lewis recognized significant differences among these four authors. Lewis criticized each of the four, and he also acknowledged a debt to each of the four. In this chapter and the next chapter we ignore some of those differences in order to focus on a few important similarities in Wells and Bergson that are relevant for the present book. Lewis himself occasionally makes the same connection, for example, in *The Discarded Image* and in his essay "The Funeral of a Great Myth." Despite our present conflation of the two authors, readers should not assume they have identical philosophies or aims in their writing, nor that Lewis's debt to them was identical. For a very good treatment of Lewis's relationship to Bergson and Wells, and their relevance for the Space Trilogy, see Sanford Schwartz's two articles "Cosmic Anthropology: Race and Reason in *Out of the Silent Planet*" and "Paradise Reframed: Lewis, Bergson, and Changing Times on Perelandra," appearing in volumes 52 and 51, respectively, of *Christianity and Literature* (Summer 2003: 523–56, and Summer 2002: 569–602). At the time of writing of this book, Schwartz was also preparing a manuscript on Lewis's science fiction.

6. Norman Wirzba, "Introduction: Why Agrarianism Matters—Even to Urbanites," in *The Essential Agrarian Reader: The Future of Culture, Community, and the Land,* edited by Norman Wirzba, 1–20 (Lexington: University Press of Kentucky, 2003).

7. Our previous book, *From Homer to Harry Potter,* explores in more depth both Lewis's and J. R. R. Tolkien's views on mythology and fairy tales.

8. J. R. R. Tolkien, "On Fairy-Stories," in *Tree and Leaf* (Boston: Houghton Mifflin, 1989), 55.

9. In one edition of *The Sparrow,* Russell explains that she chose to write a "speculative novel" about space travel in order to help readers see the world anew from a vantage point that modernity has otherwise closed off to us. Russell writes that she "wanted to show how very difficult first contact [between cultures] would be, even with the benefit of hindsight. That's when I decided to

write a story that put modern, sophisticated, resourceful, well-educated, and well-meaning people in the same position as those early explorers and missionaries—a position of radical ignorance. Unfortunately, there's no place on Earth today where 'first contact' is possible. . . . The only way to create a 'first contact' story like this was to go off-planet." "A Conversation with Mary Doria Russell," *The Sparrow* (New York: Ballantine, 1997), back matter (n.p.).

10. For example, in his essay "The River of the Mother of God" (in *The River of the Mother of God and Other Essays by Aldo Leopold,* edited by Susan L. Flader and J. Baird Callicott, 123–27 [Madison: University of Wisconsin Press, 1991]), Leopold argues that in the twentieth century a new epoch has come into being, "an epoch in which Unknown Places disappear as a dominant fact in human life" (124). This is, he says, a lamentable fact, since it is not "to be expected that it shall be lost from human experience without something likewise being lost from human character" (124). Although Leopold and Lewis were unlikely to have read much, if any, of each other's work, both identify H. G. Wells as exemplary of a dangerous vision of nature. Leopold writes in the same essay: "There is a current advertisement of Wells' Outline of History [*sic*] which says, 'The unforgivable sin is standing still. In all Nature, to cease to grow is to perish.' I suppose this pretty accurately summarizes the rebuttal which the Economic American would make to the proposal of a national system of wilderness playgrounds" (125).

11. The word for "heaven" in Russian is the same as the word for "sky" or "outer space."

12. Lewis writes in a letter to "Mrs. Hook" that this word is possibly derived from the Greek *nous,* meaning intellect or mind (*L3,* 1005, December 29, 1958). He follows the letter with a postscript: "*Nous:* The intellectual faculty of the natural man . . . employed in practical judgement, [sic] capable of being good or evil, and of being regenerated, the mind, the reason, the reasoning faculty."

13. It is interesting to note in this regard that recent finds by paleontologists suggest that this was not always the case; there have apparently been several species of humanids alive at the same time and in the same place. Were we unable to get along with other hnau? Did we violently bring other human species to an end?

14. Lewis did not necessarily oppose Darwinian or biological evolution. What he opposed was the corollary often tacked onto Darwinian evolution, namely, that just as we are changing biologically, so we are *progressing* morally, getting better all the time. Lewis held that Darwinism was not opposed to any Christian doctrine, but evolutionism was opposed to the doctrine of original sin. See Lewis's correspondence with Bernard Acworth (in his published *Letters*) for a larger view of Lewis's view of Darwin.

15. Henri Bergson, *Creative Evolution*, translated by Arthur Mitchell (New York: Modern Library, 1944), 141.

16. C. S. Lewis, "The Seeing Eye," in *Christian Reflections*, edited by Walter Hooper (Grand Rapids, Mich.: Eerdmans, 1968), 173–74; emphasis added.

17. They might also be said to "hunt" a sort of shellfish that they eat.

18. David Downing, *Planets in Peril* (Amherst: University of Massachusetts Press, 1995), 69–70. Downing's book is one of the finest written about Lewis's fiction, and we recommend it strongly as a reference for readers of the Space Trilogy.

19. C. S. Lewis, *Medieval and Renaissance Literature* (New York: Cambridge University Press, 1996), 162. In this passage he is speaking of Spenser's Neo-Platonism, which, Lewis says, makes Spenser's world both full and resplendent with being. It is infinitely full, but its fullness is always locally intimate, unlike the vast impersonal and sterile infinities of later cosmologies.

20. But contrast this with the view offered by Bill Bryson in *A Short History of Nearly Everything* (New York: Broadway, 2003): "'Space' is extremely well named and rather dismayingly uneventful." Our modern view is that space is indeed empty. In one sense, it is: there are very few objects that draw our attention as useful or attractive. Tourists visiting prairies or deserts or oceans often have the same opinion of the landscape—that it is empty—because they have not yet learned how to see what is there, nor how full the landscapes really are. It lies within the realm of possibility that one day Lewis's view will be vindicated over that of Wells and Bryson.

21. Cf. *Christian Reflections*, 169, where Lewis makes this point about wish fulfillment.

22. Richard Foster, *Celebration of Discipline* (San Francisco: Harper and Row, 1978), 70.

23. See, for example, Acts of the Apostles, 2–4.

24. Scott Sanders, "Introduction," in *For the Health of the Land: Previously Unpublished Essays and Other Writings*, by Aldo Leopold, edited by J. Baird Callicott and Eric T. Freyfogle (Washington, D.C.: Island Press, 1999), xix.

25. Postscript, *OSP*, 156. In this passage Lewis anticipates some of what Donna Haraway writes in her *Companion Species Manifesto: Dogs, People, and Significant Otherness* (Chicago: Prickly Paradigm Press, 2003). As Haraway puts it, "there cannot be just one companion species; there have to be at least two to make one. It is in the syntax; it is in the flesh. . . . .I believe that all ethical relating, within or between species, is knit from the silk-strong thread of ongoing alertness to otherness-in-relation. We are not one, and being depends on getting on together" (13, 50). Those familiar with both Lewis and Haraway will note that these two make strange bedfellows, but Lewis and Haraway plainly

agree that the human-pet relationship, when construed as one of simple domination, ownership, or mastery, impoverishes both parties.

26. But we must notice that "rational animal" does not here mean "human" as it does in the tradition following Aristotle.

27. The Spanish philosopher José Ortega y Gassett, who was not a hunter, nevertheless makes this same point in the closing lines of his introduction to *Veinte años de caza mayor* by the Count de Orgaz. Ortega points out that the advantage of the hunter is precisely the advantage of one who has learned to break free from tradition and habit and so to see the surprising and valuable things that escape the notice of the casual and habit-bound observer.

28. "Maleldil" appears to be the Malacandrian (or "Old Solar") name for God.

29. C. S. Lewis, "Shall We Lose God in Outer Space?" (Great Britain: SPCK, 1959), 10.

6. *Perelandra*

The first epigraph to chapter 6 is drawn from C. S. Lewis, *The Four Loves* (San Diego: Harcourt Brace Jovanovich, 1960), 33. Lewis does not acknowledge it here, but he is of course citing Wordsworth's "The Table Turned." We humbly acknowledge that this is not primarily directed at biologists but at literary critics—like us.

1. See *LC*, 90.

2. Lewis wrote to E. R. Eddison in 1943 and complained that "Lanes [the publishers of *Perelandra*] *are* fools. Note that they blab out my whole theme in the blurb [on the book cover], which was meant to come over the reader by stealth. Idiots!" (*L2*, 570). So obviously he didn't mean for the mask to be taken all the way off.

3. David Downing, *Planets in Peril* (Amherst: University of Massachusetts Press, 1996), 46.

4. David Landis Barnhill and Roger S. Gottlieb, eds., *Deep Ecology and World Religions: New Essays on Sacred Ground* (Albany, N.Y.: State University of New York Press, 2001), 5.

5. See, for example, Bill Devall, *Simple in Means, Rich in Ends, Practicing Deep Ecology* (Salt Lake City: Peregrine Smith Books, 1988).

6. Barnhill and Gottlieb, *Deep Ecology and World Religions*, 6.

7. Ibid., 6.

8. C. S. Lewis, *George MacDonald* (New York: Macmillan, 1948), 69.

9. Ibid., 69–70.

10. Lewis noted in a personal letter that he was unfamiliar with the philosophical school known as "Personalism," that is, the school that holds that per-

sons must be central in any account of the world, but he appears to have been something of a Personalist nonetheless. Cf. *L2,* 914.

11. The citation from Milton that occurs early in *Out of the Silent Planet* ("Happy climes that ly . . .") (*OSP,* v) shows that Lewis was thinking of Milton while writing at least one of the Space Trilogy books. See Walter Hooper, *C. S. Lewis: A Companion and Guide* (New York: Harper Collins, 1996), 221ff. Hooper writes that Lewis "had been lecturing in the University on Milton's *Paradise Lost* since 1937 and this, doubtless, furnished him with the basic plot of *Perelandra*" (221).

12. Calvin DeWitt, "Seeking to Image the Order and Beauty of God's 'House': A Scriptural Foundation for Creation-care," in *Creation-Care in Ministry: Down-to-Earth Christianity,* edited by W. D. Roberts and P. E. Pretiz (Wynnewood, Pa.: Aerdo, 2000), 9–24.

13. Steven Bouma-Prediger, *For the Beauty of the Earth* (Grand Rapids, Mich.: Baker, 2001), 74.

14. Note the similar description of mer-folk in *Voyage of the Dawn Treader.*

15. Michael E. Zimmerman, "Ken Wilber's Critique of Ecological Spirituality," in *Deep Ecology and World Religions,* ed. Barnhill and Gottlieb, 245. Zimmerman's excellent article critiques a broad range of SDEs, including forms of eco-paganism and Christian ecology, but especially argues against ecologies that attempt to reduce reality to one-dimensional "Flatland" ontologies by claiming that only the physical/natural world is real, and against those SDEs that attempt to claim that culture is the original sin, so to speak. Zimmerman argues, along with Wilber, for a hierarchical view of nature that entails human responsibility and allows for an increasing complexity in the cosmos.

16. Peter Singer, in his *One World,* has drawn criticism for suggesting that rich nations who have benefited from industrialization should be held responsible for the cost of cleaning up the effects of that industrialization in a way that is proportionate to the benefits they have received. Singer is not shy of controversy, and, as his critics are legion, we will not dwell on the criticisms here. Our point is only that Singer and others on both sides of the pollution-cost debates are aware that sacrifices such as the ones we are talking about are, clearly, sacrifices—they are economically costly and may involve other disadvantages in terms of future research, productivity, health, and so on.

7. *That Hideous Strength*

1. The passage cited is from the chapter titled "The Scouring of the Shire," in J. R. R. Tolkien's *The Return of the King.* See Matthew Dickerson and Jonathan Evans, *Ents, Elves, and Eriador: The Environmental Vision of J. R. R. Tolkien* (Lexington: University Press of Kentucky, 2006), on the connection between

the Shire in Middle-earth and the England of Tolkien's youth (especially pp. 76–80), and for a fuller exploration of Tolkien's threefold portrayal of environmental evils (especially pp. 185–213, from chapter 8, "Three Faces of Mordor").

2. Gregory Starkey has also noted similarities between Tolkien and Lewis in their portrayals of the impact of evil on nature, and argues it is evidence of Tolkien's influence on Lewis (Gregory Starkey, "Tolkien's Influence on C. S. Lewis," *Mallorn: The Journal of the Tolkien Society* 17 [October 1981]: 23–28). Starkey writes, "Concerning evil itself, in Tolkien evil is externalized and manifested in the lack of respect [for] and destruction of Nature, seen especially in the turmoil in the countryside. The chapter titled 'The Scouring of the Shire' in *The Return of the King* illustrates this effect to the full. Evil vents its rage on the trees without reason. This same idea is developed by Lewis in *That Hideous Strength*, when the countryside begins to be attacked." Although *That Hideous Strength* was published about a decade before *The Lord of the Rings*, an influence of the latter book on the former is certainly plausible, as Tolkien had read early portions of his work to Lewis long before its publication. Lewis even references Tolkien's work in the preface to *That Hideous Strength*, writing: "Those who would like to learn further about Numinor [*sic*] and the True West must (alas!) await the publication of much that still exists only in the MSS. of my friend, Professor J. R. R. Tolkien." For our purposes, no assumption of influence in one direction or the other is necessary or even important; the similarity reflects an underlying shared Christian worldview.

3. While Tolkien's region known as the Shire in Middle-earth was inspired by the England of the late nineteenth century, just a few decades before the publication of *The Lord of the Rings*, Lewis's *That Hideous Strength* takes place in England itself, in what to him would have been the very near future.

4. Readers later learn of an ulterior motive for the location of the development: top officials at the N.I.C.E. (Wither and Frost) obtain the land and cut down Bragdon Wood to provide access to Merlin's tomb and thus to Merlin himself. However, the stated reason for the cutting of the wood—the justification given early in the novel, and the one of which the majority of the members of the N.I.C.E. and Bracton College are aware and act upon—is to pave the way (literally and figuratively) for development. (The fellows of Bracton also act to eliminate the "burden" of maintaining the Wood.) Even if we consider the ulterior motive, we note that the point of the search for Merlin is to gain access to Merlin's power over nature. Thus, whether we consider the blatant agenda or the hidden one, we may conclude that the cutting of trees is for the sake of gaining power (either technological or magical) over nature.

5. As we mention in several previous chapters, this hostility seems to go along with the view that what is there in nature is, ipso facto, there for us to use as we will. Ethicists from John Locke on have reminded us that there ought

to be limitations to this kind of use, however. Chief among these limitations is that we should not take away from others what we cannot fully use and which will perish in our keeping. Later ethicists have argued that this ought to apply not only to those currently alive but to posterity as well. To destroy an ancient forest is to arrogate to a single generation the heritage of many previous generations at the expense of all future generations. The value of Bragdon Wood is not the cash value of the timber plus the cash value of the real estate. Its true valuation must take into account its history as an ancient grove, the fact that it is an example of a medieval walled garden in a time when such examples are rare, and its aesthetic, cultural, and spiritual value. We must add to that the fact that old environments wind up being repositories of the chemical history of the earth, of tremendous value for climatologists and other empirical scientists. When such woods are destroyed, irretrievable data are lost.

6. David W. Orr, "The Uses of Prophecy," in *The Essential Agrarian Reader: The Future of Culture, Community, and the Land,* edited by Norman Wirzba, 171–87 (Lexington: University Press of Kentucky, 2004), 179.

7. As we mention in a previous note, Lewis frequently played with significant names. This, of course, can be seen in the hard, cold names of the antagonists in *THS,* or the use of *hnau* (a variant of the Greek *nous*) and *Oyarsa* (a variant of the Latin/Greek *Ousiarches*) in the previous two novels. The name of this town may be significant as well: a "cure" is a parish, or a place to care for souls. So a "cure hardy" or a "hardy cure" would be a robust parish or a robust place to care for souls. Lewis's name for this small agricultural town tells us it is a robust place to care for souls—in sharp contrast with Belbury, where soul, soil, and body are all in peril.

8. See, for example, Thomas Howard's *C. S. Lewis: Man of Letters—A Reading of His Fiction* (San Francisco: Ignatius, 1990) (originally published as *The Achievement of C. S. Lewis* [H. Shaw, 1980]), as well as David Downing's excellent *Planets in Peril* (Amherst: University of Massachusetts Press, 1995).

9. Don W. King, *C. S. Lewis, Poet: The Legacy of His Poetic Impulses* (Kent, Ohio: Kent State University Press, 2001), 208.

10. For example, in a personal letter composed in April 1951, he writes, "I don't feel in a position to have clear opinions about anyone I know only from newspapers. You see, whenever they deal with anyone (or anything) I know myself, I find they're always a mass of lies & misunderstandings: so I conclude they're no better in the places where I *don't* know" (*L3,* 114). In a letter dated a year and a half later, he writes: "But don't send me any newspaper cuttings. I never believe a word said in the papers. The real history of a period (as we always discover a few years later) has v. little to do with all that, and private people like you and me are never allowed to know it while it is going on" (*L3,* 252).

11. Howard, *C. S. Lewis,* 150–51.

12. Ibid., 130.

13. Again we recognize that "Platonism" can mean a range of things. We refer to, for instance, the doctrine, which has frequently and traditionally been taken from dialogues such as Plato's *Phaedo* or his *Republic*, that the aim of the soul is to familiarize itself with Ideal Forms and thus to seek its ultimate liberation from the body and the world.

14. The full title of the poem is "Ane dialog betwix Experience and ane Courtier of the miserabill estait of the World." The poem was written in the sixteenth century by Sir David Lyndsay, who was the Lyon king-of-arms (the chief herald) of Scotland. As Thomas Howard has pointed out, "that itself may give us a clue as to how to read this and all of Lewis's fiction; there is a sense in which it is all heraldic" (Howard, *C. S. Lewis,* 122).

15. This is striking since it is usually religious believers who are accused of devaluing *this* world in favor of some *other* world—an accusation that often mystifies Christians like Lewis who believe in the Incarnation. The Incarnation, after all, may be understood as the definitive Divine statement of the value of *this* world. When Ares is wounded in Homer's account of the Trojan War, he flees back to Olympus to escape the pain of this world. He is unwilling to die here and to share in the fate of mortals. Christians regard Christ as God incarnate, that is, as the god who chooses deliberately to share human life—and death. Also important to Christians like Lewis is the historical claim that Christ appeared at a certain time and a certain place. It will not do to have Christ be a mere timeless spirit or a perennial ideal. It matters entirely that Christ chose to dwell on particular soil (though his choice of *which* soil may have been arbitrary). Lewis is suggesting that it is in fact those who worship technology who are led to reject the world and the particularities of life in contact with the earth. The N.I.C.E. intends to transcend this world altogether.

16. Macrobes, the reader may eventually come to realize, are demonic beings, or fallen angels—the eldila of our world—but Filostrato does not seem to understand this, or perhaps he doesn't care.

17. Howard, *C. S. Lewis,* 125–26.

18. We note in earlier chapters that Lewis was responding to ideas put forth in many well-known works of science fiction, such as those of H. G. Wells. This is true not only of ideas, but of specific plot elements. As Donald Glover notes, "W. Olaf Stapledon's *Last and First Men,* 1930, offers much against which Lewis might have reacted. . . . Reading it after encountering Lewis, we see possible sources for some of Weston's and Frost's scientific experiments." Glover goes on to point out that the following all happen in *Last and First Men:* (1) men invade Venus, where they "destroy all native intelligence, and justify such action on the basis that the prime directive is to maintain the human species in any environment"; (2) "early in the book there is a confrontation between a naked

native woman of another planet, an American emissary, and a Chinese emissary"; and (3) "there is a great brain kept alive with tubes and other scientific apparatus" (Donald Glover, *C. S. Lewis: The Art of Enchantment* [Athens: Ohio University Press, 1981], 76–77). Very similar or even identical plot elements to these three examples appear, respectively, in the three books of Lewis's Space Trilogy, except that the second one rather than the first happens on Venus.

19. Francis Crick, cited in Francis Schaeffer, *Back to Freedom and Dignity*, vol. 4, bk. 1 in *The Complete Works of Francis Schaeffer* (Wheaton, Ill.: Crossway Books, 1982), 366.

20. Ray Kurzweil, *The Age of Spiritual Machines: When Computers Exceed Human Intelligence* (New York: Penguin Books, 1999).

21. Ibid., 128–29. Kurzweil is quoting from W. B. Yeats's poem "Sailing to Byzantium."

22. Ibid., 134–35.

23. This is also suggested by Ray Kurzweil's Web site, www.kurzweilAI .net. As of July 2007, the top line of his Web site still reads "When Humans Transcend Biology." This is both the prediction and the goal: to escape biological bodies and eventually all of biology.

24. Kurzweil, *Age of Spiritual Machines*, 138.

25. Ibid., 141–42.

26. Ibid., 148.

27. We also believe, and could argue—and indeed many have already argued—that our minds are also dependent on nature. To keep our minds healthy we need beauty, wilderness, soil, and water. But this argument is less immediate, and the conclusion, though we believe true, is not important to the present point, which is that a rejection of our bodies will lead to a rejection of the earth.

28. Wendell Berry, "The Body and the Earth," in *The Art of the Commonplace: the Agrarian Essays of Wendell Berry*, edited by Norman Wirzba, 93–134 (Washington, D.C.: Shoemaker and Hoard, 2002), 102.

29. Ibid., 103.

30. Norman Wirzba, "Placing the Soul: An Agrarian Philosophical Principle," appearing in *The Essential Agrarian Reader: The Future of Culture, Community, and the Land*, edited by Norman Wirzba, 80–97 (Lexington: University Press of Kentucky, 1993).

31. Lewis makes it clear that he is not opposed to science, but rather respects the real scientist (as opposed to the technologist or applied scientist), as is also illustrated by the comments made by the chemist Hingest about Mark's brand of sociology, and the sociological agenda of the N.I.C.E. "There *are* no sciences like Sociology. And if I found chemistry beginning to fit in with a secret police run by a middle-aged virago who doesn't wear corsets, and

a scheme for taking away his farm and his shop and his children from every Englishman, I'd let chemistry go to the devil and take up gardening again" (*THS*, 3.4). Whether the reader agrees with Hingest or not, it is certainly the case that Lewis does, and he has this scientist (the only real scientist at the N.I.C.E.) giving (in Lewis's view) a valid assessment of what Mark is doing.

32. Ed Chapman, "Toward a Sacramental Ecology: Technology, Nature, and Transcendence in C. S. Lewis's Ransom Trilogy," *Mythlore* 3 (June 1976): 10–17, quote on 17.

33. As we have already mentioned, Lewis himself fought in the First World War. His reflections on war appear throughout his novels, and none of them seem to be accidental. As farmer and classicist Victor D. Hanson has pointed out in the appendix to his *Carnage and Culture,* in the ancient world, wars could be fought only when there was no agricultural work to be done, hence the references in the Bible, for instance, to "the time of year when kings went off to war." (See, for instance, 2 Samuel 11.1.) Hanson argues—for instance, in his *Warfare and Agriculture in Classical Greece*—along Jeffersonian lines that the small agrarian farmer is the basis of our culture. Hanson laments in several of his other books, and especially *Fields without Dreams: Defending the Agrarian Ideal,* that our age is seeing the end of privately owned family farms. Cosser's view is that this is a good thing, and that the displaced farmers can now be expended in wars that continue for years and throughout all seasons, thanks to the demise of the family farm. Lewis—and Hanson—admit with grave sadness that Cosser is right about the connection between the loss of farms and the "progress" of modern warfare.

34. In a later scene, when Mark tries to flee from the N.I.C.E., and finds himself in the midst of the destruction, the narrator notes: "Fragments of articles which Mark himself had written drifted to and fro. Apparently he and his kind had done their work well; Miss Hardcastle had rated too high the resistance of the working classes to propaganda" (*THS*, 10.2).

35. Evan K. Gibson, *C. S. Lewis Spinner of Tales: A Guide to His Fiction* (Washington, D.C.: Eerdmans, 1980), 70.

36. Glover, *C. S. Lewis,* 116–17.

37. Howard, *C. S. Lewis,* 137–38.

38. Wayne Martindale, *Beyond the Shadowlands: C. S. Lewis on Heaven and Hell* (Wheaton: Crossway Books, 2005), 171.

39. Howard, *C. S. Lewis,* 135.

40. Chapman, "Toward a Sacramental Ecology," 15.

41. Again, as we have already quoted Lewis as having written, "I have always loved real mice."

42. As the scientist and philosopher Charles S. Peirce wrote in 1898, scientists are those who are motivated by a "desire to find things out" and an equal

desire to be proven wrong in their pursuit of the truth. *Philosophical Writings of Peirce*, edited by Justus Buchler (New York: Dover, 1955), 4, 37.

8. The Re-enchantment of Creation

1. Henry David Thoreau, "Walking," in *The Selected Works of Thoreau* (Boston: Houghton Mifflin, 1975), 672.

2. Alan Jacobs, *The Narnian: The Life and Imagination of C. S. Lewis* (San Francisco: HarperSanFrancisco, 2005), xxi.

3. C. S. Lewis, *The Weight of Glory*, cited in Alan Jacobs, *The Narnian*, 189.

4. Jacobs, *The Narnian*, 188. Jacobs attributes the phrase "the disenchantment of the world" to Max Weber.

5. Gary Snyder, *The Practice of the Wild* (San Francisco: North Point Press, 1990), 8.

6. Fred Van Dyke, David C. Mahan, Joseph K. Sheldon, and Raymond H. Brand, *Redeeming Creation* (Downers Grove, Ill.: Intervarsity Press, 1996); see 14.1. Citations from 74–75.

7. We say "indirectly," because Hanson is not critiquing Lewis but a genre of writers into which Lewis may be supposed to fall.

8. Victor Davis Hanson, *Fields without Dreams: Defending the Agrarian Ideal* (New York: Free Press, 1996), xi.

9. Gregory Wolfe, "C. S. Lewis's Debt to George MacDonald," *The Bulletin of the New York C. S. Lewis Society* 15, no. 2 (December 1983): 1–7.

Recommended Reading

Recent years have yielded an abundant crop of Lewis-related books of interest to both scholars and general readers. The following are books that we have found helpful in preparing our book and that we think general readers will find both interesting and accessible. It is, of course, by no means an exhaustive list of books relevant to Lewis's ecological vision. In the general area of ecology and nature writing only, even if we exclude fiction and poetry and limit ourselves to nonfiction, there is a wealth of wonderful writing spanning at least three centuries and writers from H. D. Thoreau to Annie Dillard. Bill McKibben has suggested that the nature-writing tradition may be America's great and unique contribution to world literature. However, in keeping with an important principle of ecology, namely, the finitude of the created world and its resources, below is a minimal list of books to get the interested reader started.

C. S. Lewis: Biography

Griffin, William. *C. S. Lewis: The Authentic Voice.* Oxford: Lion, 1986.
Hooper, Walter. *C. S. Lewis: A Companion and Guide.* New York: HarperCollins, 1996.
Jacobs, Alan. *The Narnian: The Life and Imagination of C. S. Lewis.* San Francisco: HarperSanFrancisco, 2005.
Sayer, George. *Jack: C. S. Lewis and His Times.* San Franciso: Harper & Row, 1988.

C. S. Lewis: Fantasy Literature

Dickerson, Matthew, and David O'Hara. *From Homer to Harry Potter: A Handbook of Myth and Fantasy.* Grand Rapids, Mich.: Brazos Press, 2006.
Downing, David C. *Planets in Peril: A Critical Study of C. S. Lewis's Ransom Trilogy.* Amherst: University of Massachusetts Press, 1992.
Glover, Donald. *C. S. Lewis: The Art of Enchantment.* Athens: Ohio University Press, 1981.

Howard, Thomas. *Narnia and Beyond: A Guide to the Fiction of C. S. Lewis.* San Francisco: Ignatius Press, 2006. Note that this book is a new edition of a book previously titled *C. S. Lewis: Man of Letters: A Reading of His Fiction,* published by Ignatius in 1990, and *The Achievement of C. S. Lewis* (Wheaton, Ill.: Harold Shaw, 1980).

Schakel, Peter J. *Reading with the Heart: The Way into Narnia.* Grand Rapids, Mich.: Eerdmans, 1979.

Ward, Michael. *Planet Narnia.* Oxford: Oxford University Press, 2008.

Ecology and Literature

Dickerson, Matthew, and Jonathan Evans. *Ents, Elves, and Eriador: The Environmental Vision of J. R. R. Tolkien.* Lexington: University Press of Kentucky, 2006.

Finch, Robert, and John Elder, eds. *Nature Writing: The Tradition in English.* New York: W. W. Norton, 2002.

McKibben, Bill, ed. *American Earth: Environmental Writing since Thoreau.* New York: Library of America, 2008.

Ecology and Christianity

Berry, Wendell. *The Art of the Commonplace: The Agrarian Essays of Wendell Berry,* edited by Norman Wirzba. Washington, D.C.: Shoemaker and Hoard, 2002.

Bouma-Prediger, Steven. *For the Beauty of the Earth.* Grand Rapids, Mich.: Baker Academic, 2001.

Joranson, Philip N., and Ken Butigan, eds. *Cry of the Environment: Rebuilding the Christian Creation Tradition.* Santa Fe: Bear and Company, 1984.

Larsen, Dale, and Sandy Larsen. *While Creation Waits: A Christian Response to the Environmental Challenge.* Wheaton, Ill.: Harold Shaw, 1992.

Moore, T. M. *Consider the Lilies.* Phillipsburg, N.J.: P&R Publishing, 2005.

Sherrard, Philip. *The Rape of Man and Nature.* Ipswich, U.K.: Golgonooza, 1987.

Wirzba, Norman. *The Paradise of God: Renewing Religion in an Ecological Age.* Oxford: Oxford University Press, 2007.

Index

This index does not include entries for several key concepts like "nature," because they occur frequently throughout the book, and the references are too numerous to list. Entries for invented terms and proper nouns that appear in C. S. Lewis's fictional works are set in bold type.